Dilemmas of Decline

THE BERKELEY SERIES IN BRITISH STUDIES

Mark Bevir and James Vernon, University of California, Berkeley, Editors

1. *The Peculiarities of Liberal Modernity in Imperial Britain,* edited by Simon Gunn and James Vernon
2. *Dilemmas of Decline: British Intellectuals and World Politics, 1945–1975,* by Ian Hall

Dilemmas of Decline

British Intellectuals and World Politics, 1945-1975

IAN HALL

Global, Area, and International Archive
University of California Press
BERKELEY   LOS ANGELES   LONDON

The Global, Area, and International Archive (GAIA) is an initiative of the Institute of International Studies, University of California, Berkeley, in partnership with the University of California Press, the California Digital Library, and international research programs across the University of California system.

University of California Press, one of the most distinguished university presses in the United States, enriches lives around the world by advancing scholarship in the humanities, social sciences, and natural sciences. Its activities are supported by the UC Press Foundation and by philanthropic contributions from individuals and institutions. For more information, visit www.ucpress.edu.

University of California Press
Berkeley and Los Angeles, California

University of California Press, Ltd.
London, England

© 2012 by The Regents of the University of California

Library of Congress Cataloging-in-Publication Data

A catalog record for this book is available from the Library of Congress

21 20 19 18 17 16 15 14 13 12
10 9 8 7 6 5 4 3 2 1

For my parents

Contents

	Acknowledgments	ix
1.	Introduction: The Dilemmas of Decline	1
2.	Traditions and Dilemmas	14
3.	The Fall and Rise of Political Realism	29
4.	The Persistence of Liberalism	48
5.	The Fragmentation of Internationalism	64
6.	The Whigs and the Diplomatic Tradition	83
7.	The Radicals	107
8.	The Revolt against the West: Decolonization and Its Repercussions	131
9.	War and Peace	152
10.	Conclusion: British Intellectuals and the Retreat from Power	170
	Notes	185
	Index	249

Acknowledgments

This book concludes more than a decade's research on British international thought in the aftermath of the Second World War. It began with a doctoral thesis on three particular figures, Herbert Butterfield, Arnold J. Toynbee, and Martin Wight, who were central to the development of British international thought in the twentieth century. It continued through a monograph on Wight's ideas and a series of narrower studies of other thinkers, including George Orwell and Charles Webster, and particular traditions, especially political realism. This book offers something different: a synoptic account of the ways in which British intellectuals responded to world politics after 1945. The account is far from exhaustive, but it tries to bring narrative order to a very fragmented intellectual history. All historiography requires abridgement, and while some will no doubt disagree with the way that it is done here, this book aims not just to give today's professional students of international relations a better sense of their forebears, but also to explain why the British struggled to come to terms with their new place in the world in the aftermath of 1945.

The origins of this book can be traced back to the University of St Andrews, in the northeast of Scotland, but it was written at Griffith University, in the rather different climate of Brisbane. I have accumulated a number of debts on my travels in between. At St Andrews, Michael Bentley, Tony Lang, Nick Rengger, and especially Mark Imber, who donated a considerable collection of postwar international relations texts to my own growing hoard, all influenced my thinking in the crucial early stages. At Adelaide, Juanita Elias, Lisa Hill, Clem Macintyre, and Czes Tubilewicz contributed useful thoughts as my work progressed. The project also could not have been undertaken without the research funding provided by the University of Adelaide's Qantas Early Career Researcher Grant and Faculty of Humanities and Social Sciences Small Grant, both of which permitted necessary travel to archives. Finally, I thank my former colleagues at Griffith University, especially Gideon Baker, Tom Conley, Martin Griffiths, Michael Heazle, Haig Patapan, Jason Sharman, Pat Weller, and Michael Wesley.

The intervention of Duncan Bell was decisive in pushing this book to completion and for that I am very thankful. I hasten to add—in case his association with the project compromises him in the eyes of the Cambridge School—that he would almost certainly disagree with the approach I have used. The advice of Chris Brown and Mick Cox was indispensible when it came to untangling the intricacies of radicalism in the 1960s. So too, on a range of issues, were conversations with James Cotton, Richard Devetak, Tim Dunne, Jeanne Morefield, and Casper Sylvest. David Long and another, anonymous, reviewer provided a series of helpful suggestions on the original manuscript, and while I have not taken all of their advice, I hope they find the completed book much improved as a result. I am also most grateful to Mark Bevir, who first suggested that I submit a proposal for this book to the Berkeley Series in British Studies, which he edits with James Vernon. At the University of California, Nathan MacBrien was a very patient and tolerant editor. Lastly, I would like to thank Taylor and Francis for their permission to reprint parts of an article from the *International History Review* in chapter 8. Any errors of fact or judgment are my own.

Renée, Sadie, and latterly Scarlett showed immense forbearance during the time it took to get this book done, and for that they deserve and probably want an apology rather than gratitude. I offer both.

This book is dedicated to my parents, children of the postwar era, who witnessed firsthand Britain's decline and the dilemmas it posed.

1. Introduction
The Dilemmas of Decline

> Next year we shall be living in a country
> That brought its soldiers home for lack of money.
> The statues will be standing in the same
> Tree-muffled squares, and look nearly the same.
> Our children will not know it's a different country.
> All we can hope to leave them now is money.
>   PHILIP LARKIN, "Homage to a Government" (1969)

Within fifteen years of Allied victory in the Second World War, the United Kingdom was shorn of all but a few fragments of its colonial empire and displaced from its preeminent position in the international hierarchy of states. Another fifteen years on, Britain was mired in economic recession and political stasis, dependent on the United States in its finances and its security, and a supplicant to the European Economic Community.

In just three decades, Britain's relationships with the major powers of world politics were transformed. As the United States and Soviet Union rose, the European empires that had dominated modern international politics for four centuries were eclipsed, their global interests circumscribed and their ambitions curtailed. British voices could still be heard in Washington, as the United Kingdom tied itself ever closer to the United States by treaty, sentiment, and a carefully tended historical memory.[1] But this process had not occurred without resistance and resentment on the part of many Britons, for the "special relationship" barely disguised the brute fact their country had been overtaken and supplanted as the leader of the Western powers. Britain's relations with its other major wartime ally were no less complex. Although the Soviet Union had been rendered a latent enemy by the Cold War, reserves of sympathy for Russia and its political system, especially among British intellectuals, remained considerable.

By the mid-1970s, as F. S. Northedge pointed out at the time, the "British people ... found that there was little they could do in international affairs from the basis of their own strength."[2] That strength had ebbed away and with it Britain's ability to shape world politics. Whether this dramatic and unprecedented transformation of Britain's global standing constitutes "decline"—and in what sense of that term—remains bitterly contested. It was certainly thought so at the time, as the title of Northedge's 1974 book—*Descent from Power*—illustrates so well. Britain's loss of global power and influence went hand in hand with the raising of domestic living standards and extensive social reform, but whether these changes made Britain "better" and whether they compensated for that loss is still a matter of intense debate.[3]

This book sidesteps this issue. What matters, from the point of view of the intellectual history of the postwar period, is not whether decline occurred, but whether contemporaries perceived it to be occurring. Of this there can be little doubt. Almost all the intellectuals discussed in what follows were convinced that Britain—and indeed "Western civilization" more generally—was in some kind of decline, be it political, moral, cultural, social, economic, or spiritual. This "declinism" is perceptible among some British thinkers in the interwar years, but in the 1940s it became far more general, reaching its peak in the late 1950s and early 1960s.[4] It spurred a series of meditations not just on British politics and society but on foreign policy and international relations. British reactions to the changing place, power, and role of Britain in world politics were shaped and conditioned by this shared perception of decline. Where they differed—sometimes quite violently—was over where to lay the blame and what to do in response. They argued, often vehemently, about the value of their inherited ways of thinking about—and indeed practicing—domestic and international politics, as well as over novel approaches suggested by both British and foreign intellectuals.

Many British thinkers agreed that world politics posed the greatest challenge to Britain of the postwar era.[5] They were convinced that "to get . . . foreign policy right" was "the first task of British statesmanship," as the conservative historian Max Beloff put it in 1969—"a necessary precondition of every other measure directed at Britain's recovery."[6] For Beloff as for his peers, *Aussenpolitik* was primary; domestic politics were of lesser importance.[7]

Few disagreed with this diagnosis, but there was little consensus on the best cure.[8] As we shall see, some favored radical departures from past policies informed by "realism" or by more radical philosophies of international relations. Some argued that Britain had declined precisely because of such departures, urging instead the recovery of apparently tried-and-tested ways of conducting foreign policy. Some, like Northedge, even concluded that the "strength and ubiquity of... geopolitical forces" meant that "hardly any action by a British government... could have done anything to arrest or reverse the British decline."[9]

The actions that were taken have been discussed in a number of studies, and this book does not revisit them.[10] Its focus is rather on the philosophies and beliefs that underpinned and shaped those policies—and their alternatives—in the postwar period. This book offers, in other words, an intellectual history of British international thought in the postwar period. It is not a "disciplinary history" because no "discipline" of "international relations" (IR) existed in Britain until the late 1960s, at least outside the London School of Economics (LSE).[11] Thinking about world politics in the thirty years after 1945 was not confined to university departments or to professional academics, nor was it the preserve of one "discipline."[12] It was an interdisciplinary exercise and a nondisciplinary one, in the sense that much of the most interesting discussions were had outside institutions of higher learning and the pages of scholarly journals. Not for nothing did the founders of the British International Studies Association (BISA), formed in 1974, refer to their field as "international studies"—their thinking roamed much wider than a mere "discipline." It was only later, partly and somewhat ironically under the pressure of disciplinary history, that such a "discipline" of IR coalesced.

This book examines what engaged, interested intellectuals thought about world politics in the postwar years. It does so in terms of the traditions of thought about politics and international relations that these intellectuals inherited, modified, rejected, or revived. It tells the story of how these traditions developed—how they rose and fell; how they emerged and evolved—at the hands of postwar thinkers. These shifts were often quite rapid and dramatic—fittingly so, given the extraordinary transformations occurring in the wider world. At times, indeed, international developments prompted many contemporaries to call for wholesale revolutions in the ways in which the British conceived—and acted in—international relations. These demands came from the Right as well as the Left, generating extensive and passionate debate among British intellectuals about their views of the world and what ought to be done to change it. Out of this debate emerged a series of new perspectives, some faithful to key aspects of inherited traditions, and some diverging from them. Sometimes these new perspectives resulted from the application of new methods and approaches to old topics; sometimes they emerged as thinkers shifted their focus away from inherited concerns towards different subjects. Together, they sought to explain how world politics worked, why the world had changed in the way that it had, and—much more rarely, it must be admitted—what ought to be done about the dilemmas these changes had brought into being.

HISTORIES OF INTERNATIONAL THOUGHT

> UK IR never really followed the US in accepting behaviouralism and positivism has historically been much less established in the UK than in the US. There has always been resistance to the attempts of US IR to create a "science" of IR, as Hedley Bull and Fred Northedge famously argued in the 1960s and 1970s. Instead, the UK community is much more likely to analyse IR through detailed historical study.
> STEVE SMITH, "The Discipline of International Relations" (2000)[13]

> The biggest clichés about British political science define it in contrast to American positivism.
> ROBERT ADCOCK & MARK BEVIR, "Political Science" (2010)[14]

The "accepted story of a British approach to politics," as Bevir and Rhodes have called it, is a whiggish narrative about a whiggish discipline.[15] It tells of a field of study once bound to philosophy, law, and history that has become, over time, an ever more systematic and professional discipline with its own distinctive approaches. Beginning with the historical and philosophical investigation of political ideas and institutions, so this story goes, British students of politics slowly honed their own craft, adapting themselves to some of the "theoretical, quantitative and substantive concerns of American political scientists but without their concomitant theoretical self-consciousness."[16] In so doing, they retained "a concern with agency, a sense of the stability of institutions, and a suspicion of theoretical generalizations"[17] which were lost on the other side of the Atlantic in the American rush to ever-more rigorous "science." The British study of politics thus evolved into a discipline that is at once mature and unassuming, equal to its American counterpart in its professionalism but less vaulting in its ambition. It became a "self-deprecating" discipline (to use Jack Hayward's term), "sober" and "skeptical" (to use Brian Barry's), self-assured as to its subject matter and modest about its methods.[18]

A similar story is told about the development of international relations in Britain during the twentieth century. Again, there is a sense that the field has progressed from being a rather inchoate interdisciplinary enterprise between the two world wars into a professional "discipline" in its own right, complete with a rough consensus about its concerns and a common language with which to discuss them.[19] Again, too, the postwar part of the story concentrates on the responses of British specialists to American developments. The only difference concerns the manner of that reaction. While disciplinary histories of political studies tend to emphasize the extent to which British scholars adapted and adopted—cautiously but pragmatically—American ways of thinking, the accepted disciplinary history of British IR instead celebrates the wholesale rejection by British scholars of American theories, their claims, and their pretensions.[20]

In the 1940s, so this story goes, the British simply refused to countenance the power politics of "realist" theory, as professed by Walter Lippmann, Hans Morgenthau, Frederick Schuman, or Nicholas Spykman, and still less as advocated by E. H. Carr. Instead, they stuck to their traditional studies of international institutions and international law.[21] In the 1950s and 1960s, British scholars again stood firm, but this time the issue was method, not subject matter. Steadfastly they resisted the importation of a series of American scientific approaches—behavioral and otherwise—and insisted instead on the virtues of what Hedley Bull called the "classical approach."[22] Led supposedly by the "English school of international relations," British scholars in international relations maintained their fidelity to history and their concern with the normative foundations of international relations.[23] The British, Steve Smith notes with pride, "never bought into the positivist assumptions that dominated the discipline" in the United States, thereby preserving for later generations an approach to international relations unsullied by American scientism.[24]

This narrative about the evolution of IR is also unusual in that it is shared by both traditionalists and by more radical scholars with critical theoretical and postmodern tastes. Indeed, while the rise of "postpositivism" in the field has helped to stimulate a deeper concern for intellectual and disciplinary history on both sides of the Atlantic and elsewhere,[25] it has not substantively modified the basic story of the development of British international thought in the twentieth century. Instead, it remains a whiggish narrative with more than a hint of self-congratulation.[26] For nineteenth-century whig historians, British history was the story of the triumph of Protestant liberty over Catholic authority. For British students of international relations, the history of their field is the story of the triumph of native British philosophy over imported American methodology.

This narrative is, however, misleading. Just as the whiggish story of British political studies excludes from the history of the field whole areas of British political thinking—the Anglo-Marxist tradition, for example[27]—so too does the whiggish story of British international thought. The influence of continental European sociology and the enthusiastic embrace of formal modeling, behavioralism, and systems theory by some British international theorists are all omitted from the conventional narrative. And the whiggish story also obscures important divisions among British thinkers—not least, as we shall see, between philosophical Idealist historicists, on the one hand, and "modernist empiricists" on the other. As we shall see, there was a great deal more variety, and more disagreement, in British international thought in the postwar period than the conventional history suggests. It obscures, too, important links between British intellectuals and their American counterparts, many of whom shared epistemological beliefs and methodological commitments and agreed on far more than they disputed. Above all, the whig story conveys too little about the extent of change in postwar thinking and what stimulated it.

This is a problem because demands for new thinking were just as common in the postwar years—if not indeed more common—than demands for the preservation of some kind of hallowed, "classical approach" to the problems of world politics. By the late 1960s, even the staunchest conservatives—like Max Beloff—could not resist this mood. In his *Future of British Foreign Policy* (1969) Beloff argued with some passion that the novel circumstances in which Britain found itself almost rendered traditional ways of thinking about international relations defunct. "Attitudes proper to the citizens of a world power," he complained, have been "carried over into the new situation." In psychological terms, Britain's ego was out of all proportion to the country's present importance; in political terms, Britain's inherited policies and their conventional alternatives were obsolete. Arrogant imperialism had been rendered impossible by the loss of economic and military power, but liberals and radicals needed also to realize the limits of Britain's capabilities. Those "who talk of Britain's duty to set an example to the world" by unilateral disarmament or some similar moral cause, Beloff noted, are "just as much the heirs of empire as the most belligerent protagonist of national interest on the extreme Right."[28] British thinking needed to be cut down to size; Britain must abandon its striving to be "the Athens of example," as Bernard Crick put it in 1959, just as Britons had already abandoned their aspirations to be "the Rome of power."[29]

This difficult process of intellectual decolonization—conscious and unconscious, never quite completed, but nonetheless conceived by many British thinkers as an important response to decline—is one longitudinal theme of this book. So too is the opening up of British international thought to novel ways of thinking about world politics. And there are others. The first is intrusion of a variety of foreign influences and ideas into Britain and into British thinking about international politics, as well as the reactions they generated—whether welcoming, hostile, or frankly uncomprehending. These intrusions came with movements of people and money (from foundations and think tanks, mainly from the United States), as well as of ideas. In the 1930s, Britain, like America, had witnessed the immigration of a number of prominent thinkers, academics, and scientists. Some, like the German-Jewish Hans Morgenthau, who later forged a reputation as one of the foremost "realists" in the study of international relations in the United States, quickly passed through Britain on the way to greener pastures (in Morgenthau's case, first Kansas, then Chicago, and finally New York).[30] Others, such as the historian Lewis Namier (in 1907), the political theorist Isaiah Berlin (in 1921), and the philosopher Karl Popper (in 1946) joined an émigré community already prominent in British intellectual life. Indeed, if it is stretched to include the children of recent immigrants—such as the classicist and international relations specialist Alfred Zimmern, born to German parents, or indeed Max Beloff, of Central European Jewish lineage—and to scholars from various parts of the Empire-Commonwealth, especially Australians, including Keith Hancock and Hedley Bull, but also South Africans like C. A. W. Manning—this group constituted a significant proportion of those working on political and international themes in Britain in the postwar period.

Together, though emphatically not in any coordinated way, these individuals exerted considerable influence over the development of British international thought after 1945. So too did the influx of foreign finance and ideas—especially, from the 1950s onward, from the United States. Both posed their own dilemmas. American foundations, among them the highly active Rockefeller Foundation, were assiduous in cultivating British intellectuals, paying for their travel expenses to and from the United States, drawing them into conversations at august gatherings at Princeton's Institute for Advanced Studies and like settings, and funding their research endeavors, such as Herbert Butterfield's British Committee on the Theory of International Politics.[31] American political science, particularly in its "behaviorial" form, was more of a concern to the British, suggesting as it did a wholly different way of thinking about politics from that to which they were, on the whole, accustomed. While some—a greater number than is sometimes, with blinkered hindsight, recognized—embraced all or part of this new American thinking, many reacted with distaste and disgust. A few, like the historian and international theorist Martin Wight, even thought it downright demonic.[32] The impact of American political science did, however, provoke British intellectuals to consider more extensively—if not more deeply—the virtues and the limitations of their own ways of approaching and thinking about political and international issues.

Although many were unwilling to surrender the field to American methods, British thinkers did not simply retreat behind the barricades of a "classical approach." Plenty of "good old fellows," as Bernard Crick called them, could still be found well into the 1970s, the sort of scholars "who had no fancy thoughts about the epistemological problems of theory and practice." For them, the study of politics and international relations was uncomplicated and there was no need for change; they simply "assumed that if [you] lived in London or Oxford (or in Sir Denis Brogan's case could get away from Cambridge), you . . . talked to civil servants and Cabinet Ministers, as in the good old days of the war, and sat hard on committees."[33] These views were less and less common, however, as the postwar period wore on. Snide questioning of the possible benefits of asking such questions as "how far the study of international relations can be scientific . . . or . . . whether the student of international politics can learn more from mathematics or from Machiavelli?" continued well into the 1970s, if not later, but by that time they were under challenge.[34] For Beloff and for many others, they represented a "general laxness of political thinking," if not outright "decadence in thought."[35]

The thinkers doing the thinking also changed, albeit more slowly. Those who thought and wrote about world politics in Britain in the three decades after 1945 were not, on the whole, specialists, and professional "IR" scholars did not emerge until the mid- to late 1960s. The bulk of those concerned with the field were rather historians and classicists, philosophers and lawyers, sociologists and anthropologists, active and retired diplomats, politicians and journalists. Area studies—work on particular states or regions—far outweighed work on the "international system" as a whole. Very few of the intellectuals discussed in what follows worked in university departments of "international politics" or "international relations." Such departments did, of course, exist—notably at the University College of Wales, Aberystwyth (later the University of Wales, Aberystwyth, and now just the University of Aberystwyth) and, most important of all, at the LSE—but their academic staff formed only a small proportion of those who wrote about or taught the subject in one manner or another.

From the end of the Second World War to the mid-1970s, academic specialists in international relations remained a small minority of all those concerned with their conduct. The same was true, of course, in the British study of politics more generally. In both cases, the contrast with the parallel development of the academic disciplines in the United States is revealing. Whereas in 1950 the American Political Science Association (APSA) could claim over 5,000 (mostly American) members, fewer than 100 came together that same year to found its British counterpart, the Political Studies Association (PSA). Two decades later, in 1970, APSA had grown to over 13,500, while the PSA had merely doubled in size to about 200 members.[36] Of all those British scholars belonging to the PSA, only a handful were primarily concerned with international, as opposed to domestic, politics.[37] Granted, some did not join the PSA, preferring Chatham House or the International Institute for Strategic Studies (IISS, founded as the Institute for Strategic Studies in 1958), or indeed choosing no particular affiliation, but the academic field of international relations in Britain cannot be considered by any reasonable measure to have been overpopulated in the period between the mid-1940s and the mid-1970s.[38]

For much of the 1950s and 1960s, moreover, the few specialists there were—like Charles Manning, Montague Burton Professor of International Relations at the London School of Economics (1930–62), or P. A. Reynolds, Woodrow Wilson Professor at Aberystwyth (1948–62)—were frequently besieged by critics. They were repeatedly harangued for their ideological positions and especially for the intellectual claims they made for their supposed "discipline."[39] They were far outnumbered and indeed outmaneuvered, in bureaucratic and sometimes intellectual terms, in political life and in the press, by the far more numerous and powerful historians. When newspapers, serious periodicals, diplomats, or even prime ministers wanted comment on international affairs, it was to historians that they turned: to Lewis Namier or Charles Webster or even Arnold J. Toynbee during the late 1940s and 1950s, and to Herbert Butterfield, Michael Howard, and especially A. J. P. Taylor throughout the years covered here.

The public prominence of historians in British intellectual life was matched by the sway they held in academia, especially in the ancient universities.[40] At Oxford, the historians were so dominant that the specialists did not gain more than the odd foothold until well into the late 1970s and early 1980s.[41] The official history of St Antony's College captures the prevailing prejudice against pretensions of the new "discipline" well, if unintentionally. Somewhat archly, it notes that it was only "towards the end of the 1970s," some forty years after Montague Burton founded a chair at Oxford in the subject, that "it became clear" to members of the University "that international relations was an increasingly attractive area of study."[42] At Oxford, indeed, the field was not even favored in the quarters where one might expect enthusiasm, among the professors charged with the duty of studying it. The incumbent of the Montague Burton Chair from 1948 to 1970, Agnes Headlam-Morley, was a diplomatic historian and a staunch opponent of the study of contemporary international relations, let alone the use of newfangled social scientific methods.[43] It was not coincidental that the Oxford BPhil (now MPhil) in the subject was introduced only after her retirement, in 1971.

To the historians should be added the many activists, politicians, journalists, writers, and concerned intellectuals who contributed to the conversation about world politics and Britain's role. Their ideas influenced and reflected public perceptions and scholarly debate. They included campaigners for international peace and organizations like the veteran Norman Angell; the redoubtable Kathleen Courtney, the suffragette and doyenne of the League of Nations Union and United Nations Association; and the ubiquitous Bertrand Russell, amongst many others. Significant ideas on international affairs were contributed too by practitioners like Anthony Eden, Denis Healey, and, above all, Winston Churchill, whose framing of Britain's place in the postwar world was an inescapable point of reference. Of note too are the many religious voices of the time, those of churchmen or laypeople, especially during the short-lived but broad-based revival of Christian thought and practice in the 1940s and early 1950s.[44] Their ideas are scattered throughout contemporary periodicals—in the *Listener*, *Spectator*, or quarterlies—and are varied in tone, doctrine, and political orientation, from Donald Soper's radical pacifism to the neo-orthodox conservatism of V. A. Demant.[45] Finally, there are the novelists, poets, and essayists, some of whom supplied far more lasting interpretations of postwar international politics than any academic.[46]

This diversity of the intellectuals concerned with world politics combined with the ferment of new thinking and foreign influences all militate against a strictly "disciplinary" approach to the intellectual history of the postwar period and against a whiggish narrative. Neither, I argue, can adequately capture the work that was done or the ideas that emerged. Instead, as we shall see in the next chapter, this book adopts a different approach, one that aims to trace the evolution of traditions of thought as they were adopted, adapted, or abandoned by concerned British intellectuals in response to the challenges—dilemmas—they perceived. These dilemmas were sometimes political—the greatest of which being, of course, Britain's decline—and sometimes intellectual, in terms of new facts, methods, or ideas. Once they were perceived, they prompted thinkers to rethink their inherited beliefs, retrench their preferred tradition, or reject what they had once held dear. The narrative that follows is thus neither linear nor necessarily progressive, nor is it intended as a celebration of British thought in the postwar years.

DILEMMAS OF DECLINE

> Either we can abdicate at the price of renouncing our great possessions, or we can take part in the coming struggle in the hope that, if we throw our weight into the scales against the European dictatorships, then the World dominion which will be the prize of the struggle will fall, not to Germany and her confederates, but to North America. As we cannot be, and do not want to be, the World conquerors ourselves, there would be much to be said for abdicating and accepting the political impotence and economic poverty which abdication would necessarily carry with it. But I doubt this is practical politics. I am afraid that my conclusion is gloomy, but I have no belief at all in the possibility of "getting by" as the Americans say, in the next act of the tragedy.
> ARNOLD TOYNBEE to Lord Allen of Hurtwood, 11 May 1938 [47]

The biggest dilemma that British intellectuals faced in the postwar years was decline. How they addressed it—and how they failed to address it—is a core theme of this book. But British thinkers also confronted a number of other, lesser dilemmas. Chapter 3 discusses the first of these—the dilemma posed by the rise of "political realism" in the late 1930s and early 1940s. While some welcomed "realism" as a means of exposing the apparent hypocrisy of the dominant British tradition of thought and practice in world politics, liberalism, most British intellectuals were suspicious of its implications, as well as the appeal it held for totalitarian governments and those who wished to "appease" them. Rather than accept realism or modify it for their own uses, as some American contemporaries did in the 1940s, most British thinkers rejected the tradition outright, at least in the first instance, and only began to acknowledge some of its virtues in the 1960s and 1970s.

This spurning of realism was not a function of blind confidence in liberalism or internationalism. Liberalism persisted into the 1950s as the dominant tradition, as chapter 4 explains, but largely because of the longevity and energy of leading liberals. Faith in liberalism and internationalism were both shaken by the Second World War and by the emergence of the Cold War. As a result, as chapters 4 and 5 discuss, liberals and internationalists struggled hard to explain these events and to reform and retrench their inherited beliefs. While leading liberals feared that their core principles rested less on human nature or historical progress than on power and contingency, internationalists from across the political spectrum wrestled with a series of dilemmas: the corruption of nationalism, the failures of international organization, and the difficulties of maintaining cooperation on transnational challenges.

While liberals and internationalists fretted about the viability of their traditional modes of thought, they were challenged by the invention, reinvention, or revival of other traditions. On the one side, a group of diplomats and historians, beginning with Harold Nicolson and ending with Herbert Butterfield's British Committee on the Theory of International Politics, attempted to construct or reconstruct a "whig" tradition of international thought. For the "whigs," discussed in chapter 6, the dilemmas of the twentieth century were best met by recovering and then adhering to an apparently venerable tradition once lost, one that emphasized tolerance over righteousness, historical-mindedness over presentism, and the old diplomacy over the new. On the other side were the radicals, the subject of chapter 7. The radicals rejected not just the preferred responses of liberals, internationalists, and whigs to the core dilemmas Britain faced in the postwar years, they rejected also the way the dilemmas were conceived. Their focus was imperialism and anti-imperialism, directing attention not to politics but to economics, and latterly—as enthusiasts for a series of new methods—to psychology and other harder sciences.

Chapter 8 turns to one of the major dilemmas Britons faced in the postwar years: the end of empire. Far from being indifferent to decolonization, as some historians have suggested, many British intellectuals were deeply concerned with the loss of its overseas territories and dominions. This chapter traces the various reactions they had to the so-called revolt against the West and the implications they believed it had for world politics. Chapter 9 addresses the other major dilemmas of war and peace, of how best to wage war in a nuclear age, and how to maintain peace in the shadow of Armageddon. These dilemmas gave rise to two sets of academic work—strategic studies and peace research—that integrated new knowledge and approaches from indigenous and overseas sources. In the conclusion, I discuss the various ways in which these modes of thought, together with the evolving traditions addressed in earlier chapters, shaped the emergence of a discipline of international relations in British universities and influenced the direction of British policy.

Before turning to these substantive issues, however, the next chapter outlines and justifies the approach taken to their analysis, one that emphasizes the importance of traditions and dilemmas in the history of international thought.

2. Traditions and Dilemmas

> Tradition is unavoidable as a starting point, not as a final destination.
> MARK BEVIR, *The Logic of the History of Ideas* (1999)

Since the mid-1990s two parallel developments have transformed the way in which the history of international thought is understood and its historiography written.[1] On the one hand, specialists in international relations—especially those animated by postpositivist concerns—have become increasingly interested in their "disciplinary history" and the history of the field more broadly.[2] On the other, historians of political thought have begun to turn their attention to international relations, producing a series of works examining, in particular, the origins of European imperialism.[3] These two movements have helped to reconnect the fields of international political theory and intellectual history, if not quite to heal what David Armitage has called the "fifty years' rift" between the two.[4]

These two developments have also stimulated a considerable if somewhat lopsided debate over method. Both the IR scholars and the historians have tended to agree that older approaches to the history of international thought were flawed. The major complaints are that these older accounts, such as Martin Wight's "three traditions,"[5] are too often insensitive to the historical contexts within which a text was written, anachronistic in their interpretations of past theories, and Procrustean in forcing past thinkers into often ahistorical "traditions" or "paradigms."[6] When it comes to the ways in which these problems might be overcome, however, splits have emerged between the IR scholars and the historians. While the historians of political thought have tended to push one agenda—that of Cambridge School "contextualism"[7]—interested specialists in IR have been far more varied in their approaches.[8] As a result, substantive disagreement remains about how best to study past international thought.

This chapter outlines the approach taken in this book, but it also suggests a way forward for students of the field that resolves some of the major disagreements between the historians of political thought and IR scholars. The next section describes the background to these disagreements and gives a brief account of the development of the intellectual history of international thought. The remainder of the chapter explores the approach taken in what follows, an approach derived especially from Bevir's *Logic of the History of Ideas* (1999) and associated writings. In particular, it addresses the implicit concern of some IR theorists that an insistence on contextualism renders the history of international thought into a kind of antiquarianism with little or nothing to say to contemporary theory. In so doing, it restores a concern with the evolution of ideas over time, giving it equal weight to the kinds of "cross-sections" of history favored by Cambridge School contextualists, and a connection between the worlds of intellectual endeavor and political practice. Finally, it also restores the recently much-maligned concept of "traditions," not as structures or paradigms but as vital tools in comprehending the beliefs of past thinkers.

INTELLECTUAL HISTORY IN INTERNATIONAL RELATIONS

> As we looked along the perspective of history we saw a succession of isolated thinkers, and heard voices crying out in the wilderness, pointing out the right way...
> F. MELIAN STAWELL, *The Growth of International Thought* (1929)[9]

A concern for the intellectual history of thought about world politics runs back into the interwar years, if not before. In 1919, for example, D. P. Heatley published an undergraduate textbook entitled *Diplomacy and the Study of International Relations* which included substantial extracts from treaties, what he called "juristic literature," "controversial literature," works on diplomacy, and treatises on international ethics.[10] Heatley, an historian at the University of Edinburgh, was moved both by the desire to better educate the public about world politics and by the perceived need to lay out the principles by which he thought international relations were conducted. His immediate aim was to dispel the notion that the conduct of foreign policy was merely a pragmatic and reactive activity. Other writers of this period had similar concerns. Melian Stawell, an Australian who taught at Newnham College, Cambridge, wished her *Growth of International Thought* (1929) would point "the way to internationalism."[11] Her survey of European international thought from the Greeks to the present was thus heavier on cosmopolitanism and various schemes for perpetual peace than Heatley's, though it had much the same intention.

Neither Heatley nor Stawell dwelt much on their methods. Heatley's book offered a rather meandering introductory essay on the conduct of foreign policy followed by an exhaustive series of bibliographical notes on, and extracts from, canonical texts (Machiavelli and the anti-Machiavels, for example), as well as discussions of various episodes in the history of European diplomacy. But nowhere did Heatley spell out the criteria he used for the selection of texts. Stawell was only slightly more informative. Arguing that all the "best thinkers of Europe" had perceived that a "sane nationalism" must end in "internationalism," and that "a single State cannot end with the single State," she constructed a canon accordingly.[12] Beginning with Socrates, Aristotle, Pericles, Alexander the Great, the Stoics, the Church Fathers, Dante, Machiavelli, More, Erasmus, Sully, Grotius, Rousseau, Burke, Kant, and Goethe all loom large in Stawell's text, but apart from Machiavelli most of the exponents of raison d'état or *Realpolitik* are excluded, as befitted her theme.

The idea of traditions of international thought did not loom large in these early texts. Both hint at a Machiavellian tradition of amoralism, but neither discussed it in much detail. In Britain it was only in the mid-1930s that the notion of "realist" or "idealist" traditions of thought emerged, and this occurred mainly in response to a change in the terms of political rhetoric rather than scholarly thinking.[13] It was of course E. H. Carr that used these categories to greatest effect, deploying "realism" and "utopianism" to make his case for the appeasement of Nazi Germany and imperial Japan in his *Twenty Years' Crisis*.[14] Carr's account of the realist tradition—analyzed here in more detail in chapter 3—was, however, unorthodox. He distinguished between two realisms: an older realism, born of Machiavelli and elaborated upon by Bodin, Hobbes and Spinoza, and a "modern realism," of which Hegel and Marx were the greatest exponents.[15] Carr's "utopianism" was even more venerable, but no less eccentric, beginning with Plato and ending with Winston Churchill.

In the 1940s and 1950s, the idea of "realist" and "idealist" traditions of international thought, promoted initially only by self-proclaimed "realists," took hold in Britain and the United States. Considerable effort was put into establishing their core principles and the membership of both traditions.[16] This did not happen, however, without some questioning from scholars working in the field. Some, like Georg Schwarzenberger, argued that the "battles between so-called realists and idealists" were a distraction from proper scholarship; others, including Martin Wight, suggested that the categories of "realism" and "idealism" failed to capture the complexities of past international thought.[17]

To address this problem, Wight first proposed organizing the history of international thought into three rather than two traditions.[18] In a series of lectures delivered at Chicago and the London School of Economics between 1956 and 1960, subsequently published as *International Theory* (1990), Wight identified and described "realist" (or Machiavellian), "rationalist" (or Grotian), and "revolutionist" (or Kantian) traditions. Wight's effort was pioneering but not without its problems, as he himself appreciated and his critics have been keen to point out. His "traditions" were somewhat artificial and Procrustean, sometimes distorting what a text states or what an author intended in order to fit them into one or other tradition. His treatment of Kant, for example, was dubious. Wight called Kant a "revolutionist" and thereby implied that like the other "revolutionists" he included in this tradition, Kant believed that the end justified the means.[19] As Chris Brown has noted, this was hardly a fair or accurate representation of Kant's moral philosophy.[20]

In his later work, Wight moved away from his "three traditions" and toward an approach that concentrated more on what A. O. Lovejoy called "unit-ideas." His most polished essays on the history of international thought, such as "Western Values in International Relations" (1966) concentrated more on what particular thinkers had to say on particular issues, such as human nature, war, international organization, and so on, rather than trying to construct overarching "traditions."[21] In the work of Wight's followers, however, the notion of traditions proved remarkably resilient. Hedley Bull, Michael Donelan, Robert Jackson, Brian Porter, and others all contributed significant efforts to the study of particular traditions of thought, and the contemporary "English school" also retains the conviction that the "traditions" approach is a particularly valuable one.[22] It remains powerful too among "realists," who have recently published a series of works exploring that particular tradition.[23]

In the contemporary discipline of international relations, the principal competitor to the traditions approach is one that concentrates rather on "paradigms." This approach, which draws upon Thomas Kuhn's work on the history of science,[24] is far more prevalent in North America than in Europe or Australia, at least since the late 1980s.[25] In both contexts, the idea of a "paradigm" has been used in different ways. In much American work, the "paradigm" has been employed in a sense much closer to Kuhn's original intention—that is, to describe a set of fundamental precepts agreed upon by all or almost all thinkers working in a given field. Thus utilized, American scholars have sought to tell disciplinary histories that emphasize the progress or degeneration of research programs and the accumulation of knowledge about a given field.[26] By contrast, British and some Canadian scholars have tended to use "paradigm" in a looser way, arguing—contrary to Kuhn's account of scientific development—that a number of different paradigms with "incommensurable" precepts can exist simultaneously.[27]

Since the early 1990s, however, a growing number of scholars have voiced disquiet with the uses of "traditions" and "paradigms" in the intellectual history of the field. They have complained that corralling thinkers and texts into such categories does violence to the distinct meanings particular intellectuals intended to convey. With these problems in mind, historians of international thought from the discipline of both history and IR have recently tended to eschew or at least qualify the use of "traditions" or "paradigms." Instead, in the main, they have followed one of three different approaches—contextualism, poststructuralism, and "internal discursive history." In these ways, they have sought to provide a more historically accurate portrayal of the development of thinking about international relations and, indeed, to furnish better accounts of what particular thinkers intended to say.

In two of these approaches, the contextualist and the poststructural, the focus is directed at the contemporary contexts within which a thinker or thinkers worked—exploring, in other words, cross-sections or "snapshots" of history rather than developments over time. The "contextualists," inspired by the work of the Cambridge history of ideas school, especially that of J. G. A. Pocock and Quentin Skinner, have concentrated upon the political languages "available" to political thinkers, arguing that delineating the linguistic context of a text provides the best means to discerning what message the author intended to convey at a particular historical moment.[28] The poststructural school, drawing on the work of Michel Foucault, roams wider, seeking to map the "discourses" of any given field, relate them to "sites" and relationships of power, and to thus describe the ways in which discourses shape the "production of knowledge."[29] Their interests are not confined to linguistic contexts, but to political, economic and social ones, arguing that there is a direct and intimate relationship between the ways in which the structures of society are described and the functioning of those structures.

While both the contextualists and poststructuralists avoid discussion of "traditions" for fear of anachronism or essentialism, the internal discursive historians do make use of the concept, albeit it in a pared-down form. Their argument is that historians of political and international thought should concentrate only on those "traditions" of thinking that emerge from scholarly discussions, over time, about a particular topic that defines particular academic disciplines. These might be "democracy" in the case of American political science or "anarchy" in the study of international relations.[30] These topics serve as the poles around which the "internal discourses" of disciplines revolve.

In internal discursive histories "historical traditions" of work are thereby distinguished from the artificial and constructed "analytical traditions" used by political and international theorists with a tendency to cast intellectual history into "epic" narratives. For John Gunnell or Brian Schmidt, two prominent exponents of this approach, historians can thus circumvent the problems posed by R. G. Collingwood's famous historicist assertion that there cannot be a grand tradition of political theory because political theorists in every age were not providing different answers to the same question, but rather offering answers to wholly different questions. Though we should not (and arguably cannot) construct "epic" traditions, Gunnell and Schmidt argue that we can reconstruct lesser patterns of influence over time, rather than just concentrate on cross-sections of the past as the contextualists often imply we ought to do.[31] For the internal discursive historians, therefore, we can talk about a "tradition" when we can demonstrate that thinkers have the same question in mind—thus there was, for example, a tradition of political speculation about the best ordering of the Greek polis, just as there is arguably a continuing tradition, in IR, about anarchy—though not, of course, when the defining topic of a given discipline changes.

Using these new approaches—contextualism, poststructuralism, and internal discursive history—a series of recent studies have dispelled a number of self-serving or merely inaccurate "disciplinary myths" in the study of international relations and its past,[32] as well as highlighting a number of methodological problems for intellectual histories of the field. But they have not completely dislodged the notion of "tradition" from international relations. What Renée Jeffery has named the "traditions tradition"—the practice of describing past and present international thought in terms of distinct traditions—has proved tenacious, despite calls from some intellectual historians to set aside such historiographically questionable notions.[33] International relations theory, for example, continues to be taught in terms of traditions: realism, liberalism, constructivism, poststructuralism, feminism, and many others.[34] Indeed, it is difficult to conceive of a way of dispensing with the terms, providing as they do convenient shorthand for designating particular theories or positions.

Pedagogic utility is not, however, the only reason why traditions are so difficult to dispense with in writing intellectual history. As Mark Bevir has argued, traditions are indispensible concepts in explaining the formation of thinkers' "webs of belief"—the ideas they hold about the world that allow them to make sense of it which they have acquired through processes of socialization.[35] It is impossible accurately to describe a particular thinker's thought without reference to those beliefs and theories that they had inherited, still less to determine what contribution they may or may not have made to their field.[36] The concept of a "tradition" cannot but play a critical role in the interpretation of a thinker's beliefs—the question is how best to conceive them and to analyze them.

THE USES OF TRADITION

> [I]t belongs to the nature of a tradition to tolerate and unite an internal variety, not insisting upon conformity to a single character, and because, further, it has the ability to change without losing its identity.
> MICHAEL OAKESHOTT, "Introduction to *Leviathan*" (1946)[37]

This book brings traditions back into the intellectual history of international thought, albeit under particular conditions.[38] It argues that accurate interpretations of texts require understandings not merely of the contemporary linguistic context or prevailing discourse, but of the intellectual inheritance bequeathed to an author by his or her forebears and of the ways in which an author modifies, retrenches, or abandons his or her understanding of that tradition. It follows Bevir in arguing that "we should conceive of a tradition primarily as an initial influence on people" and not as "a defining presence on all one believes or does."[39] It does not aim to reduce this or that intellectual's ideas to a monolithic tradition or to test a thinker's work to see if it fits or deviates from a tradition. To do this implies—wrongly—that traditions have an existence independent of individuals. Traditions are better understood as sets of connected beliefs and theories residing in individuals, in those that bequeath them to others, or in those that inherit them from their parents, teachers, or other authorities.

Viewing traditions in this way avoids many of the problems that have arisen with the notion in histories of international thought. First, it discourages anachronism, not least in the temptation to "invent" traditions that were not understood as such by past thinkers.[40] We should only talk of a particular tradition in relation to a particular individual who saw themselves as an inheritor of that tradition or can be established as such in retrospect beyond the bounds of ordinary historical doubt by identifying key teachers or texts read or signs of influence in their work. This meets the historicist insistence that—as far as possible—past thought be seen "their way," through the eyes of contemporaries rather than those of the present.[41]

Second, it guards against the dangers that flow from what might be called the "hypostatizing" of traditions. Traditions do not and cannot exist apart from the beliefs of individuals and groups of individuals that adhere to them or reject them. It makes little sense, therefore, to write historical studies of past thinkers that attempt to demonstrate how they might "fit" a tradition or how they fail to "fit" within its boundaries. The practice of intellectual history cannot be a matter of ticking applicable boxes or seeing if a thinker "tests positive" for particular beliefs.[42] What matters, in terms of explaining what a past thinker thought, is what they inherited and how they accepted, modified, and rejected aspects of that inheritance. Seeing traditions in this light allows for us to discuss the influence of more than one tradition on a particular intellectual and requires us to acknowledge that past thinkers often inherit, during the course of their education, knowledge of a number of different traditions. In this book, for example, there are thinkers whose thought is shaped by the liberal, "whig," and indeed radical traditions and is not reducible to one or the other.

Third, understanding traditions in this way militates against the notion that they can be understood as "structures" containing or limiting thought—an idea also latent in some uses of the term "paradigm."[43] Like a financial inheritance, an individual can use the traditions of thought they inherit in many different ways. They can reconceive core beliefs or shift emphasis from one to another, thus modifying the tradition. They can even abandon an inherited tradition for another one that did not figure in their original inheritance. Liberals can become socialists; Christians can become Buddhists. In what follows, internationalists like E. H. Carr become radicals; youthful radicals like Martin Wight become conservative "whigs." As Bevir argues: "Tradition is the unavoidable background to what all we say and do, but not a constitutive process in all we say and do. Individuals can come to hold beliefs, and so act, only against the background of a social inheritance; but this inheritance does not limit the beliefs they later can go on to hold, or the actions they can go on to perform."[44] Employing the concept of traditions does not thus deny agency, but rather highlights the extent to which individuals can and do change their beliefs.

THE IMPORTANCE OF DILEMMAS

> The general war of 1914 overtook me expounding Thucydides to Balliol undergraduates ... and then suddenly my understanding was illuminated. The experiences we were having in our world now had been experienced by Thucydides in his world already.
> ARNOLD J. TOYNBEE, "My View of History" (1948)[45]

Why, then, do individuals change their beliefs? Historians of international thought offer a number of different answers to this question and some—notably the contextualists—sometimes ignore it altogether, treating it as an issue exogenous to their concerns. Two particular answers, however, stand out. Many intellectual historians argue that thinkers change their beliefs and modify traditions in response to external stimuli, to real-world events or developments. Thus Stanley Hoffmann famously argued that the emergence of the subfield of international relations, that very "American Social Science," was a function of the rise to superpower status of the United States.[46] Some—notably internal discursive historians like Gunnell and Schmidt—maintain instead that these changes come from the ordinary processes of academic discourse, the to and fro of intellectual exchange within disciplines. For such historians, "Developments in the field ... have been informed more by disciplinary trends in political science and by the character of the American university than by external events taking place in international politics."[47]

The argument that developments outside the walls of universities matter, in terms of prompting individuals to modify, retrench, or abandon their beliefs, comes moreover in both determinist and nondeterminist forms. The determinist form of the argument posits that relationships of power dictate patterns of thought, or at least that there is a connection between the material circumstances of the thinker and what they think. This argument is often derived—albeit normally second hand, through E. H. Carr's *Twenty Years' Crisis*[48]—from Karl Mannheim's sociology of knowledge.[49] In Carr's hands, Mannheim's theory about the relationship of power and knowledge was used to allege that the appeal of the liberal tradition of international thought (which he called "utopianism") rested less on the validity of its claims to universality than on British economic and military strength. This "utopianism" was not selfless, Carr wrote. Instead, "the intellectual theories and ethical standards of utopianism," he argued, "far from being the expression of absolute and *a priori* principles, are historically conditioned, being both products of circumstances and interests and weapons framed for the furtherance of interests."[50]

This kind of assertion can be found throughout much writing on the intellectual history of political science and international relations. Where Hoffmann and other nondeterminists have argued that these fields emerged and developed as what might be called the handmaidens of American power, serving particular needs of the government, military and business, others have gone further, implying that what is thought within these disciplines is a direct product of that power. The first contention, to be clear, is that disciplinary development is a result of circumstance; the second, by contrast, insists that these disciplines were determined to develop in a particular way because of some kind of necessary relationship between power and knowledge. Hoffmann's suggestion that "intellectual predispositions, political circumstances, and institutional opportunities" shaped the evolution of American IR illustrates the first of these, as Haslam's suggestion that "British decline" brought about a "decline in British thinking" about world politics after 1945, especially in British "realist" thinking, illustrates the second.[51]

There are a number of problems with the determinist argument. Above all, it is unclear whether the empirical evidence for such direct and necessary relationships between power and knowledge actually exists. Not all postwar American political scientists welcomed America's rise to power, not all American theories of IR treat the acquisition and extension of that power as a good, and not all of these alternative theories can be considered "marginal" or "marginalized" in any meaningful way.[52] Moreover, the determinists have not yet done enough to demonstrate that alternative explanations for critical episodes in the intellectual history of the field are wrong. I have argued elsewhere, for example, that the rejection of "realism" by British thinkers in the 1940s was less a function of declining British power than a result of their associating the term with appeasement and totalitarianism.[53] In the absence of good reasons to dismiss explanations like this, which rely on explanatory narratives of contingent events rather than grand sociological arguments, there are grounds to be suspicious of the determinist case.

Rather than seeking to explain changes of belief in terms of changes in power, Bevir argues that we can more reliably account for such changes by examining the responses of individuals to perceived "specifiable dilemmas" involving the modification of existing traditions or the advent of new theories.[54] This approach has a number of virtues. First, it allows us to cope better with the diversity of responses that we see, empirically, in the intellectual history of international thought. Second, it opens a space for us to tell a story about the ways in which traditions are modified over time. Third, though perhaps more important, it permits us to retain a commitment to agency.

For Bevir, a "dilemma" refers to a problem that arises when a thinker accepts some new belief to be true which does not fit with their existing beliefs, informed by inherited traditions. These dilemmas—to use Schmidt's terms[55]—can be exogenous or endogenous in origin. They can come from real-world events or academic discussion. "Dilemmas can arise," Bevir argues, "from an experience of the relationships of production, an acquaintance with a philosophical argument or scientific theory, a mystical experience, an encounter with a different culture, and so on."[56] If these experiences are judged to be meaningful, they will prompt new beliefs that will be subsumed into an individual's "web of beliefs."

These new beliefs may or may not be consistent with other beliefs. Where they are inconsistent, a "dilemma" is produced, and a thinker may rationally reappraise their beliefs better to accommodate the new one, and in so doing, may adjust and modify a tradition of thinking about a particular subject. Thus, Bevir maintains, Darwin's theory of evolution required Victorians either to reject it wholeheartedly or to modify their religious beliefs in line with the new view of the world that it suggested.[57] No particular reaction or modification, it should be pointed out, was determined by the advent of this or any other theory—individual responses could, of course, take a number of different forms, depending on the traditions they had inherited and the beliefs they held to be true. Arnold J. Toynbee's much-quoted description of the moment his perceptions of both Thucydides and contemporary world politics changed also illustrates this process well. The outbreak of war forced a reevaluation of his beliefs, but the modifications he made were not predetermined. Thucydides has moved many intellectuals to take a "realist" line, but his effect on Toynbee was quite different—it prompted him to begin a lifelong search for another way of grounding his liberalism to the one he had inherited.[58]

By reference to dilemmas, therefore, we can account for changes in the thought of individuals and for changes in the traditions that they carry within their webs of belief. We can thus tell stories of how particular thinkers developed their theories and how traditions evolved as their inheritors passed them—changed or unchanged—from one generation to the next. Without being inattentive to context, we can also be attentive to longitudinal patterns of continuity and transformation in the history of international thought.

TRADITIONS AND DILEMMAS IN POSTWAR BRITISH INTERNATIONAL THOUGHT

> I became Gladstone Professor in the year [1957] before the collapse of the Fourth Republic; I resigned my chair in the year [1974] in which a British government duly elected and enjoying a reasonable Parliamentary majority was forced to the polls; it was also the year in which an American President elected by a very large majority was obliged to resign to avoid impeachment. . . . During the seventeen years of my tenure of the chair the dissolution of the European empires overseas was brought almost to completion, and in almost every case the newly enfranchised state was able to keep going only at the price of some form of despotic rule . . . The United Nations lost its effectiveness and respect with almost every addition to its membership; its claim to represent the collective conscience of mankind was even more far-fetched at the end of the period than at its beginning.
> MAX BELOFF, "The Politics of Oxford 'Politics'" (1975)[59]

Britain's postwar decline and the wider condition of world politics in the postwar period posed a series of dilemmas: some apparent, some real, some perceived, and others woefully misunderstood. They demanded responses and, when they came, they were highly varied in form, some drawing upon inherited ways of interpreting international relations and Britain's place with them, some rejecting them and striking out in novel directions. This book explores some of these responses, agreeing with Bevir's argument that intellectual historians need both "diachronic" and "synchronic" explanations of ideas, providing accounts of change as snapshots of when, where, how, and by whom texts were composed.[60]

One major challenge, however, lurks in this endeavor. To tell diachronic stories in the way that Bevir would have it depends on identifying "traditions," and he gives little guidance in *The Logic of the History of Ideas* or elsewhere as to how to do this. He implies that all a child might learn from his or her parents and teachers might be considered a "tradition," which suggests that a tradition might be very broad indeed.[61] At the same time, however, Bevir argues that when historians analyze the thought of a particular thinker, they "can select traditions to suit their different purposes." This does not mean, of course, that one can choose any tradition at all. What matters, when it comes to explaining someone's beliefs, is the "explanatory power" of a tradition, and the narrower the historian defines a tradition, the greater that power is likely to be.[62] And, further, the tradition must have some kind of internal coherence—its beliefs and theories must be linked together in some way and there must be clear processes of transmission from person to person.[63]

Clearly, on these criteria, many traditions could be identified in British international thought. We could have Anglican or Catholic traditions (contrast, for example, William Temple's ideas about international order with Christopher Dawson's)[64] and High Tory or Trotskyite traditions. These would each yield insights into the darker corners of British international thought, but perhaps not give the kind of synoptic view required in this book. Instead, I have chosen five broad traditions—realism, liberalism, internationalism, "whiggism," and radicalism. Not all of these were what might be called indigenous traditions and not all of them had particularly long pedigrees. All five, however, had a significant and lasting impact.

Realism, in all of its varieties, was very much an import, at least as a tradition of thought. Its origins were traced by E. H. Carr back to Machiavelli, and almost all British intellectuals of the postwar period considered its evolution dependent on German political thinkers, with all the negative associations they evoked. Liberalism, on the other hand, was far more characteristically British, the product of Jeremy Bentham and John Stuart Mill and the New Liberals of the late nineteenth century rather than—as later liberals would have it—that of Immanuel Kant. So too were internationalism, which also came in a number of different forms, "whiggism," and radicalism. Postwar thinkers found for each of these a long, impressive pedigree. Depending on their tastes, the internationalists could look to the Stoics, Dante, or Arthur Balfour, the "whigs" to Bolingbroke, Burke, and Roosevelt, and the radicals to Bright and Cobden and sometimes—though not always—Marx.

To varying degrees, these traditions were "invented," most of them in the mid-twentieth century.[65] This is most obvious in the case of realism, whose canon was constructed in the 1940s, first by Carr and then by his American counterparts. Although its advocates purported to claim it as venerable, "whiggism" was also a twentieth-century concoction, put together in the 1940s and 1950s as a possible alternative to both realism and liberalism. Liberalism and radicalism had (and have) more claim to be seen as historical traditions, with clear lines of transmission from generation to generation. But even here, as we shall see, the events of the mid-twentieth century prompted their adherents to reevaluate the content and the historical development of these traditions.

These traditions were not impermeable to outside influence from other traditions of thought, nor were they incommensurable, in the manner of paradigms. Many beliefs were shared by thinkers of different traditions and there was considerable overlap between them. Some intellectuals—notably Martin Wight—were the inheritors of more than one tradition, moved between them, and served as transmitters to later generations of more than one set of beliefs. While in each case I lay out some of what were the shared precepts of that tradition, I do not argue that if a thinker modified or rejected one or more of them in some way, they ought to be "thrown out," in some way, from that tradition.

In the event, however, few thinkers in what follows substantially modified any one of the traditions on their own, as might be expected from Bevir's theory. Instead, as we shall see, the history of postwar international thought in Britain tends to confirm the view, put by Bruce Frohnen, that traditions are modified more by social interaction between thinkers rather than by actions by one thinker alone.[66] Whiggism is a useful case in point—without the collaboration of Herbert Butterfield with Martin Wight, Hedley Bull, and others, it is difficult to conceive of a way in which either Butterfield or Wight would have been able independently to come to their understandings of that tradition. Its invention or reinvention was prompted by clear dilemmas, but its modification came about by social intercourse—at the British Committee, above all, and in correspondence.[67]

This book therefore follows my earlier work in emphasizing dialogue between thinkers about issues, rather than concentrating on one intellectual's work or one text. This might involve the passing down of a tradition from a mentor to a student, as I have explored in the relationship between Arnold J. Toynbee and Martin Wight, or arguments between peers, as I have examined in a number of articles on political realism.[68] As I argue in what follows, some of the most important responses to dilemmas and reinterpretations of traditions emerged through discussion between thinkers as much as it did through one individual's actions.

In the postwar period British intellectuals faced a number of dilemmas that demanded such changes to traditions. The overarching one, of course, was Britain's decline. Oddly, however, few thinkers confronted this problem head on, and few proposed any really tangible responses. Northedge argued in 1974 that this was a function of "national arrogance" or "national pretentiousness,"[69] but I will argue it was also a consequence of more mundane developments, not least the emergence of a new set of professional academic norms that were hostile to policy recommendation. In part, this was itself the result of a reaction to another postwar dilemma: what to do about the rising intellectual power of the United

States? American thought and scholarship offered a persistent challenge to British ways of thinking, provoking responses that ranged from outright rejection to enthusiastic acceptance.

Three other sets of dilemmas stand out. The first was posed by the Soviet Union and by the Cold War. These developments required British intellectuals to reconsider their orientation toward their former wartime ally and then to consider the best means to deal with it. This produced, as I discuss in later chapters, some odd responses. Whereas some liberals pushed for a more confrontational and less accommodating response, some realists and "whigs" pushed for greater understanding of Soviet positions and interests. The second set of dilemmas concerned decolonization. The "revolt against the West," as it became known, provoked a range of reactions, from the visceral opposition of many liberals and internationalists, who feared that the fabric of "international society" would be torn apart by new states with aggressive, anti-Western policies, to the plaudits of many radicals. Finally, the changing nature of war and conflict prompted the emergence of the two scholarly subfields, examined in chapter 9, of strategic studies and peace research. These built upon existing traditions and generated new thinking that was critical to the evolution of British international thought into the "disciplinary" era.

3. The Fall and Rise of Political Realism

> Other Powers have pursued similar aims, and still do. Other Powers treat smaller countries as their satellites. Other Powers seek to defend their vital interests by force of arms. In international affairs there was nothing wrong with Hitler except he was a German.
>
> A. J. P. TAYLOR, *Origins of the Second World War* (1964)

> "Realism" (it used to be called dishonesty) is part of the general political atmosphere of our time.
>
> GEORGE ORWELL, "Who Are the War Criminals?" (1943)

In the postwar period, a series of intellectuals, beginning with E. H. Carr, argued that political realism offered the best response to the dilemmas Britain faced in an uncertain and unstable world.[1] For them, the interwar years had provided ample evidence of the weaknesses of Britain's conventional whiggish and liberal approaches to world politics. These were not just ineffective in promoting the national interest and maintaining international peace and security, the realists asserted, they were also hypocritical and unjust. If Britain was to be secure or even to prosper, it needed to learn the lessons of a realist tradition of thought about world politics British intellectuals and politicians had long derided, but which—as recent events had shown—continued to flourish in continental Europe. For as even its strongest proponents recognized, and as its critics never ceased to point out, political realism was not a British tradition but a foreign import.[2]

Partly because it was an alien tradition, realism struggled to find adherents among British thinkers and practitioners from the 1940s until at least the mid-1960s, if not later. Certainly, no realist of the stature of Hans Morgenthau, George Kennan, or Henry Kissinger emerged in Britain in the postwar era. Perhaps the only figure who might have stood alongside them, E. H. Carr (1892–1982), retreated from the field after 1945 to write his history of Soviet Russia.[3] And while a number of thinkers occasionally laid claim to the title "realist," some were sometimes labeled as such, and many more claimed to be "realistic," no systematic "realist" theory of international relations emerged in Britain until the 1960s.[4] Moreover, what realism can be found in Britain in the postwar years was usually derivative of American models, embedded in international histories, like those of A. J. P. Taylor (1906–1990),[5] or—like Carr's version—so idiosyncratic as to barely qualify for the title.[6]

The foreignness of realism was not, however, the only reason why it failed to gain purchase in British minds. In the 1940s and 1950s, realism suffered too from its associations with totalitarianism, on the one hand, and Neville Chamberlain's policy of "appeasement" on the other. In the 1930s, both totalitarian foreign policy and appeasement had been labeled "realist."[7] Thus while there were British intellectuals who espoused dark views of human nature akin to those of Morgenthau or the other American realists, and some who thought "power politics" inevitable in an anarchical world, few wished to be called "realists" for fear of the image the term could still generate in British minds.[8] For many, to espouse "realism"—in the 1940s and early 1950s at least—was not just to espouse a foreign creed, but also to align oneself with either totalitarianism or the appeasement of totalitarianism. This association drove realism beyond the moral pale for a significant number of British thinkers, or at least made them very wary of using the term to describe their work.

It had other effects, too. In particular, it prompted British intellectuals to consider just how successful realism actually was when put into practice. Whereas American thinkers like Morgenthau argued that realism was a necessary response to the existence of active or latently hostile powers in the international system, British thinkers went one stage further, pointing out that even in the hands of the most ruthless and amoral totalitarian, realism did not seem to produce the results it promised. Just as the outbreak of the Second World War demonstrated the failure of appeasement as a means of confronting totalitarians, the outcome of the war demonstrated for them that "power politics" could be defeated by whigs and liberals without the need to ape the behavior of the "realists" they had fought.

The hostile reception given to realism in Britain in the 1940s and early 1950s did not mean, of course, that realism was rejected by all or that certain realist beliefs were not taken on by British intellectuals. Aspects of realism were appropriated by inheritors of other traditions, especially by whigs and radicals. After 1960, moreover, realism began to exercise a more significant influence in academic circles, especially as the teaching of international relations in universities outside London, Oxford, and

Cambridge took hold. This "realism" differed, however, from Carr's early interpretation. The new realism was American or continental European in provenance and stripped of Carr's radicalism. One source was the influx of American textbooks, up to date with the latest modish theory;[9] another, as we shall see, was the small group of émigré thinkers working in the UK, including, in particular, Georg Schwarzenberger.

By 1960 this new realism had begun to pervade some British thinking and by 1970 it was being eagerly consumed by a new generation. Students of that time recall being fed "a form of fast-food realism," as Ken Booth has called it, in which the "complexity, sophistication and moral anguish of Reinhold Niebuhr and others" had been replaced with more palatable, but less nutritious, intellectual fare.[10] This caused irritation to liberals and whigs, as well as to radicals like Booth. When Martin Wight complained (in 1960) that his students refused to read "Thucydides or Machiavelli or Kant on Perpetual Peace" because they could "get by" in their studies "on E. H. Carr plus the latest American textbook plus last week's *Economist*," he was voicing a more general gripe.[11]

This chapter charts this fall and rise of realism, as well as its mutation from a radical creed to an American-inspired commonplace. The first part examines the legacy of E. H. Carr's attempt to import and rejuvenate realism for a British audience. The second describes the reaction to that attempt and the impact of the association of totalitarianism and appeasement on the postwar reception of realism in Britain. The third turns to the ways in which British thinkers and practitioners appropriated elements of realism into their analyses of postwar world politics and integrated realist beliefs into their own inherited traditions. The last part explores the rise of realism within the British academy, beginning with Georg Schwarzenberger's attempt to use continental sociological ideas to generate a new and more robust theory of world politics that might better ground its practice.

POWER POLITICS AND APPEASEMENT

> Because most men are dishonest, is that to say there is to be no law against thieving?
> GILBERT MURRAY to E. H. Carr, 5 December 1936[12]

Although the term "Machiavellianism" can be located in earlier scholarship and political debate, together with an appreciation of a "Machiavellian" tradition, the word "realism" did not enter general use in Britain before the mid-1930s.[13] It appeared in the midst of the fierce debate about the efficacy of the League of Nations and the wisdom of British foreign policy in the Abyssinian crisis of 1935–36. In this debate, the terms "realist" and "idealist" were not used to refer to theories of international relations. Instead, "realist" was used to refer to those critical of the League and "idealist" to those who continued to believe it could work. The publication of the previously secret Hoare-Laval Pact, which sidelined the League and gave British and French recognition to Mussolini's conquests in Abyssinia, confirmed this new divide in British political life. Supporters of the pact, convinced that the League was now obsolete, styled themselves "realists"; critics who believed that the League still had a role to play were deemed by these "realists" to be "idealists."

Looking back from 1939, Alfred Zimmern remembered this as a crucial turning point. It was the moment, he recalled, when "[t]hose who, whether by temperament or as a result of experience, were disinclined to range themselves with the believers [in the League of the Nations] were driven into a camp of their own—the Adullam of the so-called 'realists'—and a cleavage was set up in our public opinion upon lines hitherto unfamiliar. For one of the axioms of political life has always been that all who took part in it should be realists, and that neither realism nor idealism should be the monopoly of any particular group."[14] During 1936, this association of "realism" with those who believed that the League was largely incapable of functioning as an effective guarantor of international security grew stronger. For these "realists," peace with the dictators had to be sought by other means, principally by the adjustment of British interests to accommodate the demands of Germany, Italy, and Japan. Thus by the end of that year, as the historian Neville Thompson has observed, "the terms 'realism' and 'appeasement' were practically synonymous . . . and the leaders of the National Government took special pride in their claim to be realists."[15]

E. H. Carr's adoption of the word "realism" to describe one of the two modes of thinking about international relations he described in *The Twenty Years' Crisis* must be seen very much in this context. He was fully aware of its associations with Chamberlain, with opposition to the League, and with the policy of appeasement. In the *Times Literary Supplement* in April 1939 he had declared his backing for what he called, in the title of his review of the prime minister's collected speeches, "Mr Chamberlain's Struggle: The Realistic Quest for Peace."[16] Carr admired the manner in which the prime minister had sought, as he put it, to "break through the forest of words and phrases in which British policy has become enveloped and obscured."[17] Elsewhere Carr observed that Chamberlain's government had "perceived more clearly" than its critics the realities of contemporary international relations and pursued "a consistent policy of conciliation and concession . . . more in accordance with traditional British policy."[18] And in the *Twenty Years' Crisis* itself, in a footnote near the close of the first chapter that was excised from the second edition,[19] Carr described appeasement as an archetypal "reaction of realism against utopianism."[20]

Carr's own version of realism, however, went much further than Chamberlain's.[21] While he welcomed Chamberlain's realism as a necessary corrective to the League's utopianism, it did not represent his own ideal mode of conducting international relations. Realism, he wrote, is "liable to assume a critical and somewhat cynical aspect," "to emphasise the irresistible strength of existing forces and the inevitable character of existing tendencies, and to insist that the highest wisdom lies in accepting, and adapting oneself to, these forces and tendencies."[22] Carr distinguished this realism from a newer form, with which he had more sympathy, and then distinguished both from a utopian-realist synthesis, which was the position he advocated and with which he concluded the book.

"Conservative realism," Carr argued in a review of Butterfield's *Statecraft of Machiavelli* (1940)—the kind of realism one found in Machiavelli or indeed in Chamberlain—wore for him "an old-fashioned look in an age of dialectical materialism."[23] As a critical weapon, Carr preferred instead a "modern realism" that incorporated the "eighteenth century belief in progress" as well as the insights of Hegel and Marx. "Modern realism" could reveal more than just empirical facts, as Chamberlain's version claimed to do; it could "reveal, not merely the determinist aspects of the historical process, but the relative and pragmatic character of thought itself."[24] More powerful than conservative realism, it could "bring down the whole cardboard structure of post-War utopian thought by exposing the hollowness of the material out of which it was built."[25]

Two versions of "realism" can thus be found in the first half of *The Twenty Years' Crisis*: the conservative, practical, prudential "realism" of the National Government, and the radical, historicist, theoretical, "realism" of chapter five, "The Realist Critique." In the second half, Carr tried then to weld the latter to a new utopia of his own making, a "new international order" that would recognize the obsolescence of all the tenets of the liberal order it was to replace: free trade, the doctrine of the harmony of interests, the rule of international law, the nation-state, the League, and liberal morality. A utopian-realist order would instead be driven by the urgent need for "economic reconstruction" in the common interest of humanity, predicated on the recognition that "the conflict between the nations like the conflict between the classes cannot be resolved without real sacrifices, involving in all probability a substantial reduction of consumption by privileged groups and in privileged countries."[26] What was needed in the international sphere as in the domestic, Carr insisted, was "[f]rank acceptance of the subordination of economic advantage to social ends, and the recognition that what is economically good is not always morally good."[27]

In the *Twenty Years' Crisis* Carr moved through these two different versions of realism to arrive at a radical justification of a conservative policy: appeasement. The transfer of territory, populations, or colonies from the "have" powers of Britain and France to the "have-not" powers of Germany, Italy, and Japan was defended on the grounds that it was a necessary step along the road toward "economic reconstruction," large-scale economic planning, and the demise of the nation-state. Because these things were to Carr's mind inevitable—to be realized by force or by peaceful acquiescence on the part of the West—Britain needed as soon as possible to accommodate them. "Realism," on Carr's understanding, meant first and foremost the acknowledgment that the liberal, laissez-faire West represented the past, and that planning and totalitarianism represented the future, its injustices at the level of individual freedom being more than outweighed by its apparent capacity to deliver large-scale improvements in living standards.[28]

REALISM ASSAILED

> Men who allow their love of power to give them a distorted view of the world are to be found in every asylum.... Highly similar delusions, if expressed by educated men in obscure language, lead to professorships of philosophy; and if expressed by emotional men in eloquent language, to dictatorships.
> BERTRAND RUSSELL, *Power: A New Social Analysis* (1938)[29]

The appeasers' claim to be "realists" was the subject of much contemporary satire, remembered long into the late 1940s and 1950s. In one cartoon of the time, for example, David Low lampooned what he saw as the muddled logic of Chamberlain's diplomacy, his Tory antihero Colonel Blimp summing up the problem in his characteristically pithy style: "Gad, Sir, Mr Poliakoff is right. Eden is one of those sloppy idealists that want everything on a sound basis, while Chamberlain is a hard realist who will trust anybody."[30] With the outbreak of war, such lighthearted mockery was overtaken by cruder attacks. The pseudonymous authors of *Guilty Men*

(1940), for instance, ridiculed Chamberlain's version of "common sense" and portrayed him as an egomaniacal fantasist with no sense of the "real world."[31] The prime minister, they asserted, echoing the criticisms of postwar realists like Morgenthau,[32] had little grasp of "human nature." Instead, he was a prisoner of his own illusions, blind to anything he did not wish to see, including Hitler's military machine and aggressive intentions.

Such attacks continued for much of the war, to lasting effect. In 1943, for example, George Orwell lambasted the "clumsy way" in which Chamberlain had played "the game of Machiavelli, of 'political realism'" during the prewar years, noting the "cynical abandonment of one ally after another, the imbecile optimism of the Tory press, the flat refusal to believe that the Dictators meant war."[33] He feared that, despite all that had happened, realism continued to appeal to politicians and pundits alike, for "the mere fact that it throws ordinary decency overboard will be accepted as part of its grown-upness and consequently of its efficacy."[34] The record of realism in delivering what states want in international relations, Orwell thought, was hardly impressive: "In our own day, Mussolini, the conscious pupil of Machiavelli and Pareto, does not seem to have made a brilliant success of things. And the Nazi regime, based upon essentially Machiavellian principles, is being smashed to pieces by the forces that its own lack of scruple conjured up."[35] "If there is a way," Orwell wrote, "out of the moral pig-sty that we are living in, the first step towards it is probably to grasp that 'realism' does *not* pay, and that to sell your friends and sit rubbing your hands while they are destroyed is *not* the last word in political wisdom."[36]

In Cambridge, the historian Herbert Butterfield had reached a similar conclusion. Before the war, he had favored appeasement, believing that Britain has lacked the power and the will to act against Hitler. "A country relatively disarmed," as he tried to explain his position later, "must not expect its diplomacy to be effective."[37] His disillusionment, however, did not lead to a wholehearted embrace of "power politics" as an alternative. In 1940, Butterfield had observed: "The only true portrait of Machiavellism is a Napoleon Bonaparte. And he is the clearest commentary on the system."[38] Political virtuosity was not enough: the usurper could apply the lessons of the Florentine's realist "science of politics" and for a while it might work, but success at the outset would eventually culminate in abject failure. Machiavelli's politics were for Butterfield too "rigid," "inflexible," and "doctrinaire."[39] The dictators' defeat was thus inevitable, he came to believe: brought upon them by the very methods that had brought them to power.

Others were less sure. Harold Laski (1893–1950), for instance, displayed in wartime and afterward a tortured and ambiguous attitude to realism and "power politics."⁴⁰ In 1941, he was still criticizing Chamberlain in classic internationalist terms, arguing that at Munich he had "wrecked collective security," abandoned moral and legal obligations, and sought to play "the historic game of power politics" with predictably disastrous effects.⁴¹ Yet at the same time Laski considered that the British and French had "shuffled and evaded realism in negotiation" and missed their opportunity to play their "main trump card—Germany's fear of a war on two fronts."⁴² They had missed the "simple fact that the Fascist leaders were outlaws, not statesmen" and failed to appreciate that "you can only deal with an outlaw by force; as he seeks to break your will, so you must seek to break his. . . . The defeat must be decisive; his collapse must be an abject one."⁴³ Laski wanted it, in other words, both ways: he wished that Chamberlain had been at one and the same time a paragon of internationalist virtue and a Machiavellian genius, quick to sense his strategic advantage and press it home. This blend of moralism and realism was uncomfortable, but it prefigured postwar arguments to come.

After 1945, the reception of realism in Britain was also complicated by the rise of a version of the doctrine in America. Three American realist classics had been published during the war: Nicholas Spykman's *America's Strategy in World Politics* (1942), Walter Lippmann's *US Foreign Policy: Shield of the Republic* (1943), and Reinhold Niebuhr's *The Children of Light and the Children of Darkness* (1944). The years that followed brought forth Hans Morgenthau's triptych *Scientific Man versus Power Politics* (1946), *Politics among Nations* (1948), and *In Defense of the National Interest* (1951), as well as George Kennan's *American Diplomacy* (1950).⁴⁴ All of these works were self-consciously realist in style and content. They emphasized, to use Lippmann's words, the "cold calculation" required to "organize and regulate the politics of power."⁴⁵ Their authors were unflattering about human nature, skeptical about historical progress, and hostile to universalistic ethics—although often they overstated these positions for rhetorical effect and were more moderate in their policy recommendations. They were also informed by a particular reading of appeasement, which they regarded not as "realism," but rather as a "corrupted policy of compromise" wholly incapable of dealing with Nazi "imperialism."⁴⁶

While many in Britain shared the American analysis of the weaknesses of appeasement, many also remained suspicious of realism in its German or American guises. Some pointed to inconsistencies in American arguments, especially in Morgenthau's. Saul Rose observed that Morgenthau's realism, measured by his judgments of recent history, had an unfortunate tendency to be "unrealistic," and A. F. Ensor asked whether his doctrine amounted to anything more than a return to "old-fashioned diplomacy."[47] In the Chatham House journal *International Affairs*, the chemist and public intellectual C. H. Desch attacked Morgenthau's *Scientific Man* for not stating or justifying the "moral forces" that Morgenthau thought might "oppose" the "general decay in the political thinking of the Western world."[48] More enthusiastic about the American realists were émigrés— like David Mitrany, who penned a deeply admiring review of Niebuhr's *Children of Light and Children of Darkness*—and emigrants, such as George Catlin, who had left Britain for Cornell in the 1920s. For him, at least, Kennan's *American Diplomacy* was a "book of the first importance."[49]

Well into the 1950s, however, most British intellectuals remained skeptical about realism because of its associations with appeasement and with power politics, especially power politics as practiced by the Axis states. The association with appeasement was kept alive in the string of Churchillian histories of the 1930s that appeared in the late 1940s. In these works John Wheeler-Bennett, Lewis Namier, and (above all) Winston Churchill ridiculed the claim by the "French and British appeasers" to have practiced, as Namier put it, "moral and realistic statesmanship."[50] Wheeler-Bennett's *Munich* was thus presented as a "case-history in the disease of political myopia which afflicted the leaders ... of the world in the years between the wars," littered with references to Chamberlain's "blind confidence in his political intuition" and his disregard of "the signs and portents about him."[51] Lewis Namier also drew contrasts between those with a "clear-sighted" view of Nazi intentions and capabilities and those Chamberlainites mired in the "mists of wishful thinking."[52] His heroes of the prewar era, like Robert Coulondre, the French ambassador to Moscow (1936–38) and Berlin (1938–39), were praised for having "no illusions" as to the nature of dictatorship, while the villains, especially Chamberlain, were castigated for their "rigid, narrow, doctrinaire self-certainty."[53]

For this group, as for the American realists, the Second World War had been, to use Churchill's phrase, "the Unnecessary War."[54] Together they argued that if Britain had followed her supposedly traditional policy of maintaining the continental balance of power, Hitler would have been deterred from his bid for European hegemony.[55] But though they mocked Chamberlain's "realism," most of his British critics—unlike the Americans—did not assume the title "realist" to describe their own philosophy of international relations. The exception was Namier (1888–1960).[56] In 1940 he had followed Carr—whose *Twenty Years' Crisis* he called that "brilliant book"—in attacking the supporters of the League for their "faith, facile optimism and comfortable illusions of mid-nineteenth century 'utilitarian' believers in democracy."[57] Namier alone among academic commentators used "realist" as a term of praise—in his review of Coulondre's memoirs, *De Staline à Hitler*.[58] Elsewhere he declared his admiration for the "shrewd realist perception" of the Soviets and condemned Herman Göring's attempt to produce, in the late 1930s, "a counterfeit of Conservatism, devoid of realism, dignity or tradition."[59] In neither Wheeler-Bennett's *Munich* nor Churchill's *Gathering Storm* is it possible to find comparable statements.

In the main, this continued association of "realism" with appeasement and totalitarianism in memoirs, contemporary histories, and in the minds of British thinkers and the reading public militated against the use of the term even by those who might otherwise have adopted it to describe their own position. In his lectures at the LSE, for example, the otherwise "realistic" Martin Wight continued to link "realism" not just to appeasement but also to the methods of the dictators throughout the 1950s. For him, Carr's "realism" remained "the theology of appeasement" and, as Friedrich Hayek had argued in his *Road to Serfdom* (1944), implicitly totalitarian to boot.[60] In an essay on Nazi Germany for the Chatham House *Survey of International Affairs* (1952), Wight recalled the "terrible combination of realism and fanaticism" that was to be found in Hitler's own thought. The *Führer*, he observed, had made "power politics the object of his study; he understood the theory of it; and he left dicta thereon as penetrating and enduring as Machiavelli's."[61] Though "the periphery of his lens was always liable to be fogged by nonsense" and his "discernment... hampered by his creed and temperament," Hitler had succeeded in producing a "landmark in political philosophy," *Mein Kampf*, "at the point where the justification of authority was superseded by the assertion of power."[62]

The identification of realism with the diplomacy of the dictators continued to lead British scholars to an obvious conclusion. For the historian Charles Webster, Britain's principled pragmatism, its whiggish, supposedly "traditional" policy of defending "constitutionalism" while upholding the European balance of power, was clearly the superior doctrine.[63] "Nothing," as G. L. Arnold put it in 1949, was "clearer than that *Realpolitik* has failed."[64] Wight, like Orwell and Butterfield, took heart from this failure: pure realism, he concluded, for all its seductive appeal and promises of victory, brought only ephemeral, Pyrrhic success. In *Power Politics*, he looked to "a richer conception of politics, which made power an instrument and not an end, and subordinated national interest to public justice." This was the kind of politics practiced by William Gladstone or Franklin Roosevelt, "who had a moral ascendancy and a power over the public opinion of the world, evoking a trust and loyalty far beyond his own country." "Moral insight and political judgement," he implied, would triumph, but it required a redefined "realism," one that meant "absence of optimism," not an absence of morality.[65] In such a form, Wight concluded, "realism can be a very good thing: it all depends on whether it means the abandonment of high ideals or of foolish expectations."[66]

THE RISE

[O]ther things being equal, it is always "good" to be realistic...
R. N. BERKI, *On Political Realism* (1981)[67]

In the late 1940s, the mainstream view of British intellectuals was that realism, construed as amoral "power politics," was commonly practiced by other states but was not to be recommended as a guide to British foreign policy. Most agreed that it was "realistic" to recognize the shortcomings of international law and organizations to restrain those that practiced "power politics," but many observed too that those who cleaved too closely to realism in the conduct of international relations tended not to succeed, at least in the long run. An approach to international politics that tempered "power politics" with some kind of moral restraint was thus required.

At the same time, certain ideas often thought of as distinctively realist in nature—especially about the intrinsic weaknesses of human nature or the inevitability of conflict between states in an anarchical system—were voiced far more readily in the late 1940s than they had been a decade earlier. So too was the belief that circumstances demanded "empirical" approaches to problems, rather than the devising of what Geoffrey Goodwin called "optimistically fashioned Utopian devices."[68] In 1948, the veteran liberal Gilbert Murray noted this change of mood, complaining that what he considered certain "utterly repugnant" views had gained widespread currency, particularly those that suggested that "moral ideals were out of place in politics; liberalism an out-dated luxury, collective security a will-o'-the-wisp; small nations militarily negligible and bound of necessity to obey their betters; and the politics of power the only reality."[69] As evidence Murray cited the apparent popularity of Carr's *Conditions of Peace* (1942).[70]

This was an overstatement. There was pessimism among British intellectuals, especially in the late 1940s and early 1950s, about the prospect of a Third World War. This is readily apparent in Toynbee's *Civilization on Trial* (1948), with its prediction that "world unity" might soon be achieved not by peaceful means, but by a "knock-out blow" administered by one superpower on the other.[71] Toynbee's prophecies caught what Wight called the "apocalyptical" mood of the late 1940s well, as did Wight's own work.[72] On hearing of the atomic bombing of Hiroshima on 7 August 1945, in the midst of writing his Chatham House pamphlet *Power Politics*, Wight penned a dark and satirical spoof news report entitled "World War III."[73] This gloomy mood did not lift for some time. From the inaugural meeting of the United Nations in 1946, where he was acting as correspondent for *The Observer*, Wight wrote to J. H. Oldham of *The Christian Frontier*:

(a) No thorough-going cooperation between Russia and the West is possible within the foreseeable future. It may be possible however to establish a balance of power which will last as long as thirty years.

(b) Given the foregoing, the Third World War is as certain as the return of Halley's Comet. A balance of power is no substitute for international order: it is inherently unstable.

To this, Wight added for good measure: "I hope this may not seem brutally realistic."[74]

Many British intellectuals agreed with the conclusions of Wight's analysis, but few thought that international relations ought to be conducted in a realist or "power political" way as a result—even if realism was conceived, as Morgenthau conceived it, as a necessary defense of liberalism at home. In *Power Politics*, Wight traced the history of modern international anarchy from its origins in the slow demise of Western Christendom to the contemporary world, but he made no secret of his view that this was a story of the unrelenting decline of standards in political morality and conduct.[75] He doubted that it could ever be reversed. While Butterfield was consoled by the belief that pure realism was self-defeating, Wight was more pessimistic, both about the general direction in which the world was moving and about the future of liberalism. He desired, however, no compromise with realism, arguing in 1960 that it would be "better" for the "West" to show itself "capable of . . . balance, moderation and noble solicitude for the future of mankind, and lose the Cold War . . . that it should win the Cold War with a more Machiavellian philosophy."[76]

Other scholars of international relations took a more accommodating view. The most obvious were the émigrés, like Hersch Lauterpacht (1897–1960),[77] Karl Mannheim (1893–1947),[78] and Georg Schwarzenberger (1908–1991),[79] who imported with them ideas derived from continental schools of jurisprudence and sociology more amenable to realism. The last arguably had the greatest impact. Educated at the Universities of Heidelberg, Frankfurt, Berlin, Tübingen, Paris, and London, Schwarzenberger fled Germany in 1934 and became secretary of the New Commonwealth Institute, later renamed the London Institute for World Affairs. He took up a post in the Faculty of Laws at University College, London (UCL) in 1938 and there he remained until 1975.[80]

At UCL, Schwarzenberger built a department to rival C. A. W. Manning's latterly more famous outfit at the LSE. It became a significant training ground for a number of important figures in the nascent discipline, among them Fred Parkinson; the international lawyer L. C. Green; Joseph Frankel, who began his career as an assistant lecturer under Schwarzenberger and later became professor of politics at Southampton; and most notably Susan Strange, a lecturer from 1949 to 1965 and later Montague Burton Professor at the LSE. In the 1960s, it became an institutional base for the emerging school of peace and conflict researchers, including the highly energetic Australian John Burton. Schwarzenberger ensured too that he and his preferred scholars had an outlet for their work, editing (with G. W. Keeton) the short-lived journal *World Affairs* and the longer-lived *Year Book of World Affairs*.[81] His own intellectual contribution to the field was also significant; indeed, his *Power Politics* (first edition, 1941) was for twenty years the only available British "textbook" in the field, running to three editions (the second in 1951 and third in 1964).

Schwarzenberger's approach to international relations began with a rejection of the claims historians had staked in the field. Like Goodwin or Butterfield or Bull, he appealed for an "empirical approach," but unlike them he objected strongly to "the one-way road of the historical treatment of the subject." Telling the story of the historical evolution of any "topic," he argued, was of course "relevant," but he argued that it did not exhaust the ways in which that topic might be examined.[82] Schwarzenberger preferred a sociological approach that did not prejudge the method or the outcome, one that permitted "classifications or types and forms of social relations" and the "analysis of static and dynamic factors" in "international society"—such things could not be done, he argued, by history alone.[83]

To pursue his cause, Schwarzenberger imported into British international thought a set of continental sociological ideas, drawn partly from

Max Weber and Ferdinand Tönnies, as well as the German jurisprudential tradition. He had no time for indigenous British forms of "sociology" like Manning's "sociology of appreciation"—his international relations as "connoisseurship."[84] Rather, Schwarzenberger's sociology was relentlessly mundane. "Its objects," he declared, "are the evolution and structure of international society; the individuals and groups which are actively or passively engaged in the social nexus."[85] These could be studied in a number of different ways and had been, notably by those whom Schwarzenberger called "naturalist writers" and by historians. The "naturalists" took an a priori position and built an account of the workings of international relations on top. They might begin with an optimistic or pessimistic view of human nature, for example, and proceed to draw equally optimistic or pessimistic conclusions about the nature of international relations. The "realists" and the "idealists" both did this, he noted.[86] The historians, on the other hand, simply retailed the story of the evolution of "a person, people, science, age or civilization" and while this is undoubtedly relevant, it is not sufficient for a "science" of international relations.[87]

Schwarzenberger offered "empiricism" as a means of avoiding the pitfalls of the "naturalists" and "sociology" as a means of doing due "justice to the structure of present-day international society, to the typical patterns of behaviour on the international scene or to the forces by which the hierarchy of powers within international society is determined."[88] Only an empirical sociology could "provide" the kind of "synopsis" which could account for the "complex conditions of modern life" as well as the platform that would permit the usage of a number of different tools borrowed from other disciplines.[89] It "achieves this end," Schwarzenberger argued, "by the classification of types and forms of social relations, by the analysis of static and dynamic factors within any social environment and by the assessment of their relative importance within the group which is the object of inquiry."[90] Recognizing both the "danger of dilettantism" and the danger of commitment of which Butterfield and the other historians warned, Schwarzenberger argued that this sociology had to be rigorous in examining its premises and its methods, and that it had to take what he called a "relativist approach" to the examination of the possible futures for international relations.[91]

Above all, this meant giving due regard to power, which the "realists" were right to complain had been neglected by the "idealists." To explore the implications of power, Schwarzenberger thus insisted on the centrality of Tönnies's distinction between society and community as different forms of social organization. "Society is the means to an end," he argued, "while a community is an end in itself."[92] The former was "founded on distrust, whereas the other presupposes mutual trust."[93] As a consequence, he added, "[i]ndividuals and groups within a society concentrate on the pursuit of their own self-interest"—and this was the cause of "power politics" that beset international society.[94]

Like Wight, therefore, though for different reasons,[95] Schwarzenberger had come to believe that all modern international relations tended toward power politics, but that they need not do so. Unlike Wight he was skeptical that mainstream internationalism, still less a revival of Gladstonianism, was an effective way of confronting the dilemmas that were faced. Any system of law, he thought, was merely an expression of the social arrangements that produced it. Given that "international society" was a "society" and not a "community," that meant that international law was merely a "law of power," dictated by the strong to the weak, or sometimes a "law of reciprocity." It was not yet, Schwarzenberger believed, a "law of co-ordination," as it would be in a community.[96]

Even where law played a part in contemporary international relations, he argued, it was thus merely a cloak for the pursuit of interests by states. Alongside simple power politics, for Schwarzenberger, operated an equally insidious system of what he called "power politics in disguise."[97] This was the "reality" of the Cold War. "The hope that the United Nations would be the guardian of world peace," he observed, "was based on the assumption of continuing harmony between the world powers."[98] Once it was lost, the world had returned to the darkest days of the interwar period. In a bitter and sarcastic response, Schwarzenberger penned in his book a "grammar of power politics"—presumably an allusion to Laski's famous *Grammar of Politics*—setting out the means by which international law and organizations could best be used to play that game. One must, he argued, always claim to be peace loving while taking one's adversary to the brink of war, and always declare that collective security is the "only reliable guarantee of collective security while avoiding any definite commitment under the Charter, and so on."[99]

This was less realism than straightforward cynicism, but it was a view that became increasingly popular as the 1950s wore on, uniting conservatives to disaffected internationalists and indeed radicals. It can be found in international and contemporary histories, like the radical-cynic A. J. P. Taylor's *Struggle for Mastery in Europe* (1954), which opens with the assertion that "[t]hough individuals never lived in [the] state of nature" that Hobbes described, "the Great Powers of Europe have always done so."[100] It certainly lies just below the surface of Taylor's notorious argument, quoted at the beginning of this chapter, that Hitler's foreign policy was no different from any other European leaders. It can be detected too in novels of the time, in Graham Greene's *The Quiet American* (1955), for example. Greene's contrast between American and European political thought—one of the running themes of the book—is a contrast not just between jaded experience and feckless youth, but a clash of two "realisms." On the one side, is the Englishman Fowler's tired, skeptical, even cynical and corrupt realism, and on the other, the American Pyle's new realism, born of "good intentions and . . . ignorance," grounded in the fervent belief that good ends justify evil means.[101] Greene's quiet American might have found the "imaginary 'old colonialist' . . . repulsive," but he was not above planting bombs in city streets to further the local cause of his "Third Force" and the wider cause of "democracy."[102]

There remained in all of this a conviction that "realism" had, as Isaiah Berlin commented in 1954, a "sinister" sense. It recalled for Berlin, at least, Hegel's "unflinching vision of 'reality'" as well as the "more apocalyptic versions of this German creed."[103] In Britain, there remained, in other words, a sense that realism needed to be tempered by moral principle. For A. L. Rowse, writing in 1961, the 1930s had demonstrated that "empiricism carried beyond rhyme or reason" would fail—after all, he argued, that had been the fate of E. H. Carr.[104] Such views inoculated British intellectuals against a complete acceptance of realist ideas, whether American or home-grown.

CONCLUSION

> . . . if blame is to be imputed at all it should be imputed first and foremost to the philosophical Frankensteins of the 18th century, who invented the doctrine of nationalism and let it loose on an innocent and unsuspecting world.
>
> C. M. WOODHOUSE, *The New Concert of Nations* (1964)[105]

Still under suspicion in academic and intellectual circles, realism crept back into the thinking of British politicians with the onset of the Cold War. The postwar Labour government, as Cornelia Navari and others have shown, couched elements its foreign policy in quasi-realist language and conceived it in quasi-realist terms.[106] Clement Attlee's address to the Party Conference in 1945 is a case in point, urging, as it did, his government to be "realists about Japan and Germany" and to aim to curb their power, for "we cannot afford to give these people another opportunity of destroying civilisation."[107] Such "realism," indeed, provoked considerable criticism from within the Labour Party. This disquiet is evident in a resolution, proposed at the following year's conference, reproaching the government for supposedly continuing the "Conservative Party policy of power politics abroad" and in another, this time urging that it return to a foreign policy concentrating on the "support of Socialist and anti-Imperialist forces" worldwide.[108] This radical thinking fueled calls for a British-led "Third Force" in world politics—a persistent theme on the Labour left wing throughout the postwar period—but only rarely displaced the more realist beliefs at the center.[109] In the midst of the Cold War, many continued to think, as Denis Healey did, that "*Leviathan* is still a better handbook for foreign policy than *Fabian Essays*."[110]

Healey took great pains to build a vision of a "socialist foreign policy" which was "closely adapted to the power realities of the present time."[111] This did not imply, of course, an embrace of realist methods, merely an acknowledgment of parts of the diagnosis realists offered of present international ills. "In foreign as in domestic affairs," Healey argued, "socialists should aim at changing the existing system so as to realize the fundamental brotherhood of all men and to check the selfish will power."[112] It also meant realizing that international institutions could not always provide the guarantees they promised. For Healey, "the vision of a world shaped almost exclusively by Anglo-Saxon policy is fading at the very moment when it seems most likely to become reality. It is much more probably that the future will bring a return to a world of many powers in which decisions are made by the methods of traditional power politics. If this is so, conventional diplomacy will come into its own again and the adjustment of national differences by negotiation and compromise will become more urgent than the construction of international institutions or the execution of moral blueprints."[113] Few Tories could have disagreed with such a view and few did.

The change in attitudes to realism—a change to a cautious acceptance of its diagnosis of international ills, if not of its prescribed cure—came with three developments in the 1950s. The first—in importance and in chronological terms—was the emergence of a viscerally anticommunist group of thinkers in the United States, including the likes of James Burnham, who made the realists appear far more reasonable and more reasoned than they had before. The second was a straightforward improvement in the knowledge that British intellectuals had about their American counterparts, nurtured by invitations from both universities and foundations, which encouraged meetings and dialogue between them. Few of the most prominent British students of international relations failed to visit the United States during the 1950s, if they had not done so already, and, if correspondence is any measure, greater mutual understanding was the result. Over time, British scholars learned to distinguish between totalitarian and American "realisms" and to appreciate, sometimes begrudgingly, the virtues of the latter.[114]

The last of these developments, however, was perhaps the most important: the rise of a new postwar generation of intellectuals, those who came to maturity in the late 1950s and especially the early 1960s. Unlike the previous generation, who had experienced the 1930s and the war as adults, and thus retained their belief that somehow realism was bound to appeasement and Axis power politics, this younger group took a different view. They laid the blame for the calamities of the interwar years where Carr laid it, with the internationalists and radicals. To Hedley Bull, for instance, it was the weak-mindedness of the "idealists" that had allowed the dictators to disrupt international order, as well as their palpable failure to appreciate the realities of international relations.[115] In all of this, appeasement was reconfigured as an expression of "idealism" rather than—as Carr had had it—a "reaction of realism against utopianism."[116] The rehabilitation of realism was thus begun.

This process was allowed to run its course, in part, because no alternative theory of international relations emerged from Britain in the late 1940s and the 1950s. In 1964 Peter Lyon called it "a period of darkness and almost of stagnation . . . when in Britain in this field there was very little writing that broke new ground." "There were," he went on, "occasional striking essays or monographs from writers such as Professors [Denis] Brogan and [Herbert] Butterfield, and especially from Professor Beloff; but these were rare forays, peripheral to these scholars' main pursuits." Chatham House continued to publish their journals, studies, and *Surveys*; Schwarzenberger's *Year Book* appeared and his textbook was reprinted. By default, Lyon observed, "British practitioners . . . mostly followed and borrowed from American models, and this mostly meant from Hans J. Morgenthau, in particular his *Politics among Nations*."[117]

This does not quite tell the whole story, however. Though resisted by some at the LSE, Schwarzenberger's sociology of international society also helped to influence the later course of British thinking about international relations in a more "realist" or at least "realistic" direction.[118] Setting aside international and contemporary histories, by the 1960s sociological accounts of the workings of "international society" were by far the most common British treatments of that subject. Joseph Frankel's text *International Relations* (first edition, 1964) is a case in point—emphatically not a product of LSE philosophical Idealism, it is very much an expression of Schwarzenberger's sociological approach combined with a dose of straightforward modernist empiricism. Frankel took no a priori stance about human nature or the human condition. Instead he opened with a perfunctory narrative of the development of the "state-system" and quickly moved to an analysis of "international society" in terms of its "units" and "structure," "dynamic factors" like nationalism and "static" ones like sovereignty.[119] True, Frankel's treatment of foreign policy making was more influenced by American models—he had, after all, been one of the pioneers of foreign policy analysis in Britain—but his account of the "instruments and techniques" is redolent of Schwarzenberger.[120] Above all, Frankel practiced the "relativism" on which Schwarzenberger insisted—there are no flights into the normative realm; the analysis is kept strictly to the empirical.

The space for ideas like Schwarzenberger's was opened largely by the failure of the dominant British traditions of liberalism and whiggism either to address the dilemmas faced by Britain as a country or to respond adequately to scholarly developments on the continent and in the United States. In the main, as we shall see in the chapters that follow, the liberals and the whigs were either complacent or seemingly paralyzed by the pace and direction of change in world politics.

4. The Persistence of Liberalism

> In the twentieth century, philosophies that deny all moral and spiritual values ... have plunged the world into anarchy.
> LIONEL CURTIS, *World War: Its Cause and Cure* (1945)

The Liberal Party suffered a "strange death" in the interwar years, but the liberal tradition of thought about world politics lingered long after 1945.[1] Indeed, there is a strong case for arguing that liberalism remained the default position of British international thought at least until the 1960s, when it came under fresh assaults from realism and especially radicalism. It shaped and drove most British thinking about the dilemmas faced by Britain itself and by international society as a whole. This is not to say, of course, that liberalism survived the collapse of the League of Nations, the outbreak of war, and the onset of the Cold War—as well as the collapse of British power—wholly intact. Rather, it underwent a series of retrenchments forced by changed circumstance, as liberals responded to events in world politics and to developments in social science in Britain and elsewhere.

In the interwar years liberals had insisted that international law and organizations offered the best means of addressing the challenges of interstate relations and transnational issues.[2] That period, indeed, saw the farthest-reaching effort to date to realize such internationalism in the form of the League of Nations and a strengthened international legal framework. The interwar liberals viewed both of these developments as the culmination of the progressive evolution of the European system of states since the seventeenth century. They argued that the system had passed through a series of stages: from one in the eighteenth century in which the "balance of power" was the principal means by which states managed their relations to one in the nineteenth century in which there was a more co-operative "concert" of states. In the third stage, after 1919, a system of continuous and open conference diplomacy, reinforced by a more defined set of legal rights and obligations, was brought into being.[3]

The justification for this system was derived from the mainstream of liberal political thought, especially from its insistence upon the virtues of the freedom of the individual, speech, and association, and above all upon the rule of law and the need for strong institutions to uphold it.[4]

It would be a serious error, as we saw in the previous chapter, to suggest that the collapse of the League led to the wholesale abandonment of these principles by British intellectuals and practitioners, still less that they prompted a headlong flight into realism. Instead, liberal ideas were reasserted with some power in the late 1930s and 1940s. The war years saw a series of attacks on the arguments underpinning power politics and appeasement, the bulk of which were couched in terms of liberal internationalism.[5] The war itself was conceived indeed as a struggle between, as Arnold J. Toynbee put it, an international order based upon the "ideals of the democratic rule of law" and an order simply "imposed by a dominant military Power." The onset of war did not cause liberals to discard their principles; rather, they were convinced of the need to redouble their efforts to establish a "world order" with a "moral foundation."[6] A flood of articles and books in the early 1940s confirmed their commitments, rejecting the claims of "realists" like E. H. Carr that the best policy was acquiescence to the demands of power.[7] As the Allies turned the tide of the war, this conviction in the righteousness of the liberal cause became matched by a growing belief that it might again, in the postwar years, underpin international relations.

As a tradition, liberalism drew together—and still draws together—a number of distinct arguments and propositions, some of which it shares with other traditions.[8] British internationalists in the interwar and postwar years, like some realists and almost all radicals, were highly critical of the sovereign state—or, at least, of its exclusive claim to political authority. This animus was, in part, a function of the widespread conviction that there are universal moral rules that transcend mere political allegiances to states or other kinds of polity, rules deriving either from a residual—normally Christian—belief in natural law or from a humanitarian belief in human rights. It was a function too of the growing consensus among liberals that the modern world, increasingly connected by communications and information technologies and integrated into economic interdependence, required political institutions beyond the sovereign state to manage the transnational problems that thereby emerged.[9]

Together these various convictions drove two sets of liberal demands. The first was for political reform within states, leading to national self-determination, democracy, and the rule of law. The second was for the strengthening of law and institutions beyond the state, facilitating prosperity through free markets, improving relations and understanding between peoples, and leading to the creation of an authoritative and legitimate international organization to curb the incidence and ferocity of modern war.[10]

These liberal ideas, beliefs, and proposals faced significant challenges in the postwar period, shaking the confidence of all but a very few adherents to the cause. Only a very small group of liberals responded to the dilemmas that emerged by insisting that their principles be sustained without change or compromise—the Austrian émigré Friedrich Hayek among them.[11] The remainder, as Wight suggested, were unclear as to the best way to go, whether "back to natural law" or forward to "progress," or indeed to leave liberalism behind and embrace a nihilistic realism. But this is not to say that liberalism was swept aside by some kind of "paradigm shift" in British thinking.[12] While the interwar years did witness the apostasy of some liberals—E. H. Carr above all, much to the horror of friends and former allies[13]—the immediate postwar period saw instead the modification of liberal tenets and doctrines to meet the perceived demands of contemporary international politics. As a result, liberalism remained by far the strongest tradition among British intellectuals until well into the 1960s.

This chapter examines the reasons for liberalism's persistence. In part, as we have seen, liberalism remained dominant in the 1940s and 1950s because the principal alternative—realism—was unpalatable to British thinkers. In part too, the strength of liberalism in the immediate postwar period was a function of liberal victory in the Second World War. Since many British intellectuals interpreted the defeat of the Axis as a defeat for realism and "power politics," it was hardly surprising that some of them would also see the outcome of the war as a vindication of the opposing philosophy. "[N]o permanent order," wrote Lionel Curtis in 1945, "can be founded on Hitlerism, on mere physical force, on denial that right differs from wrong."[14] This kind of triumphalism could—and did—breed intellectual complacency in Britain about its inherited traditions of political thought and practice, and especially about liberalism.[15]

But the postwar persistence of liberalism also had two more prosaic and contingent—though no less significant—causes. The first was the sheer longevity and vitality of individual liberals, as well as the institutional power they continued to wield into the 1960s. The great interwar liberals lived long into the postwar period, publishing books and articles, writing for the newspapers, advising politicians and civil servants, and influencing the direction of academic studies of international relations. The second cause is less tangible but no less important: the continued influence of philosophical Idealism over British political thought in general, which carried over into thinking about world politics. While few postwar intellectuals with a concern for international relations were avowed or systematic Idealists, most continued to think about and study politics in the distinctly Idealistic categories of "ideas and institutions."[16] They remained convinced of two fundamental propositions: namely that ideas are the motivating forces of political change and that institutions the embodiment of those ideas. Thus they believed that the study of politics—including world politics—ought to combine the historical and philosophical analysis of political ideas with the forensic dissection of political institutions, especially constitutions and legal codes. Despite deep disagreements between different schools of thought, as we shall see, liberalism persisted partly because of the power of this intellectual agenda.

This chapter is divided into two main sections. The first looks at the careers of the liberals themselves, of the inheritors and transmitters of the liberal tradition. The second examines the evolution of the "ideas and institutions" approach and the tenacious influence of philosophical Idealism in British international thought in the postwar years. In the conclusion, I turn to one last reason for the persistence of liberalism: the stimulus given to liberals by the dilemmas of the Cold War.

THE LIBERALS

> I think that whatever happens to the poor Liberal Parties, the world is being divided not into Socialist V. Capitalist, but into Liberal V. Despotic, i.e. those who care for Liberty, Free Thought &c and those who are too poor ignorant and unhappy to care about such things led by ambitious groups and autocrats.
> GILBERT MURRAY to Bertrand Russell, 29 June 1948[17]

The leading lights of interwar liberalism burned well into the postwar years, most of them still writing, lecturing and campaigning. J. L. Brierly (1881–1955),[18] Lord Robert Cecil (1864–1958),[19] Lionel Curtis (1872–1955),[20] Hersch Lauterpacht (1897–1960),[21] Gilbert Murray (1866–1957),[22] Charles Webster (1886–1961),[23] and Alfred Zimmern (1879–1957)[24] each survived for at least a decade after 1945; Charles Manning (1892–1978),[25] Philip Noel-Baker (1886–1982),[26] Arnold Toynbee (1889–1975),[27] and Leonard Woolf (1880–1969)[28] saw out all or almost all of the period considered here. The generation that succeeded them as authorities on world politics in the 1950s and 1960s, most of them born in the 1910s or 1920s, were also liberals, albeit of a more chastened variety. Together, they ensured that the voice of liberalism could readily be heard in postwar Britain.

The liberals made themselves heard in books, in learned journals, and in the press. Brierly, Curtis, Lauterpacht, Murray, Toynbee, Woolf and Zimmern were all prolific in the 1940s and 1950s, publishing for the educated public as well as for other scholars. Toynbee was especially productive, producing no fewer than thirty journal articles in 1955 alone, along with a welter of other works during the 1950s and 1960s, including the four concluding volumes of his liberal theodicy, *A Study of History*, which ran to more than 2,500 pages.[29] No realist or radical came close. E. H. Carr wrote very little on world politics after his *The Soviet Impact on the Western World* (1946); Georg Schwarzberger's output, including the second edition of his *Power Politics* (1951), was far more technical, hardly designed for popular consumption. Carr, of course, still wrote for the papers, including the *Times Literary Supplement* and *The Listener*, but throughout the 1950s and 1960s the liberals had the far bigger weapon of David Astor's *Observer* at their disposal.[30] Liberal authors were prominent, too, in periodicals like *The Twentieth Century*, which replaced *The Nineteenth Century and After* in 1951 and ran until 1972, and *The New Statesman*.

These and other liberals continued to wield considerable institutional power, not least in the two most important centers for academic work on international relations: at the LSE, which remained Manning's domain until 1962, and at Oxford, where Agnes Headlam-Morley held the Montague Burton chair until 1970. The succession of Geoffrey Goodwin (1916–1995) to Manning's chair at LSE (which he held from 1962 until 1978) did little to dislodge liberalism from its position. Indeed, given that Goodwin's reputation was built on a stolid, establishment study of Britain's relations with the United Nations commissioned by the Carnegie Endowment for International Peace and aided by a study group at Chatham House, it served merely to reinforce it.[31] The liberal cause at Oxford, at the same time, was more than ably supported by a number of likeminded scholars including H. G. Nicholas (1911–1998), a fellow of New and Exeter Colleges as well as Nuffield, the Rhodes Professor of American History and Institutions, and the author of *The United Nations as a Political Institution* (first edition, 1959);[32] and the former diplomat Evan Luard (1926–1991) at St Antony's College, among whose works were *Peace and Opinion* (1962) and an unfinished history of the UN system.[33]

The liberals also remained influential outside the universities. Toynbee remained a significant figure at the Royal Institute of International

Affairs (Chatham House) throughout the period covered here; indeed, he retained an office there until his death in 1975. Successive directors of the Institute hardly wavered from a broadly liberal line, whether the former Conservative politician C.M. Woodhouse (1917–2001; director 1955–1959)[34] or the former Labour MP Sir Kenneth Younger (1908–1976; director 1959–1972).[35] At the newly formed Institute for Strategic Studies (founded in 1958 and later renamed the International Institute for Strategic Studies), liberals were equally prominent, especially in the form of its first director, Alastair Buchan (1918–1976), later successor to Headlam-Morley in the Montague Burton chair at Oxford.[36] Like Martin Wight and the international political economist Susan Strange (1923–1998),[37] Buchan had worked for the impeccably liberal *Observer* newspaper before entering into academic life; he was also the author of a biography of Walter Bagehot.[38]

At the same time, liberals within academia and in the think tanks maintained strong links to liberals in the media and public life, socializing with or simply appearing on the same platform as liberal-radical intellectuals like Bertrand Russell and politicians like the Liberal Party leader Jo Grimond. At the same time, bodies like the "Liberal Foreign Affairs Group"—which counted Grimond among its members in the early 1950s, as well as Wight, the Sinologist G.F. Hudson (then of *The Economist*, later of Oxford), the journalist and campaigner Colin Legum (then at *The Observer*), and a number of Foreign Office officials—furthered such connections.[39]

The sheer number of intelligent, eloquent, and influential liberals in the universities, the research institutes, and the policymaking community helped to ensure, in other words, the survival of the tradition well into the postwar period. But so too did the sway of a particular mode of thinking about politics that, while not exclusively liberal, was most often utilized by liberals—the ideas and institutions approach.

IDEALISM, IDEAS, AND INSTITUTIONS

> "Meta-diplomatics," then, this debutant discipline might logically, if with a smile, expect to be called.
> C. A. W. MANNING, *Nature of International Society* (1962)[40]

Carr's *Twenty Years' Crisis* apart, most interwar writing on world politics concentrated on the ideas and institutions that supposedly shaped their conduct. There was a widespread conviction that ideas played a strong causal role—that "Prussian militarism" was instrumental in driving

Germany to war in 1914, for example, or that the "obsolete" idea of the "nation-state" was one of the last major obstacles to world order and unity. Ideas were active forces in international relations, pushing in positive or negative directions, as what Norman Angell called "unseen assassins."[41] One task of the student of international relations was thus to expose the irrationality or the inappropriateness of particular ideas to contemporary circumstances and thereby to establish truths about our social condition that could then be disseminated by mass education, by schools, or by other means. For Angell, for example, the condition of "anarchy" in which states existed was straightforwardly "anomalous," but "this fact" was not appreciated by the "most educated folk" because their education had been so wayward that they could not appreciate "clear and self-evident truths."[42]

Such facts were established, by and large, by inductive empiricism. There were some, like Goldsworthy Lowes Dickinson, who preferred a more philosophical mode of establishing truths, through right reasoning displayed in Platonic dialogues, for example.[43] But in the main, facts were established either by the exercise of experienced judgment or the application of proper historical method. Like the historians, the interwar thinkers aspired to objectivity, expunging "bias" in their interpretation of evidence by the rigorous use of the techniques of professional history: cross-referencing facts, triangulating events with multiple primary accounts, and so on. In his inaugural lecture as Montague Burton Professor at Oxford, indeed, Zimmern made a particular point of saying that students of international relations should not "part company with those [i.e., historians] who have during the past hundred years elaborated new and more methodical ways for the discovery and classification of knowledge regarding the past."[44] If this knowledge were valid, then it would be invaluable in dealing with the complexities of the present.

Convinced of the motive power of ideas and confident in their burgeoning knowledge of the facts of world politics, interwar thinkers spent much time as a result constructing, modifying, or criticizing schemes for new international institutions—activities which provoked much scorn and ridicule from later scholars. These studies fall into two categories: proposals, like Leonard Woolf's *International Government* (1916), and assessments, like Alfred Zimmern's *The League of Nations and the Rule of Law* (1936).[45] Both displayed the dual conviction that institutions were the practical embodiment of ideas and that institutional reform could decisively modify the behavior of actors in international relations. They, like most other interwar thinkers, in other words, were convinced that institutions were inventions of reason that had, in some way, to "fit" with prevailing social "facts" and to change them for the better.[46]

This interwar work on international relations, emphasizing ideas, institutions, and their historical evolution, left a far greater legacy than was often acknowledged in the postwar period. The failures of the League and other interwar projects for the international reform of international relations generated among later scholars an understandable tendency to play down what achievements interwar intellectuals had made and—just as important—the continuities with their own ideas and approaches. This was especially true among postwar proponents of a new "discipline" of international relations in the universities—for they, after all, had the most to lose if academic and political opinion turned completely against them, placing the blame for the calamities of the interwar years squarely at their feet. In response to persistent criticisms—mainly from historians—that a discipline of international relations would be, as Wight put it, "symptom of a disease, not a therapy," and that it would be capable only of producing, as Butterfield argued, "dabblers in a journalistic type of thinking," its defenders were forced to distance themselves from their interwar inheritance.[47] They did this, in the main, by insisting that their work was more "realistic" than what had gone before, but not—it should be noted—by changing any of the main elements of the interwar approach.[48]

This message was promoted most vigorously by members of the LSE's department of international relations. They had, of course, a vested interest in doing so. The LSE's department remained the biggest and arguably the most intellectually significant center for the study of the field in Britain throughout the postwar years, with abiding concern within and beyond the university for justifying the new "discipline." As a result, it was at the LSE that the ideas and institutions approach was theorized most self-consciously. Elsewhere, such as at Oxford or Manchester, where there was no perceived need to corral the study of world politics within the boundaries of a discipline, its influence was more subliminal.

The new, more "realistic" ideas and institutions approach is perhaps best captured in the LSE stalwart Geoffrey Goodwin's 1951 essay on the teaching of international relations. It opened with the by-now obligatory ridiculing of the supposed "preoccupation" of interwar scholars with "the best means of promoting peace between nations, [their] . . . constant anxiety about the kind of international society that *ought* to exist and often optimistically fashioned Utopia devices to banish war from society . . . founded upon the basic humanistic presupposition of the 'brotherhood of man'."[49] For Goodwin, postwar writing was far superior, since a greater "maturity of outlook" had now been attained. Its more modest aim was merely to "lay bare the real nature of that [international] society without necessarily seeking to change it," though the "hope remains" that in the "long run" such studies might "contribute towards a reduction of the state of acute tension" that marked contemporary international relations.[50]

Goodwin was however quite vague as to the methods by which these aims would be achieved. He observed a difference between the "historical" and "analytical" approaches, noting that "the teacher with a leaning towards Sociology or Politics, as is common in London, is primarily concerned with analysis, with the similarities of occurrences and with elucidating fundamental uniformities. His method will be essentially comparative ... [and] ... there is, in some cases, a marked pragmatic element in the 'pathological' approach which he may well favour—the study of a diseased society with a mind to relieving its worst ills."[51] Goodwin thought this fit and proper, but called for the "development of a more systematized conceptual framework within which the constituent parts can form a better integrated and articulated whole." This would best be furthered, he thought, not by a substantive debate over method, which might well descend into "extravagant doctrinal claims by one teacher or another, but rather by a sensitive empiricism on the part of all."[52] In the end, what was needed was the careful appraisal of the historical development of the key ideas that have shaped the institutions of our world.

This was fine as far as it went, but it did not constitute a major change from what had gone before. Goodwin did not take issue with the focus on ideas and institutions, nor did he question the basic philosophical or historical approaches taken in the interwar period to their study. What was new was only the "realistic" tone in which he thought discussion of international relations should take place. Significant shifts in British approaches took longer to achieve. Within and outside the LSE, "ideas and institutions" remained the primary focus, despite postwar efforts to place the study of world politics on a more solid footing.

The composition of the international relations courses of the LSE B.Sc. (Econ) degree—the most developed of such degrees until the 1960s—illustrates this well. Eleven subjects in total were required for the degree; five concerned the study of international relations. As Charles Manning described them in 1957: "Economics, Applied Economics, Political History, Economic History, Government, The History of Political Ideas, and the Structure of International Society (all, thus far, in Part I), International Law (in either Part), and, in Part II, International History Since 1860, International Relations, and International Institutions."[53] Law, history, and institutions were thus the core elements, with Manning's "social mapping" of the "Structure of International Society" added for good measure.[54]

In this way Manning and his department led an effort to forge a discipline out of various disparate elements, but with the study of ideas and institutions at the core. His understandings of that discipline and of its proper method have been widely condemned by later scholars as excessively idiosyncratic, but they were consistent with the liberal and philosophical Idealist legacy.[55] What was odd was Manning's insistence on inventing neologisms to describe his subject, from "global social Topography" or "Meta-diplomatics,"[56] but these tendencies highlight the continued influence of the Idealism that had informed some of the early development of the ideas and institutions approach.[57]

Like any good Idealist, Manning "assumed," as he put it, "that of significant things that happen some have their deepest importance in their happening not in fact but in idea."[58] "Social reality," he argued, was made up of both facts and ideas, but it is ideas that are vital: "this reality includes numberless individuals nursing the images, experiencing the sentiments, thinking the thoughts, reacting to the symbols, and using the terminology, of nationhood. . . . The prevalence of the relevant ideas, the focus of emotions important for their bearing on behaviour—the mere prevalence, that is, of those ideas, irrespective of their inherent plausibility—will . . . be perceived as a fundamental datum. The facts of modern social coexistence do indeed include, and are conditioned by, these ideas, and the ideas are fostered by the accumulating facts."[59] The study of international relations was construed as the investigation of what Manning called a "world of notions" to be conducted by the interrogation of the meanings of the everyday terms used to describe or justify particular acts in international relations.[60]

Manning practiced what he preached—Hidemi Suganami notes that he divided his day into three equal parts, devoting one to the study of philosophy, one to the newspapers, and one to his students.[61] Which philosophers he read, however, is a bit unclear.[62] In his famous attack on the "English school," Roy Jones suggested Manning picked up his "idealist holism" in his youth, at Oxford, before the First World War.[63] It was certainly an outgrowth of his early work on jurisprudence and his interest in the sociology of law, which he cast in Idealist terms. Law, he argued, is an expression of the shared understandings of individuals in a society about what ought to be permitted and what ought not; comprehending a system in law, in other words, necessitated comprehending a society's beliefs, norms and rules in their totality. This view allowed Manning to argue, inter alia, that international law was indeed law, contrary to the arguments of the legal positivists, and that it was more than just a collection of unconnected rules or agreements—it was, he argued, a "body, or organic *system*, of ideas."[64]

If it is judged in terms of the followers it attracted, Manning's attempt to make his "Meta-diplomatics" the centerpiece of his "discipline" was a failure. The LSE retained its concerns with ideas and institutions, but—at least by the early 1960s—studied them in more conventional and increasingly less Idealist ways. Goodwin's insistence on being more "realistic" was clearly important here, but the main intellectual drive in this direction came from his colleague Martin Wight. When Wight—an Oxford-trained historian—first came to the subject, he thought there were "four directions in which research in international relations might profitably be pursued": "attempts to build a body of theory on the subject, like Morgenthau's 'Politics among Nations,' contemporary history like Gathorne-Hardy's,[65] re-considerations of past theorists and thinkers on international relations (of which I don't know an example, but on the lines on which a political theorist might treat Hobbes' 'Leviathan') and finally, what I can only call history written from the point of view of the questions that international relations seeks to answer: for instance, a history of the balance of power, 1815–1914."[66] Later, Wight was persuaded that "international society" might be a useful topic, albeit studied historically. And Wight affirmed that "international society" is best understood in terms of its animating ideas and the institutions through which ideas are translated into action; he did not justify this approach on metaphysical grounds.

When it came to ideas, Wight sought an account of the various international theories that had helped to shape modern European international relations akin to the "epic" histories of political theory of Leo Strauss or Eric Voegelin.[67] What he found was a jumble of ideas, "scattered, unsystematic, and mostly inaccessible to the layman."[68] Wight set about to bring order to this chaos, first, in a famous and highly influential series of lectures, by assembling these ideas into "traditions," and later by examining particularly important "unit-ideas," inspired by Arthur Lovejoy's work on the history of political thought.[69]

Wight's three traditions were taken up most notably by Hedley Bull, who transformed them into narrower Hobbesian, Kantian, and Grotian traditions, and used them to great effect in *The Anarchical Society* (1977); by Brian Porter; and by Michael Donelan, who added traditions of his own to his accounts of international political thought.[70] The influence of his work on unit-ideas is less immediately clear but was just as significant. It set precedents for a series of studies of particular ideas—Peter Lyon's study of *Neutralism* (1963), for example, which began life as a Ph.D. thesis supervised by Manning and Wight, or R.J. Vincent's work on *Nonintervention and International Order* (1974), which also had its origins in a thesis, this time overseen by Hedley Bull and J.D.B. Miller.[71] The object of these studies—as with Wight's own late essays on "international legitimacy" and "triangles and duels"—was to describe the relevant concept and then to trace its use in international practice longitudinally, through a period of time.[72]

The conviction that underpinned these efforts was that the study of international relations had to do more than simply relate the course of events, as did international history or contemporary history, and that the actions of participants in those events were best explained in terms of the ideas they held. "If a foreign policy is to win the support of a nation," Donelan argued in *The Ideas of American Foreign Policy* (1963), "if an active foreign policy is to be pursued with vigour, it must, it seems, be commanded by an idea, giving a sense of position or of direction."[73] Ideas, in other words, can explain behavior, and studying ideas allows the scholar to get beyond the mere phenomena of international relations to the "underlying" (Donelan's term) factors that matter.

How Idealist, in philosophical terms, any of this work was is hard to judge.[74] Streaks of Idealism can be found intermittently in British work on international relations in the 1960s and 70s—in Donald Mackinnon's contributions to Butterfield and Wight's *Diplomatic Investigations* (1966), for example, or in Charles Reynolds' *Theory and Explanation in International Politics* (1973).[75] The latter asked, as Wight had done more than a decade before, whether theorizing about international relations was really just "a form of historical argument."[76] In the main, however, what Wight and Reynolds sought was a return to "developmental historicism," which could have Idealist inflections, but need not have. Indeed Reynolds explicitly rejected two of the more prominent Idealisms, those of R.G. Collingwood and Michael Oakeshott, as simply impossible to realize.[77] For Reynolds, as for Wight, historical explanation concerned the beliefs, knowledge, and perceptions of historical agents; history, therefore, involved the construction of a coherent narrative of events based upon the empirical evidence of those past ideas we have in the present. Reynolds offered this mode of interpretation as an alternative to those that "depend for their validation on an internal coherence and consistency, or on some notion of an external empirical reality," for, in his view, neither of these positions could be justified.[78] "A reconstruction of past human activities or events," he went on, "is concerned not with an empathetic or systematic approach but with a coherent and consistent argument which relates events or factors to evidence of their perception of the part of those engaged in them."[79] This view led more to modernist empiricism, however, than back to Idealism.

A thicker streak of Idealism can be found in *The Reason of States* (1978), a collection of essays, mainly by former students of the LSE, edited by Michael Donelan. The editor's introduction left no doubt as to their philosophical stance: "The data of the human sciences are the product of thought," Donelan declared; "[t]he study of international relations is the study of international thought."[80] It may also be notable that of the four major articles in the first issue of the *British Journal* (later the *Review*) *of International Studies*, one addressed Idealist thought—the other topics being the law of the sea, Henry Kissinger, and the teaching of international studies at the University of Birmingham. The author of that piece, Peter Savigear (1939–1992), had not been a Manning pupil, however; rather, he had studied under the historian Herbert Butterfield at Peterhouse, Cambridge.[81]

The residues of philosophical Idealism may also be detected—albeit in smaller and smaller doses, as the postwar years wore on—in the overriding concern with institutions displayed by scholars at the LSE and by liberals more broadly. It can also be found in the way that institutions were understood by this group. As Hidemi Suganami rightly argued in his very perceptive piece on what he called the "British institutionalists" in 1983, "institutions" meant "a cluster of social rules, conventions, usages and practices: it is not a mere outwardly observable behaviour-pattern, but a set of conventional assumptions held prevalently among the society-members to provide a framework for identifying what is the done thing and what is not in appropriate circumstances. It connotes normativeness. It is to be distinguished from organizations such as NATO and UNO although these bodies come into existence through the working of institutions."[82] For the liberals—and indeed for some others, including some of the whigs—political institutions were the embodiment of ideas, whether they were tacit codes of conduct or formal organizations, and their development and workings ought to be understood and analyzed as such.

The liberals and whigs differed between each other and among themselves on exactly how ideas and institutions ought to be studied. Over time, authentic philosophical Idealists like Manning gave way to more modernist empiricist methods. In this context, Hedley Bull's work represented both continuity and disjuncture. His *Anarchical Society* (1977) and other works carried forward the argument that ideas and institutions were central to understanding the nature of international society, taking his cue from Manning but also from H. L. A. Hart's theory of law,[83] but he approached them in a thoroughly empiricist manner. In part, this shift was a function of Bull's rather different epistemological position: unlike his predecessors, he was a philosophical realist. Whereas Wight had thought that historical "facts" were different from those "facts" that "our senses give us"—that whether or not we consider a particular artifact from the past to have historical importance depends on the historian— Bull thought no such thing.[84] He might have ridiculed the misapprehension common among social scientists that historians are merely "compilers" of "data," but he did not challenge the empiricist assumption that historical "facts" exist wholly independently of observers, there simply to be gathered by the historian.[85] On this issue, as Keens-Soper observed to Wight, Bull was at one with the "positivists."[86] But by the 1960s, so were most intellectuals concerned with international relations, as philosophical realism and "modernist empiricism" took hold of political studies as a whole.

CONCLUSION

> We have a great Liberal civilization to defend and a formidable enemy to resist, alike in military power, in economic resources and in doctrine.
>
> GILBERT MURRAY, *Advance under Fire* (1951)[87]

Gilbert Murray's call to arms was neither isolated nor in vain. Just as it did with liberal political theorists, the early Cold War revitalized liberal thinkers about international relations. If victory in the Second World War had convinced British liberals of the intrinsic virtue of their cause, the challenge posed by the Soviet Union provided them with a new reason to carry it forward. This "liberal moment," as Robert Latham has called it,[88] lasted well beyond 1945, stretching into the latter half of the 1950s. As it went on, as we shall see in the next chapter, liberals and other internationalists were moved to re-evaluate, retrench, and reassert what they took to be key liberal beliefs in order to ready themselves for the new struggle.

The old liberal giants of the interwar years took to this fight in different ways. Gilbert Murray was moved simply to restate the basic principles of nineteenth century Gladstonian liberalism, and to throw himself into the good offices of the United Nations Association (UNA), as he had done, in the interwar years, with the League of Nations Union (LNU). Enraged by the repeated attacks of so-called realists like E. H. Carr, Murray vehemently denied that liberalism was some "mere vain nostalgia of old men" and pointed to the undercurrent of liberal ideas that, despite all the tribulations of the contemporary world, were nevertheless carrying it forward to better things.[89] What else, he asked, explained the aid and reconstruction efforts occurring at pace in Europe, the establishment of the World Health Organization or international cooperation on drug trafficking and slavery?[90] Nihilism, which Murray took to be Carr's preferred philosophy, could stimulate no such action for the common good.

Other liberal stalwarts took a different tack. Zimmern, for his part, set aside his earlier imperial enthusiasms and became a convert to America, which he christened the "Citadel of Freedom."[91] He became convinced that world peace would be attainable only by American leadership and by the emulation by all states of the American process of federation.[92] Toynbee also saw American leadership as crucial to the furtherance of liberal principles, and indeed to the very survival of humanity itself. But in the postwar years his work was also bitingly critical of the West and indulgent to others, including the Soviet Union, which attracted the hostility of conservative and more conservatively minded liberals.[93]

Just how these liberals and other internationalists confronted the specific dilemmas of the early Cold War period—of progress, nationalism, and international organization—is the subject of the next chapter. What is notable throughout is the centrality of liberal beliefs, if not always of the strict adherence to a systematic liberalism doctrine. In part this is due to a piece of intellectual alchemy—the transformation of "liberal" into "Western"—which gained pace in the late 1940s and early 1950s. The process was complete by the time Martin Wight published his famous essay on "Western Values in International Relations" in 1966, which "identified" them as the belief in the "freedom and self-fulfilment of the individual."[94] In a series of Anglo-American works in the 1940s and 1950s, the process was carried forward—by Frederick Watkin's *The Political Tradition of the West* (1948), for example, or Barbara Ward's *Policy for the West* (1951).[95] Throughout, the "West" was described in wholly liberal terms, standing for what the historian E. L. Woodward described in 1949: "The differentiation of the individual from the mass, the liberation of the human personality not only from the grosser servitudes of the environment—getting food, keeping warm, and so on—but also from inner bondage to ancestral fears and resentments, these great marks of progress [which] depend upon a non-materialist framework of thought."[96]

Liberalism persisted, in other words, because the pressures of the Cold War forced it to become ingrained, as British and indeed other intellectuals worked it into a new, wider narrative about the West.

5. The Fragmentation of Internationalism

> In no other field has the world paid so dearly for the abandonment of nineteenth-century liberalism as in the field where the retreat began: in international relations.
>
> FRIEDRICH HAYEK, *The Road to Serfdom* (1944)

> Do we go back to natural law, resurrect progress, or go forward to nihilism?
>
> MARTIN WIGHT, *Four Seminal Thinkers* (1959–60)

In postwar British thinking, as in the interwar period and indeed later, internationalism came in many forms. It could be liberal, conservative, or radical, and most postwar intellectuals with a concern for world politics were internationalists of one form or another.[1] Few denied that modern developments in warfare, economics, or communications technologies demanded some kind of coordinated response on the part of states. And even when, on occasion, a prominent figure suggested that Britain should go it alone, abandoning the North Atlantic alliance, ignoring the United Nations, avoiding European entanglements, and eschewing Soviet overtures, as Enoch Powell argued in the 1970s, they acknowledged that this must come at a price.[2] Most recognized that some kind of international action was needed to defray the cost of transnational challenges in an era of growing "interdependence." The question was: what sort of action was needed?

While there was near unanimity on the problem, there was very little agreement on the preferred solution. Even the United Nations failed to unite internationalists. Instead, the composition and powers of the Security Council, in particular, split them into reluctant supporters and harsh detractors, the latter issuing dire warnings of impending tyranny should the organization work as designed. Anticolonial clamoring in the General Assembly, growing in a crescendo by the end of the 1960s, did little to sustain the support of even those British internationalists who initially favored the UN and its aims. But the UN was not the only feature of the postwar international order that created schisms in internationalism.

National self-determination, especially in the context of decolonization, public opinion, and even the standing and worth of democracy provoked similar—and similarly visceral—disagreements. These issues in particular split liberal internationalists and divided the liberals from conservatives and radicals. In response some—like the functionalists, following David Mitrany's lead, or the federalists—moved to try to achieve liberal ends by the illiberal means of planning; others, like Hayek, warned of the dire consequences that would result if international as well as domestic economies were brought ever more strictly under the control of states.

This chapter examines the fragmentation of internationalism as internationalists adapted their beliefs and theories to meet the major dilemmas posed to that tradition in the postwar period. Three dilemmas, in particular, were especially challenging: the shaking of Western confidence in progress, the resurgence of nationalism in both Europe and the emerging "Third World," and the seeming inability of international organization to deal with key transnational challenges. The final section addresses the various ways forward for Britain and for world politics that internationalists favored in the postwar years. Throughout, the chapter takes the "internationalist" tradition to stand for the belief that the world is moving toward greater social and economic integration, as well as the conviction that some sort of international political solution is needed to address this process and its consequences. Internationalism is also understood to involve some kind of belief in the fundamental moral unity of all peoples which may be "thin" or "thick," but which is ever-present.[3]

PROGRESS AND PESSIMISM

> The eighteenth and nineteenth centuries were a brief interlude in the normal savagery of man; now the world has reverted back to its usual condition. For us, who imagined ourselves democrats, but were in fact the pampered products of aristocracy, it is unpleasant.
> BERTRAND RUSSELL to Gilbert Murray, 9 April 1943[4]

The criticism most commonly leveled at liberal internationalists, in particular, are that they were "progressivists" and that their supposed faith in progress was unwarranted, rendering them naïvely idealistic about human nature and the prospects for lasting peace, prosperity, and justice. E.H. Carr's use of the term "utopian" to describe interwar defenders of the League has tended to reinforce these perceptions. Paradoxically, this was not what Carr intended, for while he did wish to label his opponents naïve, his overall aim was to portray the "utopians" as hankering after a past world that was lost rather than pursuing an unrealistic world they thought would emerge in the future.[5]

The equation of internationalism with progressivism was in fact made not by Carr but by the postwar American realists, notably Hans Morgenthau, John Herz, and Kenneth Waltz.[6] It is their influence that shaped later British views of interwar thought.[7] Hedley Bull's 1969 essay on the development of the theory of international politics demonstrates this well. Bull took for granted the American realists' argument that the field had passed from an "idealist" stage to a "realist" one in the "first great debate" of the late 1930s, that this move was a good thing, and that heaping opprobrium on interwar writers to remind readers of their follies was a desirable and necessary act. He singled out Sir Alfred Zimmern, S. H. Bailey, Philip Noel-Baker, and David Mitrany for particular abuse, especially for their supposed progressivism. Indeed, for Bull, the most distinctive characteristics of these writers was what he saw as their "belief in progress" and their conviction that, in the aftermath of the First World War, "progress could now be sustained only by radical changes in the system of international relations."[8]

Like Carr's earlier attempt at the intellectual assassination of liberal internationalism, Bull's account distracted attention from the continuities in beliefs that exist between the interwar British liberals and postwar intellectuals in the field, and—just as importantly—from the subtleties of internationalist thinking. It is highly questionable, in fact, whether liberal internationalism should be thought "progressivist" at all or in its entirety.[9] There was considerable disagreement among inter- or postwar liberals that human nature could indeed be "improved" or "perfected" in any essential way. True many argued—and at length—that education might address sources of misunderstanding that might give rise to conflicts, but rarely did a liberal internationalist assert that it could transform human nature itself.[10]

For Gilbert Murray, at least, the issue was not whether human nature could be changed but whether the thin crust of civilization that overlays, disciplines, and constrains it could be sustained or even strengthened. He wrote thus to Bertrand Russell in 1940: "I some times think that we are like a savage tribe which has had all its customs and tabus broken up by an inrush of white civilisation, and has gone to the dogs in consequence. I meant that we have had more profound changes in thought and habit than we are able to digest. We are like the Scotchman who learnt that the Sabbath was in origin only the Babylonians' unlucky day, and consequently thought we could break all ten commandments."[11] Much the same sentiment is at work in other liberal internationalist writings of the period, in Lionel Curtis's insistence (1938) that the "essential disease is a failure *in the system* to develop in men the sense of duty they owe to each other," for example, and indeed in Norman Angell's view (1947) that "the 'natural' forces within men," if "given free play," will always end in "fanaticisms and ferocities."[12] For them, as for Alfred Zimmern, writing in 1948, "Human nature is a permanent and predisposing cause of the present unhappy worls [sic—"world"] situation."[13]

What is critical in this context is not that these accounts of human nature are unflattering and uncompromising, but how little these supposedly "idealist" views of the subject diverged from those of postwar "realists." There was little disagreement on the subject: that human nature was flawed in some way was a commonplace belief, even accepted truism. It was shared by classical liberals like Murray and Zimmern, radicals like Russell and Taylor, by conservatives like Namier, and by pessimistic Christian international thinkers with whig or liberal leanings like Butterfield and Wight. Indeed, the core theme of Herbert Butterfield's *Christianity and History* (1949)—namely that a thin crust of civilization separates modern society from "barbarism"—was an almost universal message of political and international thought of the late 1940s and early 1950s, regardless of whether it was realist/realistic, internationalist, whig, or even radical.[14] What united whigs like Butterfield and liberals like Murray, at least when it came to human nature, was much more substantial than what divided them. The outlier—on this issue as on so many others—was the "realist" Carr, whose unabashedly "progressivist" views were markedly different from the norm.[15]

This convergence of beliefs about human nature and progress was, of course, a product of the traumas of the late 1930s and of the war. Although, to their minds, liberalism and internationalism had triumphed in these trials, they also chastened liberal internationalists to an extent, forcing them to revaluate their assessments of the possibilities of international organization, education, and peace. But it would be wrong to suggest that what occurred was a wholesale shift in views from "idealistic" assessments of human nature and the prospects of historical progress to pessimistic and "realistic" ones.

The internationalists themselves emphasized the continuities in their views from the interwar to the postwar years. Liberals, as Gilbert Murray argued in 1951, were never ignorant of the existence of a Nietzschean "will to power" in human beings, they were just opposed to it.[16] This was indeed the whole point of liberalism: to restrain that will, and thus to protect the weak from the strong. For Murray, the threat to liberalism and thus also to the West came not from its own intrinsic failings—its supposed lack of appreciation of human nature or political or economic realities—but from a "revolution in thought" which cast out liberal verities, arguing not just that they were wrong, but that they were not worth defending.[17]

Murray's principal concern was that this revolution in thought would stir up uncontrollable passions in the "common man." "[W]e have to admit...," he noted, "that the mass of common men when in power... does not make a good ruler."[18] He feared—as did many liberals—that these passions were everywhere being unfettered, first by democracy in the West and then by self-determination in the Third World. These developments imperiled internationalism at just the moment at which, they argued, nation-states were so evidently obsolete. Mass passions found too obvious an outlet in nationalism: "[u]ncivilised nations and unenlightened masses of 'common men'," Murray argued, "tend to look on foreign nations as enemies; the aggressive ones call them enemies until they are subjects."[19]

Liberal internationalists, then, became more "realistic" in the immediate postwar years, especially about the failings of human nature and the prospects for progress, but they made only a few concessions to their critics. Contrary to later assertions by Bull and others, they were not at all united in a "belief in progress," still less in the perfectibility of human beings.[20] Rather, their work shows them to be acutely aware of the significant threats to their ideals posed by human nature. In the postwar period, most internationalists agreed, the greatest of these was the appeal of the nation-state to its emotional and irrational components.

NATIONS AND NATIONALISM

> As an agency of destruction the theory of nationalism proved one of the most potent that even modern society has ever known.
> ALFRED COBBAN, "The Nation-State" (1944)[21]

If postwar internationalists were united on any issue it was that in their present circumstances nationalism and national self-determination were dangerous, highly seductive, but inherently flawed ideas.[22] This represented both a departure from earlier liberal and conservative beliefs that were more positive about both the nation and the state, and a point of contention with radicals, who welcomed nationalist movements, especially those that aimed at dismantling imperial rule.[23] Keith Hancock's attack (made in 1943) on what he called "this sundered world of snarling nationalisms" stands in stark contrast—for example—to Guiseppe Mazzini's mid-nineteenth century enthusiasm for the realization of all nations' "mission" or "vocation."[24] So too does Arnold J. Toynbee's youthful, though qualified, enthusiasm for the principle of "nationality" (1915) and his more mature and straightforward condemnations of what he called the "idolatry of nationalism" (1930).[25]

In the interwar years, liberal internationalist views of the nation and the state underwent a radical revision. Prescient in this respect was Murray, who as early as 1922 penned a highly critical essay on the self-determination of nationalities in what became the Chatham House journal *International Affairs*. Murray thought nations a good thing and certainly preferred them to empires, but he was not so keen, as most internationalists were soon to be, on nations becoming sovereign states. Self-determination was fine, he argued, if it banished political oppression and especially war, but if self-determination led to circumstances in which the risk of war was actually increased, then clearly it had to be opposed.[26] Murray's essay demonstrated well, in other words, what might best be called the internationalists' hierarchy of preferences. At the top was the abolition of war, then of illiberal politics—only after that came the liberation of nations. If the latter conflicted with the former, the former would always trump.

In the postwar period, the internationalists were forced to make exactly that choice, partly by events, as we shall see, and partly in the face of conservative critics who suggested that liberalism was too indulgent to nationalism and that this indulgence had brought about the calamities of the twentieth century. Lewis Namier was particularly ruthless in this regard in the 1940s; Elie Kedourie was likewise in the 1960s.

Namier was actually a firm believer in nationality and was convinced that "true" nations ought to be translated from social entities into political ones. It all depended on whether the nations in question were "territorial" (true) or "linguistic" (false).[27] Whereas the former were bound to a certain patch of soil, evolved slowly and organically, and were inherently conservative, the latter were unbounded and inauthentic. For Namier, the problem was that liberal internationalists had since the French Revolution allowed and encouraged linguistic nations to flourish, to the great detriment of territorial nations. Indeed linguistic nationalism was, for Namier, a pure invention of liberalism, prompted by the nineteenth-century transfer of sovereignty from monarchs to peoples—to the "'sovereign' hordes," as Namier dismissively referred to them—in the name of liberty and self-determination.[28]

In his *Nationalism* (1960), Kedourie concurred. Again, nationalism was "invented" rather than natural; again, its origins were to be found in the Enlightenment and the French Revolution. Its consequences were dire. Kedourie argued: "What the new principles did was to introduce a new style of politics in which the expression of will overrode treaties and compacts, dissolved allegiance, and, by mere declaration, made lawful any act whatever. By its very nature, this new style ran to extremes. It represented politics as a fight for principles, not the endless composition of claims in conflict.... The ambitions of a state or the designs of a faction took on the purity of principle, compromise was treason, and a tone of exasperated intransigence became common between rivals and opponents.... Terrorism became the hallmark of purity..."[29] This argument had the happy result of explaining the rise of totalitarianism and the twentieth-century crisis of international relations, both traced to a single source: the liberal doctrine that the national self-determination of peoples should be the highest political good.

Liberal internationalists could marshal few responses to such assaults in the postwar years. They had, of course, long lamented the negative effects of nationalism. In the 1930s, for example, Toynbee had devoted extensive efforts to demonstrating that the fundamental cause of the contemporary international crisis was what he called the "struggle between oecumenialism [sic] and parochialism," between the demands imposed by the unity of the global economy and those of "political nationalism and race-feeling."[30] His monumental *Study of History* was in one sense just a greatly extended essay on the evils of nationalism, as well as of imperialism, but the explanation for why nationalism had become such a problem failed, in the end, to stand up to Namier and Kedourie's criticisms.

Rather than seeing it as an unintended consequence of liberalism, Toynbee and a number of other interwar liberal internationalists conceived nationalism in terms of a quasi-religious or spiritual failing. For Toynbee, nationalism was merely a modern form of idolatry; for Zimmern, too, it represented a failure to render to Caesar only those things that are Caesar's.[31] It was, in other words, some kind of collective spiritual error rather than the outcome of a particular way of thinking about politics. This argument held up as long as contemporaries were moved by religious rather than political modes of thought, but as the religious revivalism of the 1930s and 1940s began to fade in the 1950s, it persuaded fewer and fewer British intellectuals.[32]

At the same time, the onset of the Cold War and the beginnings of decolonization brought about yet another re-evaluation of their thinking on the nation. Internationalist conclusions were grim. The rise of anticolonial nationalism, as we shall see in later chapters, was met with consternation and hostility by many liberals: it signaled, after all, another setback to the realization of their principles. They continued to resist the notions that nationalism was either an outgrowth of liberal beliefs or their unintended consequence. Instead, some blamed democracy. The "ignorance" of the "masses" had been a prominent theme in interwar internationalist writing—it is latent in Toynbee's Bergsonian conviction that the progress of societies is driven by "creative minorities," not the mass, and it is explicit in Angell's complaints about the ignorance of "John Smith" to the realities of international relations.[33] In the postwar period, these complaints were often shrill. In 1955, in correspondence with Bertrand Russell, Murray argued that "the danger" in domestic and international politics "comes from excessive Democracy," in which "[t]he mass of stupid ignorant and prejudiced people, with no respect for their 'betters,' howl down intellectuals and carry everything before them."[34]

This marks a low point in internationalist thinking and, in effect, an admission that internationalists were struggling to explain what their theories failed to predict: the resilience of nationalism in an otherwise technologically and economically united world. This confusion is evident in later British work in the field. F. H. Hinsley's *Nationalism and the International System* (1973), for instance, struggles to locate the origins of nationalism and to account for its persistence. For Hinsley as for his liberal predecessors it was clear that there was a problem of reconciling nationalism with internationalism, but though he argued that the creation of a system to address it was urgent, he provided precious little guidance as to how it might be constructed, except to urge "reflection" upon "history."[35] By this stage, as we shall see, concerns about nationalism had been overtaken by wider worries about the imminent unraveling of international society itself.

One symptom of this decline was the patent inability of international organizations to restrain poor behavior on the part of states and other actors. As with nationalism, however, British internationalists struggled to explain why these failures were occurring. Some blamed the design of the institutions themselves; some the conduct of states and other actors. Disagreements on these points further fractured internationalism, as we shall see below, giving rise to a number of accounts of the way forward for the cause.

INTERNATIONAL ORGANIZATION

> The Great Powers will impose the law, but are themselves above it. The emphasis in the Charter is on the maintenance of security, that ambiguous word, not on justice or a rule of law.
> MARTIN WIGHT, on the United Nations in *Power Politics* (1946)[36]

British intellectuals played a critical role in drafting the Charter of the United Nations, which is best seen as a composite of British and American models with late Soviet additions. The historian Charles Webster was especially important.[37] At the outbreak of war in 1939 Webster had joined Arnold Toynbee's Foreign Press and Research Service (FRPS)—in effect Chatham House in miniature, transferred from London to Oxford—before moving to the United States to promote Britain's image to skeptical Americans in late 1941 and early 1942. Thereafter he returned to Britain to establish himself within the Economic and Reconstruction Department of the Foreign Office (FO), under Gladwyn Jebb. There he aided the composition of "The United Nations Plan for Organising Peace" that was presented to Cabinet in July 1943. Webster traveled as part of the UK delegation to Dumbarton Oaks in 1944, where the initial model for the UN was built by the Allied powers, and he attended the San Francisco sessions at which the UN Charter was negotiated and agreed. Webster's redraft of Jan Smuts's original preamble to the Charter formed the basis for the final version.[38]

Given his intimate involvement in the creation of the UN, it is not surprising that Webster was one of its more prominent postwar supporters. In theoretical terms, he conceived that institution in classically internationalist terms, as the natural culmination of the historical development of European diplomacy and, indeed, of progress already achieved. In the FO, he fought hard to ensure that the British did not backslide through this history, as it were, from its prewar commitments to conference diplomacy, the involvement of small powers, and the possibility of judicial or arbitral settlement of disputes enshrined in the League of Nations Covenant. He opposed, therefore, both Churchill's plan for a three-power council charged with the responsibility to maintain peace and security and to punish what they determined as aggression, and Jebb's scheme for a four-power international condominium managed in periodic summits.[39] For Webster, these plans made too many concessions to "power politics" and were insufficiently attentive to the positive aspects of the League. He set himself the task, therefore, of finding "new methods of harmonising the Great Power Alliance Theory and the League Theory" and of educating the prime minister and the Foreign Office about its merits.[40]

In Webster's work for the FO, the most important dilemma facing internationalists in the postwar period was posed at its most stark: should liberal means—the rule of international law guaranteed by institutions—be compromised for liberal ends? Like most liberal internationalists, Webster made that choice, though he did not find the decision easy. He remained a champion of constitutional government and of parliamentary control of foreign policy. The "democratic way of life," he wrote in 1950, must be defended, both for its own merits and because "the establishment of international peace and security [is] closely bound up with the acceptance of democratic institutions and individual rights."[41] But Webster also acknowledged that compromises had to be made in a world in which those things were not universally accepted.

One such compromise was the composition and the powers of the Security Council, which, like the wider issue of the provision of the UN Charter, deeply vexed internationalists during the immediate postwar years. For Webster, the Security Council was not an ideal means by which to ensure international peace and security, especially when its permanent members held the veto power over resolutions judged inimical to their interests. He called the veto "a blot" and wished it "was not there,"[42] but he did not think, as the liberal international lawyer J.L. Brierly did, that the nature of the Security Council, its powers, and its limits was "too heavy" a price to pay to ensure "prompt and effective action" in international relations to prevent war and confront aggression.[43] In any case Webster did not believe that an institution's form determined its success or failure. He was highly critical of those who spent their time carping about this or that aspect of the Covenant or the Charter rather than applying themselves to practical efforts for change. In 1944, in a telling passage, he observed that "there can be no future for institutions, whether national or international, unless men are prepared to accept them with all their imperfections and limitations, and transform them by action."[44] "Practical work," he argued in 1950, was what was needed; not endless debate over revising the letter of the law.[45]

Not all internationalists agreed. The League of Nations had garnered and maintained support from liberal internationalists for most of its existence; the United Nations, by contrast, divided internationalists from the start. For many liberals, as for the veteran campaigner Gilbert Murray, the UN was "clearly the right thing," and its failings attributable to external factors beyond its control. In Murray's judgment, those factors were many and varied, as he observed to Bertrand Russell in 1955: "the national ambition of Russia, the eternal discontent of poor against rich, unsuccessful against successful, coloured against white, etc., and the old liberal half-truths about equality, 'self-government better than good government,' rights of nationality etc. . . . all being dangerously misapplied."[46] Other internationalists, while acknowledging the validity of some or all of these problems, insisted that the UN was not at all the "right thing"; indeed, that it was fundamentally flawed in its design. Some even welcomed the freezing of its core institutions by the Cold War, fearing a functioning Security Council, in particular, to be far more dangerous to international peace and security than an unworkable one.

Brierly's criticisms were eagerly taken up by Wight, for example, who used them to develop a pungent critique of the UN in a series of papers and in his LSE lectures on "International Institutions." For Wight, the UN represented not an advance on the League but retrogression to the more "conservative" and "oligarchic" principles of the Congress of Europe. The Security Council was, in effect, the "Directory" of the Great Powers.[47] Wight's principal complaint concerned what he called the "basic antilegalism" of the Charter, which produced, to his mind, a "quasi-totalitarian institution." The Charter reified the balance of power between the Great Powers of 1945 and, more insidiously, gave the "great concentration of political power" in the Security Council a patina of legal respectability.[48] There were, he noted, no legal limits on its power—it was "not bound to observe rules of law or existing treaties"—and the smaller powers were merely bound to accept what it determined.[49]

The opinion of most British internationalists—indeed most British intellectuals interested in the subject—ranged between Wight's position that the UN was fundamentally illiberal and Webster's more pragmatic stance. Immediately after the war, Geoffrey Goodwin recalled in 1961, "the prevailing temper of popular opinion" toward the UN "was less one of hopefulness than of an uneasy and sceptical goodwill tinged with nostalgia." This contrasted, he thought, with official opinion, which was far more skeptical about its capacity to mitigate "power politics."[50] Alongside the skeptics stood Schwarzenberger, as well as Brierly and Wight, who was heavily critical of the structure of the UN and, as we have seen, convinced by 1951 that it was merely a forum for the pursuit of "power politics in disguise."[51] On the other side were doughty veteran internationalists like Murray or Kathleen Courtney,[52] but even they, by the early 1950s, had come to have doubts. Zimmern's view that the Charter was in effect a global "constitution" was not widely shared.[53] More common was

Murray's conviction, expressed in 1952, that the UN "faced a great difficulty" in the sense that the institution clearly could not provide what it had promised in terms of universal collective security. Only a balance of power, sustained not by the UN but by NATO, Murray concluded, could work, and this went against all internationalist instincts.[54]

THE WAY FORWARD

> I would have men forget their quarrels for a moment and reflect that, if they allow themselves to survive, there is every reason to expect the triumphs of the future to exceed immeasurably the triumphs of the past.
> BERTRAND RUSSELL, *Portraits from Memory* (1956)[55]

The revaluation of human nature and of the idea of progress forced upon internationalists by the war, together with resurgent nationalism and the paralysis of international organizations, required internationalists to seek new means of realizing their principles. The forms these new internationalisms assumed were many and varied. Some found solace in cosmopolitan religions, particularly in universalist religious beliefs ranging from relatively orthodox versions of Christianity to radical creeds like Arnold J. Toynbee's syncretic religion of Love.[56] Indeed, the flourishing of the ecumenical movement in the late 1940s and early 1950s was in part a response to failures of political internationalism, as well as revival in belief.[57] The influence of his movement was considerable—many liberals, including those like Murray who had hitherto been staunchly atheist, came to voice support for the idea and the reality of "Christian civilization."[58] It provided, moreover, a bridge across which British internationalists could speak to more religiously inclined American audiences, a principal determinant of—among other things—Toynbee's popularity in the United States in the 1950s.[59]

At a more earthly level, internationalism divided in the postwar years into three main branches: federalism, functionalism, and hybrid forms of liberal realism. The first—federalism—originated well before the Second World War as a specific solution to European or Western ills.[60] It was highly fashionable in the late 1930s and early 1940s as a response to the dilemma created by the collapse of the League; indeed, the rise of federalist commitments among internationalists was a major source of concern for the classical internationalists.[61] The federalists drew upon two principal traditions of thought, one that informed the formation of the United States (the Federalist Papers) and one—derived from the first but distinct—that had earlier called for the federation of the British Empire.[62] Together, these ideas led federalists to argue that the existence of international law and institutions alone could not prevent the outbreak of war, which they regarded as the pre-eminent international problem. Only the federation of sovereign states into a wider state could suffice.

In Britain, the Federal Union group, founded in 1938 and finally disbanded in 1963, became the focal point of the movement and attracted a significant body of inter- and postwar intellectuals, among them Lionel Curtis, a longstanding federal enthusiast; Arnold Toynbee, who flirted with the movement in the early 1940s before moving on to higher religious concerns; the pacifist C. E. M. Joad; the constitutional historian Kenneth Wheare; and the constitutional lawyer Ivor Jennings.[63] It attracted too some notable practitioners, not least Lord Lothian, who became one of the most prominent federalists, and even—for a moment—Winston Churchill, whose proposal for an Anglo-French federation in 1940 was prompted, in part, by Federal Union advocacy.[64]

In the postwar years, federalism had mixed fortunes. In the late 1940s, federal arrangements became attractive to some Western Cold Warriors, motivated by the belief that an "Atlantic Union" would be the best response to the Soviet domination of Eastern Europe and the failures of the UN.[65] This proposal helped split the old federalist movement. Some early proponents, like Schwarzenberger, who had once been a prominent member of Federal Union, drifted away when it became clear that a federation might not be universal and might instead be a means of yet again playing "power politics in disguise."[66] Others were enthused by the possibilities that it presented for a reformation of European international relations. In *Policy for the West* (1951), for instance, the assistant editor of the *Economist*, Barbara Ward, called for a "practical federalism" in Europe to curb nationalism, secure prosperity, and resist Soviet incursions into the West.[67] True to Churchillian precedent, however, Ward was ambivalent about British membership of such continental arrangements. This inability to agree or commit to a federal Europe remained a defined feature of British discussions of the subject for all of the postwar period.[68]

If the crisis of internationalism in the late 1930s and early 1940s had prompted some to embrace federalism in a bid to attain liberal ends, others went in a functionalist direction. In essence, functionalism represented a means of pursuing liberal international ends—especially the abolition of war—by alternative means, eroding state sovereignty rather than signing it away in one single act. It was informed by developments in the social sciences that seemingly made large-scale social and economic planning possible and by the general suspicion of laissez faire. In Britain, it was stimulated by the importation of insights from continental sociology and economics in the baggage of the interwar émigrés.

Karl Mannheim was only the most prominent of many who attempted in the 1930s and 1940s to harness the insights of modern sociology and the technologies of planning for the defense of liberal democracy—the explicit aim of his *Man and Society* (in German, 1935; in English, 1940). His diagnosis of the causes of the crisis of liberalism was uncompromising. It was, he argued, the very "planlessness of the liberal order" which turned politics and international relations to "anarchy."[69] Recognizing this fact made Mannheim, by his own estimate, a "Realist"—what qualified one for that title was the recognition that the "only chance" for the West was "to grasp . . . in time" the need to "find a form of planning . . . which will allow a maximum of freedom and self-determination."[70]

Mannheim thus pursued an "empirical" study of the social processes and structures shaping our social development—processes and structures which, left unchecked, would generate further and further conflict. It demanded a "historical or sociological psychology" that was the superior of the totalitarian versions (like Ortega y Gasset's *Revolt of the Masses*, which Mannheim cited, or the work of Georges Sorel or Vilfredo Pareto on crowds and collective social psychology, which he did not).[71] This psychology, like that of Gasset or Sorel or Pareto, was intended to address the irrational in human behavior at the individual and collective levels—irrationality being the greatest threat in mass democracies, often producing "its own antithesis" and providing "its enemies with their weapons."[72] Mannheim's project was to produce a means by which the "planner" might transcend both the social prejudices imposed on him by his material circumstances and insulate himself from individual and collective irrationality. Since irrationality was a product of insecurity, Mannheim argued, and insecurity a product of a lack of organization, planning was necessary. The freedoms of liberalism, by contrast, merely created a situation in which "conflict and competition prevails," preventing long-term thinking, producing insecurity, and provoking irrationality.[73]

Mannheim's quest to find the means of "transforming man" was, as he recognized, matched by other schools of thought similarly dedicated, from pragmatism to behaviorism and psychoanalysis.[74] In so far as all of these approaches were committed, in essence, to the depoliticization of political decision making, they were joined by perhaps the second most influential tradition: functionalism. This tradition came in two forms: one purer form, closer to the academic theories of its pioneers, and another, more pragmatic form, which offered more a commonsensical account of its premises and was thus far more palatable to British tastes. The academic form was developed first in anthropology, then in America by the sociologist Talcott Parsons, and finally in political science by systems theorists like David Easton, although it owes intellectual debts to both Benthamite utilitarianism and Spencerian sociology.[75] Its initial influence in Britain, as we have seen, was limited: it drew much criticism from the institutionalist establishment but returned later, in the 1960s, in the work of Roy Jones and others on the fringes of the academic world of international relations.

The more pragmatic form of planning is best demonstrated in the functionalist work of David Mitrany, especially in his Chatham House pamphlet *A Working Peace System* (1943). Mitrany's argument has been aptly summarized as "peace by pieces." His case was straightforward: when faced with a problem that required a transnational solution, states took pragmatic decisions to give up an element of their sovereign right over the relevant area and pooled it in an international agency designed to perform the function that the state could not, on its own, perform. This kind of behavior, Mitrany argued, was near-natural—its incidence and its success were evident not merely in functional agencies created in the international realm, such as the International Postal Union, but in those designed to address domestic political issues. Roosevelt's "New Deal" was the ideal illustration of his point—Mitrany characterized it as a series of ad hoc and pragmatic responses to discrete problems: unemployment and the collapse of the banking system, as well as natural disasters. He wrote: "The significant point in that emergency action was that each and every problem was tackled as a practical issue in itself. No attempt was made to relate it to a general theory or system of government. Each function was left to generate others gradually, like the functional subdivision of organic cells; and in every case the appropriate authority was left to grow and develop out of actual performance."[76] Functionalism entailed, in other words, "an original use of conservative ingredients."[77]

Mitrany's appeal rested very much on the apparent meliorism of his approach, which fitted well the prevailing view that liberalism's ends were desirable but its means inadequate, either because it put too much faith in the invisible hand or because its institutions were overly formalistic.[78] He cast functionalism as a *via media* between outright power politics and a world-state, recognizing that a "measure of centralised planning and control, for both production and distribution, is no longer to be avoided," and pre-empted the criticisms of Hayekian adherents to laissez faire by arguing that his agencies posed little risk of becoming tyrannical because their powers were limited by their functions.[79] Gradually, he argued, they would "acquire a purely technical form of management," ceasing to have a political character altogether.[80] These aspirations were shared both by some of the architects of European unity and by some academic internationalists—functionalism, indeed, enjoyed a significant but short-lived vogue in universities in the 1960s, in the work of Ernst Haas and others in the United States and Roy Jones and a few others in Britain.[81]

CONCLUSION

> It is indeed only since 1945 that it has been possible to imagine that the price of justice may literally be the ruin of the world.
> MARTIN WIGHT, "Western Values" (1966)[82]

By the time that functionalism came into vogue in Britain, classical liberal internationalism was all but defunct. For Wight, liberalism could only be sustained when underpinned by natural law, on the one side, and by the belief in progress, on the other. Once both had disappeared—natural law with the decline of Christianity and progress with the rise of the various political ideologies that had replaced traditional religion—liberal internationalism could no longer survive. What was left was an intellectual world divided into conservative cynics and millenarian radicals—what Wight thought of as "realists" and "revolutionists."

This was not, of course, a completely fair account of what occurred in the postwar period. It neglects the extent to which federalists and functionalists saw their preferred approaches as ways of realizing internationalist ends by different means; just as, indeed, the religious internationalists, like Curtis or Toynbee, had conceived their missions. It overlooks too a certain ingrained liberalism which may be found in the writings of committed and unwavering internationalists like Goodwin or Luard. Perhaps most important, it ignores the broader attempt to rebuild liberalism on more modest (but more stable) foundations that took place in the 1950s, one that recognized the weakness of natural law and progress as bases on which to construct a liberal position. This liberal realism took seriously the various criticisms leveled at liberalism in the 1930s and 1940s, but argued that no acceptable alternative had been or could be found to liberal (and therefore internationalist) ways of doing politics or international relations. This argument can be located most obviously in the work of Isaiah Berlin or Karl Popper,[83] but it was prefigured, with direct reference to matters international, in Friedrich Hayek's *Road to Serfdom* (1944).

Like Mannheim, Hayek moved to Britain in the early 1930s and took up a post at the LSE; he did not leave for the United States until 1950. His *Road to Serfdom* is perhaps his best-known work, celebrated and denigrated for its attack on socialist planning, but less often noted is Hayek's trenchant critique of contemporary international relations in the book's final chapter. "In no other field," he began, "has the world paid so dearly for the abandonment of nineteenth-century liberalism as in the field where the retreat began: in international relations."[84] In this realm, the nationalization of economic activity and the imposition of planning had their most deleterious effects, exacerbating and generating conflicts between states that would, in a liberal order, remain conflicts between firms or individuals fought not with armies, but with less destructive weapons of the marketplace. "If the resources of different nations are treated as exclusive properties of these nations as wholes," he argued, "they inevitably become the source of friction and envy between whole nations."[85] A "contest of force" rather than a "'struggle' of competition" could be the only result.[86]

For Hayek, the remedy often proposed for this predicament—planning on an international scale—was similarly fraught with danger. The economic life of a family can be planned, he argued, but as we move up the scale from families to communities to states and to the world, "the amount of agreement to order of ends decreases and the necessity to rely on force and compulsion grows."[87] Thus "[p]lanning on an international scale ... cannot be anything but a naked rule of force" comparable to that required to make the Nazi *Grossraumwirtschaft* work, albeit in the deeply dysfunctional manner that it did.[88]

It was not only the "moral enormity" which was troubling, Hayek argued, but also the political un-realism of planning's proponents. Hayek railed against the proposition that economic planning could be insulated from the political realm, as many internationalists, federalists, and functionalists argued. In thrall to Roosevelt's New Deal, for example, some maintained—like Mannheim and Carr—that a Tennessee Valley Authority for the Danube Basin might be created at the end of the war, international rather than national, and concerned only with the economic development of Southeastern Europe. Hayek had no time for such plans: "The belief that this is a practical solution rests on the fallacy that economic planning is merely a technical task, which can be solved in a strictly objective manner by experts, and that the really vital things would still be left in the hands of the political authorities. Any international economic authority, not subject to a superior political power, even if strictly confined to a particular field, could easily exercise the most tyrannical and irresponsible power imaginable."[89] It was even more difficult to conceive that such an authority could remain benign, Hayek went on, when states were incapable "of enforcing a simple Rule of Law" in international relations, let alone something as complex and powerful as an international organization charged with planning the world economy.

The irony in all this was that these schemes were most ardently supported by those intellectuals who took the most pains, Hayek noted, to "pose as the most hard-boiled realists."[90] Above all, there was the "Red Professor of Printing House Square," E. H. Carr, who had argued in both *The Twenty Years' Crisis* (1939) and *Conditions of Peace* (1942), as well as in his wartime leaders for *The Times*, that economic planning on an international or at least a supranational level was needed to address the root cause of conflict in international relations, the clash between the "haves" and the "have-nots." Hayek recognized that Carr's "realism" consisted not of a realistic appraisal of power and its constraints, but of a willingness to accept the doctrine that the ends justified the means—the ends being a planned economic international order and the means being the subjugation of the rights of individuals and "small nations" in the pursuit of that order.[91] This kind of "realism," he observed, bore an uncanny resemblance to totalitarian diplomacy.

In Hayek's view, what was needed in international relations was the extension of the "Rule of Law," which he called "a safeguard as much against the tyranny of the state over the individual as against the tyranny of the new super-state over the national communities."[92] He recognized that such law would be ineffectual without an enforcer and he proposed one: an international government constituted by federation. Hayek argued:

> We must not allow the numerous ill-considered and often extremely silly claims made on behalf of a federal organisation of the whole world during the height of the propaganda for "Federal Union" to obscure the fact that the principle of federation is the only form of association of different peoples that will create an international order without putting an undue strain on their legitimate desire for independence. Federalism is, of course, nothing but the application to international affairs of democracy, the only method of peaceful change man has yet invented. But it is a democracy with definitely limited powers. Apart from the more impracticable ideal of fusing different countries into a single centralised state . . . it is the only way in which the ideal of international law can be made a reality.[93]

Hayek even admitted that within the bounds of an international federation, with properly balanced powers, some limited planning might be necessary or desirable. The crux was to make political arrangements that would not allow such concentrations as power as planning could encourage to become overbearing or threatening to individuals or small political communities. For Hayek, none of this was "unpracticable and utopian" as the self-styled "realists" or the practitioners of "*Realpolitik*" claimed.[94] His ideals, he argued, had been shared by most liberals for a century and they were no less possible or valid in his own day.

Hayek's thinking is important not so much because it was influential from the late 1940s until the early 1970s, but because it illustrates both the strengths and the weaknesses of British liberal internationalist thinking about international relations in the postwar years. To Hayek's mind, as indeed to Murray's, the problem was not that liberalism or internationalism was intrinsically wrong. Its decline was rather a result of a loss of faith among British intellectuals faced by dilemmas they came to think were intractable or at least unanswerable by exclusively liberal means. As a consequence, they turned to alternatives they thought might fulfill their aims, but which actually—in Hayek's view, at least—placed the internationalist project at greater risk of failure.

Under pressure to confront a series of dilemmas, internationalism thus fragmented, losing much of its earlier power. It remained a default setting for most British intellectuals, many of whom continued to believe that the world was becoming increasingly integrated and that there was some kind of basic moral unity among all peoples, but there were considerable divergences on the best way forward. This weakness, as we will see in the next two chapters, opened the space for challengers, for a reinvented whig tradition and a revitalized radical one.

6. The Whigs and the Diplomatic Tradition

> Let us praise as a living thing the continuity of our history, and praise the whigs who taught us that we must nurse this blessing—reconciling continuity with change, discovering mediations between the past and present, and showing what can be achieved by man's reconciling mind.
>
> HERBERT BUTTERFIELD, *The Englishman and his History* (1944)

In *The Spirit of British Policy* (1931), the German lawyer Hermann Kantorowicz described what he perceived to be the "English" way in international relations. He found it "an admixture of chivalry, objectivity and humanity," cut through with a streak of pure "irrationality." German readers, Kantorowicz urged, should think twice before supposing that British policy was as far-sighted, unswerving, and masterful as they often thought it was. He warned them of the "irrational nature of English life in general." It was wrong, Kantorowicz argued, to see British policy as a "masterpiece of cool, clever, consistent calculation," still less to see it dedicated in any kind of way to any particular policy, like the "Encirclement of Germany."[1] The British were not in fact the diplomatic geniuses Germans—or indeed the British themselves—often supposed: their diplomats were frequently ignorant of foreign peoples, unable to speak foreign languages, even lacking in "professional skill."[2]

Kantorowicz's study is a standing rebuke to one of the more persistent myths about the British, perpetuated by British authors and by foreigners, namely that their politicians and diplomats are unusually adept at their crafts. It is a myth which predates the Second World War, but it was given great impetus by that conflict, by Britain's survival and victory. It is a myth that, as many historians have shown, was manipulated to great effect by British politicians, especially Churchill, who used his histories as well as his political utterances to entrench it.[3] In terms of foreign policy, it cast Great Britain as the defender of European—indeed global—liberties and as the "holder" of the balance of power. In terms of diplomacy, it praised what was presented as an age-old tradition of practical wisdom cultivated by an "aristocracy of talent."[4] Most important of all, this "whig" or "diplomatic" tradition in British foreign policy was lauded by many postwar thinkers for its supposed capacity to guide practitioners along the *via media* between cynical realism and moralistic internationalism.

This invented tradition was "whig" in that it rested upon the whiggish convictions that "English constitutional liberty and representative institutions" were unique, even "exemplary," and that English history was also particular in its continuity.[5] Both beliefs had been shaken by the First World War and its aftermath, but in a more modest form they were reinforced by the Second World War. Together they underpinned a "constitutional" conception of international order or "international society" distinct from the more legalistic version of internationalism and the more revolutionary order envisaged by radicals as well as realist, power-oriented theories.

There is, in addition, a more specific sense in which the "whigs" of the postwar years are worthy of the title. Their preferred foreign policy was derived quite self-consciously from the eighteenth-century whigs. It was at that time, they argued, that British foreign policy reached its highest stage of wisdom and sophistication. The eighteenth-century whigs secured European liberties, including those of Britain, with shifting patterns of temporary alliances and with occasional, limited interventions, throwing their weight against attempts to gain hegemony by continental Great Powers. Thereby the whigs had maintained the order necessary to develop a modicum of civilized international discourse and to achieve a measure of justice in European international relations, not least in terms of protecting the Protestant cause.[6] Interest and virtue were thus aligned. Whether this is or is not a fair assessment of the foreign policy of the eighteenth-century whigs, this was at least the way in which their twentieth-century followers conceived it.[7] And most important of all, they rendered that policy as Britain's *traditional* policy, implying that all deviations from a "whig" approach were aberrant.

In large part, this return to whiggism was a reaction to realist power politics and appeasement on the one hand, and to overconfident internationalism on the other. The whig policy of maintaining a continental balance of power was advocated as the polar opposite of appeasement and as a more "realistic" approach to foreign policy than blind faith in international institutions that avoided the worst excesses of "realism." Appeasement, realism, and liberal or radical forms of internationalism were cast as deviations from the norm. This argument was best expressed by Churchill, beginning with a speech of March 1936:

For four hundred years the foreign policy of England has been to oppose the strongest, most aggressive, most dominating Power on the Continent, and particularly to prevent the Low Countries falling into the hands of such a Power . . . Moreover, on all occasions England took the more difficult course. . . . [I]t would have been easy and must have been very tempting to join with the stronger and share the fruits of his conquest. However, we always took the harder course, joined with the less strong Powers, made a combination among them, and thus defeated and frustrated the Continental military tyrant, whoever he was, whatever nation he led. Thus we preserved the liberties of Europe . . . Here is the wonderful unconscious tradition of British Foreign Policy.[8]

For Churchill, in 1936, the collective security provisions of the League of Nations "harmonises perfectly" with these "past methods and actions" as well as those "broad of right and wrong" held by the British. "We wish," he went on, " for the reign of law and freedom among nations and within nations, and it was for that, and nothing less than that, that those bygone architects of our repute, magnitude, and civilization fought, toiled, and won."[9]

Appeasement, realist power politics, and blind internationalism were, in this context, nothing less than betrayals of a national tradition, rather than merely a shift in policy. The argument that appeasement—or at least the adjustment of British assets and principles to the demands of rising powers—might in fact have been more "traditional" was, in such circumstances, impossible to countenance.[10] The connected argument that British foreign policy and diplomacy were just as mired in power politics as that of continental powers was also anathema, for, as Churchill and many others argued, it was the very fact that Britain had been unbending in its opposition to such behavior that had delivered its successes.

This revival of whiggism in the 1930s and 1940s went hand in hand with a renewed emphasis on diplomacy, especially the "old diplomacy" of the world before 1914.[11] In the diplomatic system, particularly as practiced by British diplomats, scholars and politicians found similar virtues to those supposedly inherent in whig practices of politics. In best forms of both, a premium was placed upon toleration and compromise, as well as measured adaptation to change. Diplomacy itself, as an "institution" of "international society" could thus be conceived as English whiggism writ large.[12] In international as in domestic politics, the whig-diplomats emphasized the importance of rules, institutions, and constitutional form as the means by which the disruptions caused by radical change might be mitigated while evolutionary development is permitted.[13] These rules, institutions, and constitutional forms are not valued, however, purely for themselves, but for the political wisdom they supposedly embodied.[14] In the same way, the offices, rituals, and protocols of diplomacy were valued by some British intellectuals not simply because they were useful, but because they expressed a deeper set of assumptions and ideas about human nature, politics, and international relations.

This chapter traces the development of these convictions. It explores the attempt to build—or, as its enthusiasts wished to see it, to reclaim—a whig tradition of diplomacy that might avoid the pitfalls of both liberal internationalism and power political realism. The first part examines the role of diplomatic and international history, in its dominant modern empiricist forms, in grounding this work in the interwar and immediate postwar period. It looks especially at the critical role played by Harold Nicolson in contriving a conception of diplomacy capable of bearing the weight of the whig project. The second section explores the efforts of Herbert Butterfield to bridge the gap between English whiggism in political and historical thought and the study of international relations. The third turns to the work of Martin Wight and to his attempt to set out an account of "Western values" in the conduct of international relations infused with whig assumptions. The conclusion discusses the decline of the whig tradition and its legacy for the more conservative, "pluralist" wing of the "English school of international relations" that grew out of that tradition.

DIPLOMATIC INVESTIGATIONS

> Their procedure has been . . . empirical and inductive. Their point of view has on the whole been historical. They have tended to suppose that the continuities in international relations are more important than the innovations; that statecraft is an historical deposit of practical wisdom growing very slowly; that the political, diplomatic, legal and military writers who might loosely be termed "classical" have not been superseded as a result of recent developments in sociology or psychology, and that it is a useful enterprise to explore the corpus of diplomatic and military experience in order to reformulate its lessons in relation to contemporary needs.
>
> HERBERT BUTTERFIELD and MARTIN WIGHT,
> preface to *Diplomatic Investigations* (1966)[15]

The 1920s and 1930s saw the heyday of diplomatic history and the beginnings of diplomatic theory.[16] The opening of the British and continental state archives to researchers had fueled the earlier rise of diplomatic history, from the 1890s until 1914, and easier access to the private papers of many of the protagonists in nineteenth-century European diplomacy intensified interest in the 1920s and 1930s. The availability of materials was not, however, the sole reason for the burgeoning interest in the interwar period: diplomatic historians also had practical concerns with improving the conduct of contemporary diplomacy and international relations. They found an unusually receptive audience among diplomats and politicians who read their work and even invited their participation in practical matters: the peace negotiations at Versailles, in particular, were thick with historians, among them E. H. Carr, Lewis Namier, Harold Temperley, Arnold J. Toynbee, and Charles Webster. New sources and new experiences thus produced a series of major works of classical diplomatic history during the 1920s and 1930s, not least of which were Temperley's study of Canning's foreign policy and Webster's of Castlereagh's.[17]

In the postwar period, diplomatic histories gave way to "international histories" and then "contemporary histories" which, though they took broader views, were no less popular or influential.[18] Indeed, it is fair to say that these studies of international relations were far more common in Britain than theoretical or social-scientific works on the subject. No text on international relations had the reach or the sales of A. J. P. Taylor's *Origins of the Second World War* (1961), for example, and no such text arguably had the same effect on public and academic thinking about appeasement and "power politics."[19] The sources on which such work was based were, of necessity, quite different from those used by diplomatic historians: newspaper reports, eyewitness accounts, and educated conjecture, rather than official documents, which were generally subject to secrecy for at least thirty years. Both kinds of historiography were central to the British study of international relations in universities and were used widely as textbooks for courses in recent international history, as well as being fodder for debate among concerned intellectuals.[20]

In methodological terms, these historians were all broadly committed to versions of "modernist empiricism"[21]—with the obvious exception of the methodologically heterodox Toynbee. An approach shared by both historians and many British students of politics, modernist empiricism can be detected in a slew of significant works from the late 1920s to the 1960s—in Lewis Namier's prosopographical studies of parliamentarians, for example, or in S. E. Finer's work on comparative government.[22] Among contemporary studies of international relations, modernist empiricism is similarly common—see Geoffrey Goodwin's *Britain and the United*

Nations (1957) or F. H. Hinsley's *Nationalism and the International System* (1973).[23]

Modernist empiricists assumed a straightforward relationship between the scholar-as-observer and the world they observed. They assumed, too, that a real world of phenomena existed and that it could be observed and explained if the scholar strove to eliminate "bias" and to pursue "objectivity." These objectives were achieved partly by the application of the correct method and partly by upholding related "professional" norms.[24] Modernist empiricist historians set themselves the tasks of extracting the truth of historical events from the evidence, establishing facts, and correcting the errors of past historians. Modernist political scientists differed only in what they did with their facts once they found them—comparing and contrasting them, sometimes quantifying them, organizing them into types—instead of constructing them into a narrative. Indeed, for scholars of politics, modernist empiricism thus opened up, as Bevir argues, "an epistemic space in which . . . [politics] . . . might be explained by the discovery of laws or regularities based on quantitative analysis of opinion and behaviour or on the creation of suitable typologies."[25] At the same time, modernist empiricists eschewed the kind of "theory" that dragged them into ontology or epistemology. In the main, they saw themselves not as philosophers, as Michael Bentley argues, but "as practical people doing a practical activity."[26]

Modernist empiricists studying international history and international relations thought in much the same terms. In Britain, they might not have been interested in "laws," as they were in America, but they were certainly concerned with persistent "regularities" and typologies, and in relationships between agency and structure.[27] The work of the historian Herbert Butterfield illustrates this well. A classic modernist empiricist, Butterfield was drawn by his concern for international relations into more theoretical territory.[28] In a series of works—especially *Christianity and History* (1949), *History and Human Relations* (1950), and *Man on His Past* (1955)—Butterfield developed something that approached a modernist philosophy of history, albeit one that sprung as much from religious as professional concerns, which informed his view of the theory and the practice of international relations.[29] What Butterfield sought was typical of modernist empiricists: a "technical history" or a narrative of past events that all parties would accept as substantively true. To achieve this, the "technical historian" had thus to blend rigorous training in the handling of sources with a cultivated sense of what Butterfield called "imaginative sympathy." Applying both, this historian could, he argued, produce as near to an unbiased account as possible of what was done by human agents within the context of the "structure" in which they acted.

This "technical history" was part science and part art—scientific in the sense that the rigorous application of a method grounded in inductive empiricism allowed the "facts" of an historical episode to be found in the evidence; artistic because the bare narrative of facts needed to be abridged in order for a coherent historical story to be told, and this abridgement could only be the product of "impressionism."[30] This impressionism was kept in check by what Butterfield called "self-emptying"—"severe measures of self-discipline and self-purification" combined with the suspension of moral judgment.[31] "For the historian," he observed in his inaugural lecture as professor of modern history in 1944, "the only true morality is a wide catholicity."[32] These were not, of course, methodological propositions, still less philosophical ones; rather, they were attempts to establish professional norms to delimit the concerns of the "technical historian," lest they stray into areas they should not, such as political advocacy or advice. Above all, they were attempts to render the study of the past scientific—in the sense of "value-free"—to defend it from criticism and to maintain professional autonomy.[33]

The counterpart of Butterfield's ideal of professional "technical history" in the study of international relations may be found in Hedley Bull's "case for a classical approach," published in *World Politics* in 1966.[34] The bulk of the article was actually taken up by a case against American scientific approaches,[35] but when the defense of Bull's preferred approach came, it was couched in impeccably modernist empiricist terms. The classical approach did not mean, he argued, "the study and criticism of the 'classics' of international relations, the writings of Hobbes, Grotius, Kant, and other great thinkers of the past." Instead, what the "classical approach" entailed was "something wider than this." It referred to "the approach to theorizing that derives from philosophy, history, and law, and that is characterized above all by explicit reliance upon the exercise of judgment and by the assumptions that if we confine ourselves to strict standards of verification and proof there is very little of significance that can been said about international relations, that general propositions . . . must therefore derive from a scientifically imperfect process of perception and intuition, and that these general propositions cannot be accorded anything more than the tentative and inconclusive status appropriate to their doubtful origin."[36] What this amounted to, however, was little more than a call for caution when dealing with facts rather than a denial that facts can be established—an issue less of methodology than of professional norms of conduct. The appeal to "philosophy, history and law" was, in that context, quite empty, since it assumes that the study of these fields involves no methodological challenges or that the best method (i.e., inductive empiricism) has already been agreed upon.

Bull admitted that "general propositions" about international relations were indeed possible and may even be desirable, and that "systematizations of international theory" were similarly possible and desirable, albeit only in the form that Zimmern, Carr, Morgenthau, Raymond Aron, and Wight had rendered them.[37] These were significant admissions. Neither could or would be made by a philosophical Idealist or a thoroughgoing historicist, who must argue that all ages are different from each another and that, as a result, there is no proper basis for the kinds of comparison between historical events that could generate the "general propositions" that make up "systematizations of international theory."

Bull's seven objections to what he calls the "scientific approach" moved him no further in a historicist direction or away from an essentially empiricist position. Instead, he appealed for a space to be left, alongside what could be mathematically or logically proven, for "judgment," especially on normative questions, suggested that the insights of the scientific approach might be arrived at by other routes, and cast doubt on the prospects for theoretical progress. He objected to the fetishization of models—arguing that their axioms and assumptions might better be cast as "empirical generalization[s]"—and of measurement, asserting that "rigor and precision" was not the sole preserve of the "scientific approach" and that its practitioners were unreflective and uncritical about their methods.

At no point did Bull challenge the epistemological assumptions of the "scientific approach" or the notion that "facts" might be distilled from "history" and compared, contrasted, classified, and organized into general propositions. Indeed, he insisted that "[t]he theory of international relations should undoubtedly attempt to be scientific in the sense of being a coherent, precise, and orderly body of knowledge, and in the sense of being consistent with the philosophical foundations of modern science."[38] Though Bull explicitly eschewed the term at the outset of his article, his case was actually an empiricist call for "science" against what he perceived as mere "scientism," rather than a call to revive earlier historicist or philosophical Idealist modes of political or international thought. His preferred approach was not to moralize or simply narrate accounts of events, and still less to narrate accounts laden with what Bull dismissively referred to as "providentialism,"[39] as the interwar "idealists" had done, but objectively to analyze international politics with those "techniques of quantification, comparison, classification and the search for regularities" central to modernist empiricism.⁴⁰

For Roy Jones, Bull's reaction to American social science was best "equated with Caliban's howl of horror and rage on being confronted with his own reflection" rather than viewed as true disagreement about substantive philosophical or methodological propositions.⁴¹ There is much truth to this. The difference between the proponents of modernist empiricism and those of behavioral theories lay not in ontology, epistemology, or even in method, but in what they took to be the professional norms of conduct for students of international relations, as well as in what might be called their proper dispositions with regard to their subject-matter and practical politics.⁴² Bull's complaint was not that David Easton or Thomas C. Schelling misconstrued or mistreated the materials to be studied in international relations, but merely that they overstated the possibilities of their work for improving the practice of international relations. Bull's reasons for believing this did not derive from his appraisal of their methods, however, but rather from a deeper political or moral conviction that academics must assume the mantle of skepticism and profess disinterest in worldly things if they are to maintain their professional objectivity. Again, the object was to preserve autonomy and authority with an insistence that scholarship be "value-free"—at least until the "facts" are established and "judgment" can be reached.

This robust approach underpinned the whig tradition, though it was not exclusive to it. There were radical modernist empiricists—including very significant figures like A. J. P. Taylor—and there were liberal ones, like Geoffrey Goodwin. But it helped especially to sustain a way of thinking about foreign policy and international relations which prided itself on being commonsensical and down to earth.

THE INVENTION OF A TRADITION

> The general decline, in this century, of artificial manners is rather worse than interesting; and in no sphere has the downward curve been so steep as in diplomacy.
> LORD VANSITTART, "The Decline of Diplomacy" (1950)⁴³

> ... we should be on stronger ground if we made our case more diplomatic and less ideological.
> HERBERT BUTTERFIELD to Max Beloff, 15 June 1950⁴⁴

The modernist insistence on "professional objectivity" did not preclude the idea that the findings of their historical studies could inform the practice of diplomacy. The British diplomatic historians of the interwar and immediate postwar years, in particular, thought this was not just proper but essential. Charles Webster, for example, argued that the "more scientific" their work was the more it would generate knowledge for "men of action."[45] Webster's own lessons were that British diplomacy (which was almost always right) must (if it was to remain so) be as broadmindedly European as possible, recognizing Britain's inextricable links to the continent and its obligations to the maintenance of the European international order and to the prospects of constitutional government abroad as well as at home.[46]

Diplomatic history could thus be a cipher for the prejudices of the historian, but often it went deeper. From about 1930 onward, historians and others—notably former practitioners—contributed to a wider reappraisal of contemporary practices of diplomacy that had more significant results. This involved a reassessment of the virtues of the reforms to diplomacy brought about by the advent of the League of Nations and a new appreciation of the value of earlier forms of diplomatic conduct. This reassessment was—in turn—a function of a more general tendency, detected by Harold Nicolson in 1934, "to react against the unctuous inertia, the flood-lit self-righteousness, the timid imprecision, the appalling amateurishness of democratic diplomacy, in favour of the more efficient and professional methods of the old."[47] In part, too, it was driven by a growing sense that diplomacy was in decline and that the loss of the better diplomatic practices would have grave consequences for international order. The result was an upsurge of interest in the techniques and mechanics of diplomacy as an "institution" of "international society" that prefigured the better-known work of the "English school" in the 1960s and 1970s.[48]

Nicolson[49]—as a historian and as a former diplomat—contributed significant early efforts to this cause, beginning with his study of his father's role in the prelude to the First World War (1930), and continuing in his dissection of *Peacemaking 1919* (1933), his classic *Diplomacy* (1939), and finally in his portentous *Congress of Vienna* (1948).[50] In these works Nicolson utilized diplomatic history to distill something like a theory of diplomacy, guided by the belief that there are, as he put it in the second edition of *Diplomacy* in 1950, "necessary and immutable" principles of diplomatic practice.[51] Diplomacy, he asserted, was merely the process of negotiation, not the process of policymaking, which was properly the role of politicians and their advisers. It was properly a "continuous process," as he put, albeit one subject to disruption.[52]

For Nicolson, the practice of diplomacy had been severely affected by the First World War and its aftermath, developments which had given rise to a "new diplomacy." This "new diplomacy" was not simply the product, as often assumed, of the shift from "absolutism" to "democratic control" over foreign policy, nor was it a straightforward process of moving from "secret diplomacy" to an "open" version. Nicolson noted that other factors were at work: "first a growing sense of the community of nations; secondly an increasing appreciation of the importance of public opinion; and thirdly the rapid increase in communications."[53]

While Nicolson acknowledged that some change was necessary, he railed against those who insisted that democratic control over foreign policy—"a legitimate subject"—ought to extend into democratic control over the manner of negotiation.[54] Open covenants, once negotiated, were one thing; open negotiations were quite another. Nicolson was deeply skeptical as to whether negotiations could be conducted in the full glare of publicity, not least because of what he termed the "irresponsibility of the sovereign people."[55] This irresponsibility had two parts: one was straightforward fecklessness, the other born of ignorance as to the extent and content of the responsibilities of states in international relations.[56] Whipped up by equally irresponsible journalists, peoples were prone to push for the disavowal of agreements and the repudiation of treaties, behavior that, if encouraged, would lead to literal "anarchy" in international relations.[57] These basic problems were exacerbated by a number of others. Delay, imprecision, and excessive emotion were all characteristic of the "new diplomacy." Finally, an even "more dangerous innovation in diplomatic practice," Nicolson judged, "is the tendency of democratic countries to allow their politicians to take a personal part in negotiation."[58]

True to the whig tradition, Nicolson acknowledged that changes had to be made, but he insisted these changes be limited. In both the new and the old diplomacy he thought the ideal diplomatist ought to be truthful, reliable, precise, calm, modest, and loyal. There was no need to modify those essential qualities. He also suggested that British diplomacy might serve as a model of the ideal form. British diplomatists might "display little initiative" and "take no pains to impress others with their intellectual brilliance," but they remain "exceptionally well informed" and "almost always" succeed.[59] The explanation for this apparent anomaly was deeply rooted: "British diplomacy is but the expression," Nicolson argued, "of those principles of policy which, owing to history, geographical position, imperial responsibilities, liberal institutions and national character have, in the course of centuries, been found best suited to British requirements."[60]

These principles were best expressed, Nicolson wrote, in Sir Eyre

Crowe's famous memorandum of 1907. British foreign policy and diplomacy was, as Crowe described it, above all a function of geographical isolation. In turn, that isolation shaped two primary interests for the nation: independence and free trade. To secure both, Britain was bound to ensure the independence of the small states of Europe and the maintenance of the balance of power between the great ones. Together the pursuit of these interests "imposed upon British policy a peculiar quality of empiricism, or even of opportunism" that distinguished it from the German tendency to "planned ambitions" or the French to a "preoccupation with a hereditary enemy."[61] This empiricism did not preclude "idealism," Nicolson acknowledged; indeed, for the British, he thought that normally the "first impulse is one of humanitarianism and it is only at a later stage that the motives of self-interest or of self-preservation come into play."[62]

The best British diplomatists reflected, Nicolson thought, the merits of these policies and impulses, as well as their failings: "The good British diplomatist is tolerant and fair; he acquires a fine balance between imagination and reason, between idealism and realism; he is reliable and scrupulously precise; he possesses dignity without self-importance, demeanor without mannerisms, poise without stolidity; he can display resolution as well as flexibility, and can combine gentleness with courage; he never boasts; he knows that impatience is as dangerous as illtemper and that intellectual brilliance is not a diplomatic quality . . . and that the foundation of good diplomacy is the same as the formulation of good business—namely credit, confidence, consideration and compromise."[63] By contrast, Germans tended toward a "heroic" or "warrior" mode of diplomacy befitting their cultural heritage. Their guiding philosophy was one of *"Machtpolitik"* or "Power policy," with the object of inspiring "fear" rather than "confidence" in their interlocutors.[64] French policy, on the other hand, was "tense, rigid and inelastic" and French diplomatists—while "honourable and precise"—essentially superior and intolerant.[65]

What Nicolson did, in other words, was to construct an image of the ideal diplomacy that was almost wholly shaped by an idealized account of British practice informed by whig principle and inductive empiricism. In this, he was not alone; indeed, in the postwar years his lead was followed by a number of intellectuals and not a few diplomats-turned-writers, whether of memoirs or of reflection on international politics. In some of their hands, Nicolson's account of ideal diplomacy was transformed, indeed, into something close to a theory of international politics: a whig theory which drew as much on historical interpretation and on moral argument as on diplomatic experience.

THE DEVELOPMENT OF WHIG THEORY

> [The] essential diplomatic object [is] the establishment and preservation of an international order which shall comprehend conflicting ideologies and rival cupidities.
> HERBERT BUTTERFIELD, "The Balance of Power" (1959)[66]

The scourge of whig historians in the interwar years, Herbert Butterfield (1900–1979) was one of the most significant progenitors of the whig theory of foreign policy in the postwar period.[67] In his mind, there was no inconsistency between these two positions. The "whig interpretation of history" was bad history from a professional point of view, Butterfield thought, but it promoted good political thinking.[68] Its excessive moralism and over-abridgement of historical events produced distorted accounts of the past, of past acts, and of the contexts within which they occurred.[69] But the effects on British political thinking of whig history more than outweighed these historiographical failings. It produced, Butterfield argued, "an attitude to the historical process, a way of co-operating with the forces of history, an alliance with Providence" which permitted the "Englishman" to avoid revolution at home and conquest from abroad.[70]

Butterfield thus pitched the whig tradition against contemporary whig historians with the aim of producing better history and reminding the British of its political virtues. At the core of this tradition, as he described it, was a peculiarly humane stance toward others. This stance was key to both sound history and sound foreign policy, but Butterfield thought it had been lost among contemporary whig historians. "The primary assumption of all attempts to understand the men of the past," he argued, "must be the belief we can in some degree enter into minds that are unlike our own."[71] If they are properly to understand the past, therefore, historians must promise not to judge at all, or at least suspend judgment for a time, before they attempt to "enter into minds unlike our own." "Real historical understanding is not achieved by the subordination of the past to the present" by judging it by our moral standards, Butterfield wrote, "but rather by our making the past our present and attempting to see life with the eyes of another century than our own."[72]

Butterfield's concern with this point was rooted as much in his religious views as with his historical thought. He was convinced that modern political evils were in part the product of a devaluing of what he called "human personality," and that devaluing was a product, in turn, of progressivism as much as of straightforward secularization. Viewing all generations as equidistant from eternity, as the historicist should, was both good history and a sound footing for moral and political conduct. In turn, history properly done could have a beneficial influence over society, since, as Butterfield put it, "the historian deals with historical events not as though they were things which could be mechanically and externally explained but as they come out of personalities and run into personalities."[73] History and Christianity were thus complementary in this regard: "The historian begins ... with a higher estimate of the status of personality than thinkers in some other fields, just as Christianity itself does when it sees each individual as a creature of eternal moment."[74]

None of this implied that the historian or the Christian ought to be unrealistic about human beings or politics. "Having made this splendid start," Butterfield went on, "the historian proceeds—like the tradition of Christian theology itself—to a lower view of human nature than the one commonly current in the twentieth century."[75] For him,

> [t]he plain truth is that if you were to remove certain subtle safeguards in society many men who had been respectable all their lives would be transformed by the discovery of things which it was now possible to do with impunity; weak men would apparently take to crime who had previously been kept on the rails by a certain balance existing in society ... A great and prolonged police-strike, the existence of a revolutionary situation in a capital city, and the exhilaration of conquest in an enemy country are likely to show up a seamy side of human nature amongst people who, cushioned and guided by the influences of normal social life, have hitherto presented a respectable figure to the world.[76]

The problem was that although historians witnessed the realities of social and political life in their everyday work, not all historians appreciated them as they should. "Some of us," wrote Butterfield, "have become so accustomed to a humane form of society, which cushions the conflicts between men and mitigates the self-aggression, that we imagine its virtues to spring straight out of nature with no more cultivation than the wild flowers on the bank of a stream."[77]

Such assumptions were not only wrong, they were positively harmful. Among historians, this naïve view of human nature led to the righteousness of the whig interpretation. In both domestic and international politics, it led to similar forms of "moral indignation,"[78] but with even more dire consequences. For Butterfield, the taproot of the international crisis of the twentieth century, of revolution, mass murder, and wars unprecedented in their destructiveness and savagery, was this moralism.

Butterfield's argument is best expressed in two articles, "The Tragic Element in Modern International Conflict" (1950) and "The Scientific versus the Moralistic Approach" (1951).[79] In both, he brought what he called his "historical thinking" to bear on contemporary problems, wielding it to combat moralism, for "[w]hile there is battle and hatred men have eyes for nothing save the fact that the enemy is the cause of all the troubles; but long, long afterward, when all passion has been spent, the historian often sees that it was a conflict between one half-right that was perhaps too wilful, and another half-right that was perhaps too proud; and behind even this he discerns that it was a terrible predicament, which had the effect of putting men so at cross-purposes with one another."[80] Butterfield's message was simple and clear: if we take the historian's—and, of course, what he considered to be the Christian's—view, we might avoid moralism and practice better international relations.

This "historical thinking" led Butterfield to interpret the Cold War—and implicitly also the Second World War—not as a struggle between good and evil or even a better polity and a worse one, but as a "tragic" predicament in which "each side [is] locked in its own system of self-righteousness."[81] The conflict had arisen, he implied, merely out of the workings of what he called "Hobbesian fear."[82] For those who truly understood this kind of predicament—historians, some Christians perhaps, and certainly "hard-headed eighteenth-century masters of *realpolitik*"—such a situation ought not to pose problems. But for those who did not, the outcome was likely to be worsening relations, with each side "shrieking morality of that particular kind which springs from self-righteousness."[83]

Sometimes, and somewhat tentatively, Butterfield called his position "realism," but it bore little obvious resemblance to its American or continental cousins.[84] He offered it as a self-conscious response to what he—and Nicolson—called the "new diplomacy" of some radicals and internationalists. In "The Tragic Element" he called its advocates "specialists in wishful thinking" for believing that a problem that was "a standing feature of mankind in human history" could be solved by "referring it to a conference or sending it to the United Nations."[85] In later essays, Butterfield extended his attack. In *Christianity, Diplomacy and War* (1953) he acknowledged that "new techniques" to "oil the wheels of diplomatic intercourse" might be—and, in the past, had been—found, and that such changes had nurtured a certain "moral code" among diplomats, not least with regard to truthfulness.[86] Diplomacy could thus become, as he put it, more "urbane"—moving away from a "purely technical diplomacy" governed by the rules of *Realpolitik*.[87] At its height, such diplomacy could attain great things—the Vienna settlement of 1815, for example, which Butterfield argued "worked miracles in the effective reconciliation of victor and vanquished."[88] Such high points of the "European diplomatic tradition," he mused, could be "regarded as a highly elaborate projection of the idea of saving the world by an exercise of charity . . . [or] . . . forgiveness of sins."[89]

Shorn of its Christian subtext, this argument reappeared in a more elaborate form in "The New Diplomacy and Historical Diplomacy" included in the book Butterfield edited with Wight, *Diplomatic Investigations* (1966). The essay was also stripped of any footnotes or references, but Butterfield's account of the "new diplomacy" relied heavily on Nicolson. Like Nicolson, Butterfield portrayed the new diplomacy less in terms of new techniques and more in terms of the emergence of new attitudes to international relations. The new institutions, in other words, were less important than the new ideas that animated them. Conferences were not in themselves the problem; rather it was the rejection of a set of what he considered sensible attitudes about the ways in which international affairs are best managed by any state, regardless of its political predilections. Butterfield argued: "If it is unwise to exploit a victory over-much, or to forget that the enemy of today may be needed as an ally tomorrow—if it is wrong, through reliance upon the virtue of a certain power, to allow that power to get into a position where it can behave with impunity—these things do not become more admissible when practised by democracies rather than by monarchies."[90] What was imperative, then, was the recovery of these elements of wisdom that together formed the "experience of centuries" and their reconstruction into something akin to a "science of diplomacy."[91]

Butterfield's preferred "science" was a whiggish leavened *Realpolitik* partly derived from his early work on eighteenth- and early-nineteenth-century diplomatic history and partly from his reading of Machiavelli and Guicciardini.[92] Butterfield disliked the Florentine's inflexible historical methods, but greatly admired the audacity of his attempt to build a science of statecraft composed of political maxims of enduring validity. As an historian and political scientist, he preferred Machiavelli's contemporary Guicciardini, who developed a similar method but avoided the twin pitfalls of becoming "doctrinaire" and of shifting, as Butterfield put it, from a valid inductive approach to an invalid deductive one.[93] Indeed, Machiavelli's failing, in Butterfield's eyes, was that he was insufficiently realistic in his understanding of what happened around him: he was "a student and writer defective in his contacts with the actual world."[94]

Butterfield's own problem was that in seeking to take the historian's—and what he took to be the Christian's—view of contemporary international politics, he too often lapsed into a kind of relativism that could only paralyze both thought and action, taking him also a bit too far from reality. The fact that his arguments are so frequently expressed in opaque language also suggests that he himself had doubts as to their veracity. In "The Tragic Element," for instance, he implied—but did not spell out—the *ex post facto* argument that the Allies should have negotiated peace with Nazi Germany rather than, as in fact occurred, insisting on that regime's absolute surrender. Butterfield's reasoning was consequentialist; his conclusions were confirmed by his appraisal of the present world, as he argued in 1951: "In respect of the great diplomatic problem of the twentieth century, we may wonder sometimes whether Russia was so much more virtuous than Germany as to make it worth the lives of tens of millions of people in two wars to ensure that she (as a Communist system—or even as a Tsarist empire) should gain such an unchallenged and exclusive hold over that line of Central European States as Germany never had in all her history, and never could have had unless Russia had first been wiped out as a great State."[95] This kind of reasoning probably informed Butterfield's earlier support for Chamberlain's policy of appeasement and for the Munich settlement of 1938. Certainly, those events were uppermost in his mind just over a decade later when he contrasted Allied acquiescence in "our moment of victory" to the Soviet takeover of Eastern Europe to the alternative countenance at Munich.[96]

Righteousness, in other words, produced far worse outcomes than the pursuit of self-interest. Given Hobbesian fear and the predicament that it produces, the best that Butterfield thought we could hope for is a "tolerable balance of forces."[97] Better, then, to concentrate on the possible consequences of competing courses of action than, in Kantian fashion, on the purity of the principles avowed by the protagonists. This, for Butterfield, was the wisdom distilled from diplomatic experience. "In times past," he argued, "it would have been realised that the most essential thing of all is to guard against the kind of war which, if you win absolutely, will produce another 'predicament' worse than the one you started with."[98]

The difficulty here is whether what Butterfield recommended as an adequate guard against such dangers really was the distillation of European diplomatic wisdom or a later interpolation—conscious or unconscious—of other values into that tradition. In much the same way as his understanding of the historian's proper stance toward the past was an extension of his understanding of the Christian's proper duties to others, Butterfield's preferred mode of diplomacy looks very much like a further extension of the same ethical code. The suspension of judgment, the extension of understanding, the insistence on mercy and the conviction that "the principle of love . . . is the final touchstone" holding all in "harmonious relationships"—these underpinned not just his religion, but also the history and the diplomacy he favored.⁹⁹

These informed what Martin Wight called—in marginalia scribbled during an early meeting of the British Committee—"H.B.'s dogmas," namely that:

1. "Historical" thinking is more international than "political" [thinking].
2. West must accept *status quo:* not promote revisionism.
3. International politics must be undoctrinal.¹⁰⁰

Throughout the 1960s, Butterfield struggled—without much success—to put flesh on these bare bones. In *International Conflict* (1960) he tried to establish the basics of what he called the "geometry" of international relations, opening the door to a more "scientific" treatment of the field. In the mid-1960s, in search of such a "science," he began to explore the works of various American theorists of international relations, including those of Karl Deutsch, Morton Kaplan, and Thomas Schelling.¹⁰¹ Indeed, by 1968 Butterfield had come to the view that his British Committee had perhaps unjustly neglected social scientific theories of international relations, even if he remained convinced that "wisdom-literature" was preferable to "geometry" when it came to counseling policymakers.¹⁰²

Butterfield's attempt to construct a whig theory of international relations thus ground to a halt. His project was taken up, however, by others in his circle—most notably by Martin Wight and later by Butterfield's former student, Adam Watson. Their efforts broke the link—or at least attenuated it to the point where it was no longer visible—with Butterfield's religion and philosophy of history. In Wight's case, this break was effected by reconnecting the whig tradition of diplomacy with the whig tradition of government; in Watson's, it was achieved by returning to the detail of diplomatic practice.

THE WHIG AND THE WESTERN TRADITION

> There has always existed a theory of international relations which asserts the primacy of common conceptions of justice, right and law. There was an ancient tradition, dating back through the jurists and theologians of the Middle Ages to the jurists and philosophers of antiquity, of Natural Law or the Law of Nations. . . . But it was eclipsed by the new revolutionaries' creed of progress at the end of the eighteenth century, just at the time when the European Powers . . . were beginning to establish the material unification of the world.
>
> MARTIN WIGHT, *Power Politics* (1946)¹⁰³

The original title of Martin Wight's famous account of "Western Values in International Relations" (1966)—the essay that best captures his mature view of the history of international thought—was "The Whig Tradition in International Theory and Western Values."[104] Quite why he later changed the title is not clear, but it ought not distract attention from the intimate connection in Wight's thought between whiggism and the "Western tradition" of thinking about international relations that he sought to recover.[105] The whig tradition and what has been called the "international society" tradition of the early English school were, at this point at least, one and the same.

Wight's concern with the whig tradition was first expressed in the final chapter of *Power Politics* (1946) and it remained a central theme in all of what followed. For Wight, the tradition lay at the very core of Western civilization, an amalgam of Classical political thought and Christian principle, but it had been, he feared, in decline since the eighteenth century. "It is the main influence," he wrote in *Power Politics*, "that has modified, and can yet modify, the operations of power politics, and it still gleams faintly in the Charter of the United Nations."[106] It clung to life, Wight argued, in "countries whose culture and politics are favourable to its survival"—by which he meant the United States and Britain, though he did not name them.[107] He explored its central arguments in action, as it were, in his essay on "The Balance of Power" in the *Survey of International Affairs* for March 1939 (1952), and in theory in a series of pieces, culminating in "Western Values" in 1966.[108]

For Wight, Western values were not "what all Western men believe in or ought to believe in," but rather the much more restricted "highest common factor of the range of beliefs by which Western men live." In political thought, he observed that such values are taken to inform and underpin "the development and organization of liberty, especially in the form of the tradition of constitutional government which descends from Aristotle through Aquinas to Locke and the Founding Fathers."[109] In international relations Western values were manifest in what Wight called "the Whig or 'constitutional' tradition in diplomacy."[110] They underpinned the "endeavour" of Western states to "turn the former anarchy of international relations into a reign of law and order and a reasonable measure of justice," first by means of the League of Nations and then—albeit in a flawed manner—the United Nations.[111]

In Wight's famous international theory lectures at Chicago and the LSE in the late 1950s, this Western tradition was also called the "rationalist" or "Grotian tradition," after the Dutch theologian and philosopher

Hugo Grotius.[112] Such has been the interest in Grotius' thought among the members of the latter-day "English school," and such has been the fascination with Wight's lectures, which were reconstituted and published in 1990,[113] that this identification of his preferred tradition as "rationalist" or "Grotian" has overshadowed its other "whig" or "Western" appellation.[114] The result has been the close examination of one part of the tradition—the "Grotian" part—and the neglect of the whig aspect.[115] What gets lost, too, is Wight's identification of the "Western tradition" with a specifically *British*, or even *English*, way of thinking about and conducting international politics.[116]

Wight's apparently "purely illustrative" list of thinkers and practitioners he thought had contributed most to the Western tradition did not, of course, just include British names. In full, it ran: "Suarez, Grotius, Locke, Halifax, Callières, Montesquieu, Burke, Gentz, Coleridge, Castlereagh, Tocqueville, Lincoln, Gladstone, Cecil of Chelwood, Ferrero, Brierly, Harold Nicolson, Churchill, Spaak."[117] But a majority of these—a bare majority, admittedly, and one that depends on including Burke—were British. For Wight, "Western values" were very much Anglo or, at a stretch, Anglo-American values; his boundary between the West and the rest was not even at the Rhine, as it often was in the interwar years, but rather at the English Channel. Moreover, the inclusion of Gentz or Ferrero has a slightly token quality to it. And whether Callières, Montesquieu, or Tocqueville can be considered representative of the mainstream of French political or international thought is questionable.

Wight did declare that "the tradition of British diplomacy is by itself a weak authority for Western values," acknowledging that the "French or ... American" traditions "have as much right as the British to be the bearers of Western values."[118] But for "preliminary identification," he suggested that this Western tradition might be best understood as having an "explicit connection with the political philosophy of constitutional government."[119] *Prima facie*, this seems to rule out any long-standing connection to French modes of political thought or practice, and indeed on a narrow interpretation precludes any intimate relationship to American republican thinking. That Wight went on to claim this tradition had the "quality of a *via media*" merely stirs further suspicion about how "Western"—and how British—this tradition actually is.[120] Repeated appeals to Gladstone's standing as an unimpeachable exemplar of Western values or Grotian thinking merely deepen that suspicion.[121]

Betrayed by the lingering influence of philosophical Idealism, Wight located the central ideas of his tradition in the institutions of international society. He distinguished between two kinds of institution, formal—including institutions like the United Nations—and what Barry Buzan has called "primary" institutions, like war or diplomacy or international law.[122] Unusually, in the context of later work on international institutions and later usages of the term, he dismissed formal institutions as uninteresting and largely incapable, on their own, of modifying the conduct of international relations. The United Nations was just a "complicated bit of . . . diplomatic machinery," Wight judged in 1956, and not "an energizing force." Its existence and its prominence in commentary on international relations, Wight thought, tended "to obscure the abiding conditions of international life."[123] By contrast, primary institutions could change those conditions. In Wight's early work on international relations, dating from the late 1940s and early 1950s, only the balance of power and international law appeared as such institutions; in later writings, "diplomacy, alliances, guarantees, war and neutrality" were added.[124]

As we have seen, Wight analyzed these institutions not in terms of their structures or even their rules, but in terms of the various ideas that animated them—or rather, to be more specific, the various ideas that individuals held when they used these institutions to achieve their ends. The idea of "international society" was for Wight "manifest in the diplomatic system; in the conscious manipulation of the balance of power to preserve the independence of member-communities; in the regular operations of international law . . . ; in economic, social and technical interdependence and the functional international institutions established . . . to regulate it."[125] "International society" and the "balance of power" existed, in other words, only when the relevant, involved individuals think they exist and act according to their understandings of how they can and should act. They do not exist, however, as material forces or structures supposedly determining, as realists have it, what actors do. Indeed Wight rejected such materialism outright, first as an inadequate explanation of how and why actors act in the way they do, and second as a doctrine corrosive to morality.[126]

This notion of institutions as the vessels for ideas is played out most clearly in Wight's international theory lectures. Although the lectures are best known for presenting his "three traditions" of realism, rationalism, and revolutionism, it is significant that Wight did not organize the lectures into straightforward expositions of each tradition, in the manner of later undergraduate texts.[127] Rather, aspects of each tradition were examined in terms of how they conceived of foundational assumptions (human nature, mankind) and primary institutions (diplomacy, war, international law). Wight's object was to demonstrate how each institution functions under the influence of the different traditions.[128]

Wight's preferred tradition was the whiggish one—"rationalism"—which he thought of as the international equivalent of constitutionalism in domestic politics. He rejected the realist denial of what he called the "irrefragability" of the "bonds" of "international society" and, at the same time, what he took to be the Kantian conviction that "international society" "conceals, obstructs and oppresses the *real* society of individual men and women, the *civitas maxima*."[129] He supported instead the dominant—Western or whig—tradition's four core beliefs:

1. That international society exists and survives by virtue of some core of common standards and common custom, difficult to define, but having its partial embodiment in international law.
2. That the tranquillity of international society and the freedom of its members require an even distribution of power . . .
3. That international society has a right of self-defence and of coercion . . .
4. That the exercise of this right of self-defence and coercion is most fully justified when it is undertaken by the members of international society collectively, or by the majority of them, or by one of them with the authorization of the others.[130]

These beliefs were institutionalized both formally and informally, the latter in the sense of being acted upon in the primary institutions of international relations. They were present in the League of Nations' attempt to "combine the Grotian doctrine about the enforcement of law against a delinquent state with the system of the balance of power" and in the United Nations Charter's collective security provisions.[131] They are present, too, in diplomacy practiced as Nicolson or Butterfield conceived it—honest, moderate, restrained, respectful, and sympathetic[132]—and in war when fought in accordance with the principles that its ultimate object is peace and that it is a necessary evil, and nothing more.[133] Above all, these beliefs were expressed in commitments to international law and to an idea of natural law that underpins it, in obligation and the upholding of treaties, and in the adherence to an ethic of the lesser evil.[134]

CONCLUSION

The diplomatic dialogue is . . . the instrument of international society: a civilized process based on awareness and respect for other people's points of view; and a civilizing one also, because

the continuous exchange of ideas, and the attempts to find mutually acceptable solutions to conflicts of interest, increase that awareness and respect.
ADAM WATSON, *Diplomacy* (1982)[135]

The present appeal of the English school of international relations bears witness to the persistence of whig thinking among British students of international relations as much as it does to a continued concern with ideas and institutions. It should not be assumed, however, that the whig tradition exercised widespread influence among scholars throughout the postwar period. By the time *Diplomatic Investigations* appeared, later than originally planned, in 1966, there were more than a few British voices who lamented what they saw as an outmoded way of thinking about the subject. Its publication was delayed partly because of unfavorable reports from referees, who complained that the chapters were old-fashioned in tone and approach; indeed that some said "nothing new." That referee observed of Wight's "Western Values" that "the contemporary literature dwells upon values with a good deal more insight than was possible a century ago" and urged the author to pay more attention to contemporary developments in "sociology and psychology."[136] When the book did appear, it was given a warm but not glowing review in *International Affairs* by the University of Southampton's Joseph Frankel—a contrast to the much more effusive praise from Hans Morgenthau in *Political Science Quarterly*.[137] In *History*, Frank Spencer of Hull merely noted that the volume took a "high moral tone" and was not "sullied by discussion of power politics."[138]

While the concept of "international society" did continue to appeal to British scholars of the later 1960s and 1970s, leading to the slew of publications on the subject noted by Roy Jones in his assault on the "English school" in 1981, by then the whiggism once linked to it had clearly lost much of its luster. "International society" was thus separated from the whig or Western values that Wight thought sustained it. Bull's classic account of the *Anarchical Society* illustrates this well. Where once "international society" was a singular product of the Western civilization, now, in Bull's hands, it could emerge and be sustained without any common cultural inheritance simply by way of states recognizing that their existence depends on establishing common rules for their relations.[139] Bull transforms "international society" from something contrived—a self-conscious creation informed by particular principles of political and moral action, as Butterfield or Wight took it to be—to something almost natural or even mechanistic.

The older whig account did not, however, disappear. It continued to hold great appeal for practitioners—for politicians and diplomats. This is clearest of all in the work of Adam Watson, the spy-turned-diplomat-turned-scholar who became a significant force in Butterfield's British Committee, especially after Wight's death in 1972. Watson's work will be discussed in more detail in later chapters, but it is of note here because of his success in integrating the various elements of postwar whiggism into one coherent story. On the one hand, Watson returned to the study of diplomacy, left comparatively fallow after Nicolson; on the other, he concentrated attention on the historical "evolution" of international society and its various informal "institutions."[140] He reemphasized the place that diplomacy ought to have as a "civilizing" influence and warned, as Butterfield had done, of the dire consequences of righteousness and ideology. Above all, Watson restated the relevance of the Western, whig tradition at the point at which many—including, as we shall see, Wight and Bull—believed that it was on the verge of disappearing from international relations altogether, swamped in the 1960s by the incoming tide of realism and radicalism.[141]

7. The Radicals

> He spoke not of the decline of the West, but of its death by greed and constipation. He hated America very deeply, he said, and Smiley supposed he did. . . . For a while, after forty-five . . . he had remained content with Britain's part in the world, till gradually it dawned on him just how trivial this was. . . . He often wondered which side he would be on if the test ever came; after prolonged reflection he had finally to admit that if either monolith had to win the day, he would prefer it to be the East.
> "It's an aesthetic judgment as much as anything," he explained, looking up. "Partly a moral one, of course."
> "Of course," said Smiley politely.
> JOHN LE CARRÉ, *Tinker Tailor Soldier Spy*

The book of which A. J. P. Taylor was most proud was *The Troublemakers* (1957), a study of British "dissenters" from their country's foreign policy. Somewhat immodestly, he declared in the preface that it was his "favourite brain child" and that it contained his "wisest and most original work."[1] *The Troublemakers* was certainly a celebration of "dissent" as much as a dissection of its workings, and Taylor was happy to imply that he was an inheritor of what he conceived as one of the great traditions of British thought about international relations.[2]

Taylor called this tradition "dissent" because he balked at using the term "radicalism," but he acknowledged that—in the abstract—radicalism was probably the more accurate term. The problem for Taylor was that "radical" implied to him some kind of association with "a wing of the Liberal party," which meant that an alternative word had to be found.[3] "Dissent," to Taylor's mind, offered a good compromise, allowing him to include as "dissenters" figures like Charles James Fox, who predated the formation of the Liberal Party and thus also Liberal Radicalism,[4] and Philip Noel-Baker, who belonged to Labour, not to the Liberals.

Taylor was not, however, consistent in the use of even his own terminology. In the book, he also talked of a "radical tradition"—that phrase was the title of the first chapter of *The Troublemakers*—that was not reducible to late-nineteenth-century Liberal Radicalism and had a longer pedigree. This approach, this chapter argues, makes much more sense. As a descriptive term, "radicalism" best captures the overtly oppositional nature of a tradition of thinking that conceives itself as engaging systematically in departures from convention, everyday verities, and inherited patterns of behavior. The alternative terms—Taylor's "dissent" or Wight's "revolutionism"—are, as we shall see, not up to that task.

This chapter traces the evolution of postwar radicalism. In the first place, it tries to define the key elements of the radical tradition, arguing that its theory of international relations is grounded fundamentally in a thoroughgoing suspicion of all centers of power and interest. With this theory in mind, the bulk of the chapter examines the three major radical attacks on British foreign policy and the contemporary international order seen in the postwar years. It looks at the campaign to transform Britain's place in the international order in the late 1940s; then at the movement for unilateral nuclear disarmament, which flourished in the late 1950s and early 1960s; and third, at the international thought of the New Left in the mid- to late 1960s. The conclusion discusses the radicals' legacy for later thinking about international relations in Britain. First, however, some further explication of the radical tradition is needed, as well as a discussion of the legacy of interwar radicalism inherited by postwar thinkers.

THE TRADITION

> ... the rebels have as great a part in our political tradition as those who have argued the case for the claims of prescription and established authority.
>
> ALAN BULLOCK and F. W. DEAKIN (1952)[5]

Many have recognized that a radical tradition of international thought exists, but most have struggled to trace its historical development with any accuracy. International relations theorists have frequently argued that having just two main categories of thought—realism and internationalism or idealism—does not sufficiently reflect the variety of ideas, beliefs, and traditions that exist in past and contemporary thinking. Some, like Stephen Walt and Ole Wæver, have suggested that adding a third "radical" category may be helpful, echoing Martin Wight's earlier argument for the use of a "revolutionist" tradition alongside the realist and rationalist ones.[6] There are, however, a number of problems with the ways in which these categories have been constructed.

Above all, in the hands of Walt and Wæver, "radical theory" is less a historical tradition and more a catch-all for all nonrealist and nonliberal thinking, whether Marxist, critical-theoretical, or poststructural.[7] Being radical, in their sense, implies being extreme or marginal or unconventional rather than being part of a self-conscious tradition of thinking or holding specific beliefs. While it cannot be denied that many British radicals could be extreme or marginal or unconventional, it is also the case that British radicalism constituted a clear example of what John Gunnell has called an authentic "historical tradition."[8] The work of mid-twentieth-century British radicals harks back to earlier radical thinkers and theories in a self-conscious way, lauding earlier radicals as exemplars and drawing upon their thinking to further their own. The English communist historians of the 1940s and 1950s, for example, displayed a veritable obsession with popular revolts in late medieval and early modern England, implicitly associating their own radicalism with that of earlier generations.[9] Taylor's concern with "dissent" should be seen in a similar light, as an attempt to locate and extend a tradition that might ground his own criticism of contemporary developments, as well as to pay homage to what he thought of as his "Tribal Gods."[10]

These "Gods" of the British radical tradition are united in their shared commitment to four key beliefs. Above all, Taylor's "dissenters" objected to what they understood to be the fundamental underpinnings and presuppositions of "British policy" as manifest throughout the modern era.[11] Taylor captured the nature of this opposition and the underlying reasons for it by analogy. In the Church of England, he argued, a "conforming member . . . can disagree with the Bishops" but only a "Dissenter believes that Bishops should not exist."[12] The same was true of dissent from foreign policy:

> A man can disagree with a particular line of British foreign policy, while still accepting its general assumptions. The Dissenter repudiates its aims, its method, its principles. What is more, he claims to know better and to promote higher causes; he asserts a superiority, moral or intellectual. Sometimes the Dissenters have accused the Foreign Secretary and his advisors of ignorance, sometimes of corruption—usually by class-selfishness rather than personal dishonesty. The Dissenters have differed widely in their practical conclusions. They have advocated everything from complete nonintervention to universal interference. But they have all been contemptuous of those in authority.[13]

This contempt was informed by the remaining three positive beliefs about the nature of politics and international relations.

The first is that "kingcraft" and "priestcraft," to use Thomas Paine's terms, ought to be regarded with the utmost suspicion, if not opposed outright.[14] Radicals oppose these activities on the grounds that the practice of holding power over others in such a way that depends not upon the consent of the governed, but on force or fraud (or both), is wholly unjust. This conviction flows from earlier civic republican beliefs, inherited by radicals, that unfettered power corrupts rulers and the ruled, and that democratic government grounded in civic equality is a superior mode of political organization.[15]

Second, radicals match their hostility to politics with an equally vehement hostility to "special"—or, to use Bentham's term, "sinister"—interests.[16] At the most fundamental level, these special interests consist of any minority interests that clash (or might clash) with the general will, whether they may be the particular interests of a monarch or those of a group of individuals like merchants or clergy. Since those special or sinister interests put the satisfaction of themselves above those of others, they cannot but come into conflict with the interest of the majority and thus must be opposed and, for Bentham at least, coerced into accepting the superiority of the general will. This belief underpins radical hostility to capitalism in general, and, when it comes to international politics, to those economic interests deemed to play a malign role in the conduct of relations between states, like global financiers, arms manufacturers, or, latterly, multinational corporations.

Third, radicals generally share the belief that government ought to be as limited as possible. "Society in every state is a blessing," as Paine put it, "but government even in its best state is but a necessary evil."[17] We might need government for certain limited tasks, but in general its scope should be strictly curtailed. This ought not be taken to imply that all radicals have an idealistic view of human nature as pliable, perfectible, or intrinsically good and innocent[18]—some do, but many do not—rather, it displays the conviction that that society is better served by a minimum of political activity and by a severely restricted, or even absent, state. For radicals, in other words, politics is best done when decision-making is done by as direct a democracy as possible, so as to avoid the possibility that the general will, expressed by the majority, might be distorted by representatives, interests, or even parties, and decisions are carried out by a small, restricted government.[19]

For radicals, the scope of foreign policy should also be closely circumscribed. In general, radicals lean toward Trotsky's desire to do away with foreign policy altogether, by issuing a few revolutionary proclamations and then shutting up shop.[20] Although radicals often recognize that desire to be overly idealistic and impractical, it has sometimes been an obstacle to the development of systematic radical ideas about foreign policy. Part of the problem in distinguishing a radical tradition in international thought, indeed, lies in the lack of sustained attention radicals have devoted to international politics. Gordon Lewis's observations about Fabian disinterest in the "outside world" beyond the boundaries of the state, made in a notable postwar study of attitudes to America, stands for radicalism more broadly, at least until the 1950s.[21] Until then, as Lewis pointed out, British radicals had merely "assumed the continuing existence of an international world economic system based upon the London financial market. They had little insight into the possibility that a socialist Britain might have to conduct its experiment within a world subject to economic and financial forces over which it had only slight control, or that the very furtherance of freedom for colonial peoples would in fact increase the difficulties it would have to face."[22] These problems did, in the event, serve as a stimulus to radical reflection about international politics in the postwar years.

These basic assumptions of radicalism were overlaid, in the postwar period, by some particular prejudices. Above all, radical opinion was (at this time and long after) anti-American—a far more widely shared and consistent radical view than pro-Sovietism or pro-communism. Lewis described it as "the expression of a half-conscious sense of shame that a people traditionally proud of its independence now discovers itself, both in the economic and strategic fields, increasingly dependent on American aid and increasingly influenced by American desires."[23] But while there is much to be said for this observation in a general sense, there were particular factors fueling radical anti-Americanism. The first, unquestionably, was sheer ignorance of American society and politics—this Lewis also recognized.[24] The second was resentment at the usurpation of Britain's world role. Although radicals commonly opposed empire and Great Power behavior, many still perceived a world-leading role for Britain, as a moral exemplar. When even this role was usurped, radical resentment was obvious, as John Le Carré's fictional double-agent Bill Hayden made so very clear.

The postwar years saw a continuation of two interwar trends: the gradual marginalization of liberal and socialist radicalism by Marxist variants and the progressive exploration by radicals of alternative methods of studying politics. Liberal and socialist radicalism intermingled and even collaborated with each other well into the 1950s, most clearly in the antinuclear campaign in the last years of that decade, which drew together the "high-minded" radicals, as Taylor called them, with the outright "Dissenters."[25] In the Campaign for Nuclear Disarmament (CND) a Bertrand Russell could still stand alongside an E. P. Thompson, but such unity between the liberal and Marxist wings of the radical tradition did not persist into the 1960s. The rise of the New Left after 1956, and especially after the founding of the *New Left Review* in 1962, with its explicit attempt to reconnect British socialism to contemporary continental and American Marxist thinking, exacerbated this trend. Although the influence of New Left thinking played almost no role in the development of the academic discipline of international relations in Britain until well into the 1980s, it set the scene for many developments to come. In particular, as we shall see, elements of the New Left and other fringe radicals formed a vanguard for the exploration of new approaches to thinking about and practicing international relations.

DEATH AND REBIRTH

> The hero of Munich was not Attlee or Cripps or even Pollitt, the leader of the Communist party. He was Duff Cooper, erstwhile champion of Baldwin...
>
> A. J. P. TAYLOR, *Troublemakers* (1957)[26]

As Taylor recognized, his dissenter-radicals did not acquit themselves well in the interwar years. Admittedly, they did succeed in establishing themselves as the dominant voices on foreign policy—Taylor notes that when called upon to teach the contemporary history of European international relations, the books he chose as texts, in the absence of any others, were all by dissenters, by Bertrand Russell, Lowes Dickinson, G. P. Gooch, and H. N. Brailsford.[27] But when the dissenters were faced with the great challenges of the 1930s, their confidence—and sometimes also their judgment—failed them. In the 1920s, they turned themselves against the League of Nations and collective security, which "accorded ill with the Dissenting outlook." The League was tainted by its association with Versailles and victor's justice, both of which were famously excoriated by J. M. Keynes in *The Economic Consequences of the Peace* (1919).[28] It lacked universality and thus legitimacy; it did little or nothing, radicals argued, to address the real underlying sources of international tensions, which they saw (variously) as international anarchy, capitalism, and imperialism.

As a result, when the time came for the radicals to confront the problem of Nazi Germany, they had too far to travel to arrive at the point of supporting the League and upholding collective security even in the face of obvious aggression. Taylor rightly observed that the most staunch opponents of appeasement were the liberal and whig establishments, not the dissenter-radicals: men "who knew their way to the Athenaeum," like Toynbee or Seton-Watson, as well as distinctly un-high-minded individuals like Cooper or Churchill.[29] Radical thinking had, in effect, led radical politics astray. Taylor noted, too, that Munich pushed the dissenters into positions that they would never have contemplated before: advocating defensive alliances with the Soviet Union, for example, which went against all prior radical warnings against such "power political" behavior.[30]

In effect, the challenges of the interwar years brought about a bifurcation of the radical tradition into, on the one hand, an increasingly high-minded idealism and, on the other, an increasingly instrumentalist "realism"—a divide which threatened to tear radicalism apart and which provides the backdrop for postwar radical thinking to follow. Harold Laski's work best exemplifies the first of these moves and E. H. Carr's clearly demonstrates the other. Both had long-standing interests in world politics—Laski as a proponent of international organization and Carr as, in turn, diplomat, scholar, and journalist. By the 1930s, both had come to regard Marx as an indispensible guide to the contemporary world, although neither became a fully fledged, intellectually committed communist.[31] Both, moreover, made significant—if ultimately fruitless—attempts to shape Britain's postwar foreign policy.

Laski's international thought revolved—as did his political thought—around his animus toward states and state sovereignty. In disliking the state, Laski was hardly alone among British thinkers: the view that the state was "discredited" had been circulating among pluralists, liberal internationalists, radicals, and indeed many imperialists since well before the First World War.[32] For the pluralists, the state was more than an "entity," it was an "idea"—it was one "organising idea of order" among many.[33] Many internationalists and radicals held much the same view. This was not to say, of course, that the state did not exist or continue to operate; indeed, the pluralists, internationalists, and radicals all recognized, especially during and after the war, that the state was extending its powers over individuals. Rather, it was to imply—at least to the cruder readers of the theory—that the state could be changed or done away with if we change our ideas of political order.

In his first book, *Studies in the Problem of Sovereignty* (1917), Laski attacked in particular John Austin's legal positivist theory of the state and sovereignty that conceived the state, in Hobbesian terms, as a coercive enforcer of law.[34] For Laski, this idea of the state was simply too threatening in its authoritarianism. In its stead, he offered an alternative idea that disaggregated the state into functional components, each addressing a particular field, issue, or problem. This kind of disaggregated state satisfied, for Laski, not just the "is" of the demands of the contemporary world but the "ought" of his normative vision of politics.[35]

In Laski's later writings of the 1930s and 1940s, these arguments are overlain with a Marxian argument as to the causes and consequences of modern industrial capitalism. In turn, both informed an evolving account of international relations. In "Nationalism and the Future of Civilization" (1932), Laski argued that there was in the nation-state an "egoism . . . which bodes ill for mankind."[36] He went on: "The nation-state, having come to be, yearns to be strong. It adopts policies the impact of which upon other nation-states must cause any observer misgivings of which I cannot exaggerate the gravity. It seeks security from attack; and there comes the problem of armaments and strategic frontiers. It seeks an outlet for its surplus population; and there are restless experiments in colonization. Its merchants reveal anxiety about their markets; and we are plunged into imperialist and mercantilist adventures about which the spirit of nationality throws a dangerous glamour."[37] This argument led Laski to an essentially internationalist conclusion. "Modern science," he wrote, "means a world-market; a world-market means world-interdependence; world-interdependence means world-government."[38]

This vision, of course, differed very little from the standard interwar internationalist argument, expressed by the "high-minded" Murray, Toynbee, or Zimmern. It was similarly vulnerable: once it had become clear by the late 1930s that the "abrogation of national sovereignty" leading to the creation of international government was highly unlikely, at least in the near future, its appeal as a practical response to the dilemmas of international relations ebbed away.[39] Laski recognized this relatively early. When "Nationalism and the Future of Civilization" was reprinted in 1939, he added an appendix admitting as much. The destruction of "Hitlerism" and the causes of "Hitlerism," he wrote, had to come before any reform of international relations; "thoroughgoing reconstruction of the internal order of each state" to foster greater equality between individuals was critical to the eventual realization of his wider vision.[40]

Laski's conclusions indicated a broader shift in radical thinking away from the ideal to the empirical and pragmatic. Two other significant texts also pointed in that direction. The first was Russell's *Power: A New Social Analysis* (1938); the second Carr's *Twenty Years' Crisis* (1939). Both were efforts to make radicalism more realistic. Russell's objective was not the perfection of power politics but rather their taming, firm in the belief that the "ultimate aim of those who have power . . . should be to promote social co-operation" rather than competition.[41] True to Paine, Russell argued that power ought to be tamed by democracy, which, though it "does not insure [sic] good government," can prevent "certain evils" when constrained by the rule of law.[42] This would work, however, only if democracy was harnessed to socialism, to the state ownership of the means of production and finance; and vice versa, because Russell recognized that "State Socialism divorced from democracy" could itself breed tyranny, as it had in the USSR.[43] Above all, Russell was concerned with the psychological conditions necessary to tame power, and this meant removing the "hatred and destructiveness" that caused, as was caused by, war.[44]

Russell's method of achieving this last aim was hardly original. To combat common hatreds and "power philosophies," he pointed to their irrationality—a tactic employed by many radicals and internationalists then and since—and placed his hopes in better education.[45] To address what he perceived to be the insanities of realism, Russell called for the cultivation of a skeptical spirit among the young that would inoculate them against "mass hysteria and mass suggestion."[46] His earnest wish was for a "liberal education" that gave a "sense of the value of things other than domination" and "help to create wise citizens of a free community."[47]

Carr started from a similar premise—namely that power had been neglected in internationalist thinking and practice—but ended up with rather different conclusions. In part, this explains his enduring appeal: radicals were not the only constituency to which his work spoke.[48] Carr's radical realism was—as Hans Morgenthau and the American realists recognized[49]—highly unorthodox. His argument in the *Twenty Years' Crisis* was classically radical: his core complaint was that liberal verities like the "harmony of interests" and the "rule of law" were being used as Machiavellian cloaks to disguise special interests—namely, the financial, economic, and colonial interests of the West, especially those of Britain.[50] "International morality, as expounded by most contemporary Anglo-Saxon writers," Carr argued, "is now little more than a convenient weapon for belabouring those who assail the *status quo*."[51] This was both hypocritical and unfair, for it prevented "have not" powers from getting their proper due. Carr called, therefore, for the "haves" to cease preaching and engage in some pragmatic "give-and-take" with the "have nots"[52]—

thus suggesting, as Morgenthau summarized the position, that the "last word in international morality is the demand for self-sacrifice."[53]

The problems with this kind of reasoning are readily apparent, even outside the specific context in which Carr wrote. *The Twenty Years' Crisis* was—and is—a clarion call for the appeasement of "have nots" by the "haves," regardless of the means by which they prosecuted their claims and regardless of the nature of their governing regimes, Nazi, Communist, or otherwise. Realism, for Carr, meant "recognising" two fundamental "realities" about the contemporary world: first, that liberalism and democracy were obsolete, outmoded, and incapable of coping with the challenges of the twentieth century; and second, that the social and economic welfare of the majority is and should be the ultimate political objective.[54] "Frank acceptance of the subordination of economic advantage to social ends," Carr argued, "and the recognition that what is economically good is not always morally good, must be extended from the national to the international community."[55]

These "recognitions" and "acceptances" led Carr to believe that the totalitarianism and thoroughgoing planning of modern society, especially in its communist variety, represented the future of politics and international relations.[56] In *The Soviet Impact on the Western World* (1946) Carr argued: "The missionary role which has been filled in the first world war by American democracy and Woodrow Wilson has passed in the second world war to Soviet democracy and Marshal Stalin. In 1919 democratic institutions on the model of western democracy were installed in many countries: in 1945 the new political institutions which arose in eastern Europe—not to speak of those which had arisen ten or more years earlier in parts of China—conformed, though rather less slavishly, to the Soviet pattern."[57] Soviet "democracy" was not merely benign, Carr went on, it was also an offshoot of Western thought and practice, and should be welcomed as such. True, it stood in contrast to the "English conception of democracy," which was political, rather than "social democracy," but its origins lay in France and its revolutionary tradition.[58] In practice, it meant a combination of "highly concentrated, and—necessarily, in time of war—somewhat autocratic, central authority" together with "local and informal democracy" at the level of the "masses."[59]

Such autocratic "social democracy" was not the only gift the USSR had for the West. Carr was even more enthusiastic about planning, which he had long thought the future of economic policy.[60] Its postwar popularity, he argued, was "largely the result, conscious or unconscious, of the impact of Soviet practice and Soviet achievement."[61] In turn, planning implied the expansion of government far into the social lives of citizens—for Carr, the old radical-liberal view that "governments were a necessary evil and that the less positive action they took, the better" had been consigned to the dustbin of history.[62] The West, he argued, was as bound to follow the Soviet lead in this area as in the promotion of social democracy and planning. In theory, this meant an acknowledgment of the superiority of Marxist thought, particularly of its materialism, dialectical reasoning, and relativism; in practice, this implied the West must emulate Soviet policies.[63] "Of modern political philosophies," Carr wrote, "Marxism is the most consistently totalitarian and has the widest appeal; the country which has officially adopted it . . . has dazzled the world by its immense industrial progress, the spirit of its people and the rapid development of its power."[64]

The interwar failure of internationalism in its liberal or radical forms thus drove radicals in one of two directions: either, as Laski and Russell wished, to an emphasis on the prior need for the reform of domestic societies, or, as Carr desired, to an admission of defeat, coupled with an acknowledgement that totalitarian power politics represented the future of international relations. Both courses were, in their own ways, far more "realistic" than earlier radical enthusiasms, at least insofar as they took seriously the obstacles to the realization of internationalist aims. But neither, in the event, were sufficiently adequate to meet the challenges of Nazi aggression and the postwar settlement.

THE THIRD FORCE

> We were a generation of agnostics: neither optimists nor pessimists but skeptics. Zeal was not our line.
> ANTHONY HARTLEY, *State of England*[65]

The Second World War had paradoxical effects on the radical tradition, at once energizing certain elements and muting others. Radical pacifism, both secular and religious, suffered most, having sustained a prolonged onslaught from writers on both left and right.[66] But between the end of the war and Suez there was a more general malaise. As Edward Shils observed in 1955 in a notable essay on British intellectuals for *Encounter*, the predominant postwar mood was one of self-satisfaction, even among radicals, and "[d]eeply critical voices became rare."[67] "Never," Shils went on, "had an intellectual class found its society and its culture so much to its satisfaction."[68] In part, this mood was a product of a general conviction that the war, the postwar domestic reforms, and the grant of independence to India had together confirmed Britain's "moral stature" as unimpeachable.[69] In part, too, the diminution of radicalism was a function of the skepticism, empiricism, and "realism" of the postwar years—that "flight from idealism" provoked by the realization that, as Anthony Hartley put it, "ideology had visibly proved itself to be the curse of the twentieth century."[70]

This "realism" set the tone for mainstream left-wing argument about international politics in the "long" decade of 1945 to 1956, a period in which radicalism was simultaneously nurtured and stifled. It was nurtured by the achievement of some long-standing radical objectives, not the least of which was an independent India in 1947. And although many on the Left supported a redoubled commitment to the remainder of the empire, especially to what would later be called the "development" of the African colonies, in retrospect it was at this point that the radical argument against imperialism may be seen to have won.[71] Similarly, the creation of international economic and financial institutions designed for the management of the global economy and the maintenance of as near to full employment as possible were also significant achievements, in part inspired by socialist principles.

At the same time, radicalism was stifled by, on the one hand, the general lack of "zeal" that marked postwar intellectuals and the public at large, and on the other, by the onset of the Cold War, which required many on the Left to make compromises that ill-matched their instinctive sympathies or principles.[72] Laski was an early victim of these moves. His ill-judged attempts to influence the course of Labour foreign policy, like his suggestion that Clement Attlee observe but not participate in the Potsdam conference in 1945, led to his exclusion from the policy process.[73] Continuity with the foreign policy of the wartime coalition, rather than change, was the objective of both Attlee and Bevin, combined with a pragmatic stance toward new developments on the world scene.[74]

With empiricism and pragmatism as the watchwords, the mainstream Left succeeded in defining its preferred course in international relations in terms not unlike those of the whigs. Denis Healey's position, expressed in the *New Fabian Essays* (1952), was representative: "Three predictions at least are fairly safe. Britain's influence on world affairs in the immediate future will depend more than ever on her material power to help a friend or harm an enemy. Britain's fundamental interest in unity with the United States will remain supreme. And an understanding of power politics will be more than ever necessarry [sic] to a successful socialist foreign policy."[75] Little of this appealed to radicals. In response, they staked out two positions, one Marxist and one not.

The Marxist alternative was more straightforward. Marxists deplored and denounced Labour's betrayal of the Left, the international proletariat, and the Soviet Union. In the short run they favored what Carr had proposed in the *Soviet Impact:* "a state monopoly of foreign trade, and comprehensive economic planning."[76] In the long term, as the communist historian Eric Hobsbawm put it in 1954, they desired "world peace, independence for Britain (from American domination), which is essential if Britain is to pursue a policy of peace and economic development, and the unity of the labour movement in the fight for peace, independence and improved conditions for the people."[77] Their strenuous claims that they did not seek to "introduce Soviet Power in Britain" marked a recognition of the broad skepticism in Britain about the merits of Soviet communism, if not a lack of sympathy among British communists with the USSR.[78]

This alternative was espoused by only a handful of British intellectuals prior to 1956. Few intellectuals, indeed, were members of the Communist Party of Great Britain (CPGB) or avowed communists; fewer still were principally concerned with the analysis of international relations.[79] Many were scientists, like J.D. Bernal (1901–1971)[80] or J.B.S. Haldane (1982–1964),[81] but some were more directly or professionally concerned with the study of politics or history. The Marxist historians—among them Maurice Dobb (1900–76),[82] Christopher Hill (1912–2003),[83] Eric Hobsbawm (1917-),[84] V.G. Kiernan (1913–2009),[85] and E.P. Thompson (1924–1993)[86]—were especially influential in this context. In the 1930s, the Marxist historians had prompted the beginnings of a revolution of historiography, shifting the locus of historical study away from the political and diplomatic activities of elites and toward the social and economic aspects and to the lives of the masses.[87] In 1946, some of them formed the Communist Party Historians' Group to further this project and to promote their political causes.[88]

The lasting impact of these historians on thinking about international politics—as opposed to on history[89]—came principally from their analyses of capitalism and imperialism and the relations between them. Especially after the Soviet suppression of Hungarian dissent in 1956, when most of the Marxist historians split with the CPGB and, in ideological terms, from Moscow, they built upon and developed earlier radical critiques of imperialism into a potent weapon with which to menace the conventional liberal and whig defenses of British and Western foreign policies. The ways in which the post-Hungary New Left wielded this weapon will be discussed in the next section.

In the postwar years radical dissent was also forthcoming from the noncommunist Left. This group had little sympathy for the Soviet Union or for the determinism some found in Marx and opposed the kind of slavish devotion to both found in the thought of some communists. The veteran Fabian socialist G. D. H. Cole (1889–1959) argued, for instance, that Marx was best understood not as a deterministic or even a scientific materialist, but as a "realist" who, in the final analysis, allowed that individuals could and did make history.[90] Such beliefs underpinned the radical Left's alternative to both the Attlee–Bevin consensus foreign policy and the communist option.

In essence, this alternative amounted to what later became known as "nonalignment." In practical terms, at least by 1950, it meant unraveling the ties that bound Britain to the United States and placing Britain more evenly between the Cold War rivals. In many ways, this was the instinctive position of Labour activists, who desired a socialist and internationalist approach to foreign policy above all else and deplored the compromises made with "power politics."[91] It was best expressed by Richard Crossman, Michael Foot, and Ian Mikardo in their 1947 pamphlet *Keep Left*, which argued that Britain, together with other like-minded Europeans, form a "third force" in international politics equidistant from the USA and USSR.[92] What informed this proposal was the conviction—held most firmly by Foot—that Britain ought to conceive of its "international role" as a "product of the success of its socialist achievement at home." Britain would thus provide "moral leadership" to the world rather than military might.[93]

Although the "Keep Left" movement was relatively short lived, undermined by the practical realities of Britain's worsening economic and financial situation and by the United States' Marshall Plan, the "third force" idea recurred throughout the postwar period.[94] It was fueled as much by anti-Americanism as by any socialist principle, although it was arguably true to the spirit of radical opposition to unaccountable power and special interest. Aneurin Bevan (1897–1960) voiced this position most clearly in his call for British "world leadership" in his book *In Place of Fear* (1952).[95] For Bevan, the key problem of the postwar world was America and, to be more precise, American fear of communism.[96]

The United States, Bevan argued, was wrong about the Soviet Union—they have "mistaken the nature of the menace, and so they not only prescribe the wrong remedy, but their remedy itself feeds the danger."[97] Big business and the military had played their sinister part in this, distorting even Britain's limited experiment with socialism into something threatening, and causing unnecessary alarm at Soviet strength.[98] The origins of the Cold War, in other words, were to be found in American anxieties, not Soviet motives. The right British response to all of this, Bevan thought, was to take on the moral leadership of world opinion. Britain must, he thought, "align [itself] with the inevitable"—upholding communist China's right to sit in the UN, upholding the claims of colonial peoples, and bolstering the UN itself. "Idealism" was the key; "Nothing nearer than a distant horizon will beckon us from where we are now bogged."[99]

1956

> If you disapproved of Hungary but condoned Suez you were a Conservative. If you disapproved of Suez but condoned Hungary you were a Communist. If you disapproved of both you were a Radical.
> BRIAN MAGEE, *The New Radicalism* (1963)[100]

Bevan's idealism set the scene for the veritable chorus of radicals that appeared after 1956. The Suez crisis shook the British from their complacency about their political leaders and their place in the world; the Soviet invasion of Hungary shook British communists from analogous complacency about the USSR. Suez stirred radicals into thinking about domestic issues, producing a series of books decrying "what's wrong with Britain" and calling for thoroughgoing change in the political, social, and economic order.[101] It soured relations, too, with the United States, as Britain's dependency on which was painfully exposed by American actions during the crisis.[102] Hungary stirred communists to rethink their assumptions and to come up with a more rigorous foundation for political praxis. Curiously, however, few decried British foreign policy and called for equally comprehensive reform. Instead, radicalism found outlets in two areas: in government policy toward decolonization, discussed in the next chapter, and in the emerging movement for unilateral nuclear disarmament.

The central conceit and modus operandi of the British movement for nuclear disarmament stood foursquare within the radical tradition, even if, for a time, its strongest advocates were not wholly radical in their politics. British radicals had long deplored states' expenditure on arms, arguing that they impoverished the working man and woman and helped to bring about the very conflicts they were purportedly supposed to deter.[103] In this spirit Britain had been very active in the interwar period on disarmament and British writers like Philip Noel-Baker were among the best-known advocates of the cause.[104] In this sense—and in others—

the nuclear disarmament movement was, as Raymond Williams noted in 1965, "the main bearer of the long moral tradition in British politics."[105]

The nuclear disarmament movement drew succor from this well-established radical tradition but derived strength, too, from two other sources. The first was the widespread, straightforward horror of many at the destructiveness of nuclear weapons.[106] Few if any British intellectuals were willing to think of such weapons as anything like ordinary instruments of war, as some American civilian strategists were able to do in the 1950s. The second was the conviction that Britain had a particular role to play in providing a moral lead to the world, as it had done in the campaign against slavery in the nineteenth century or for conventional disarmament in the twentieth.

In the mid- to late 1950s, nuclear disarmament was thus able to unite the high-minded, the pacifists, and even some self-declared "realists" and conservatives in this radical-led cause. In Bertrand Russell, the high-minded and the radical went hand in hand; in Herbert Butterfield—who had a brief and somewhat crabbed engagement with the movement[107]—"realism" and conservatism were more clearly represented. The tone of Russell's 1957 open letter to US President Dwight D. Eisenhower and Soviet Premier Nikita Khrushchev and Butterfield's *International Conflict in the Twentieth Century* (1960) are quite different, but the message was the same: that nuclear weapons posed a grave risk to the very survival of life on earth and that their continued possession—let alone their use—could not be anything other than an evil.[108]

Such logic informed the Campaign for Nuclear Disarmament launched in London in February 1958, which drew together Russell (but not Butterfield) with Stephen King-Hall and A. J. P. Taylor,[109] as well as the veteran *New Statesman* antinuclear radicals like its editor Kingsley Martin and the playwright J. B. Priestley onto a common platform.[110] "Our programme," wrote Taylor in his autobiography, "was simple and we never wavered from it: unilateral nuclear disarmament first in our own country and then for everyone else."[111] But the CND faced two problems. The first was that in earlier ages British moralism had been matched by British power. As Taylor observed: "Ironically we were the last Imperialists. If Great Britain renounced nuclear weapons without waiting for international agreement, we should light such a candle as would never be put out. Alas it was not true. No one cared in the slightest whether Great Britain had the bomb or did not have the bomb. The Russians were not frightened because we had it. The rest of the world would not be impressed if we gave it up."[112] Britain's irrelevance became clear in 1962, if not before, in the midst of the Cuban missile crisis, but by then the CND had lost its momentum and had been captured, in the main, by the emerging New Left.[113]

THE NEW LEFT

> [I]t must be clear that, from the record at least, recent East–West negotiations have been concerned to perpetuate the *status quo* of the Cold War, to preserve the spheres of influence, and to maintain the balance of terror: and that Britain has been wholly imprisoned within this framework.... We come back, then, to the role of *positive neutrality,* which is the only position from which Britain can be in to exert pressure in the right direction. And unilateralism and the renunciation of NATO are the preconditions of a foreign policy based upon active neutrality.
> JOHN REX and PETER WORSLEY,
> "Campaign for a Foreign Policy" (1960)[114]

The New Left was a response to the general dilemmas posed by Hungary and Suez and to the particular dilemma of how to revitalize mainstream left-wing and more radical thinking about politics and international relations in their aftermath. The movement involved some of the finest British intellectuals of the generation that came to maturity and influence in the 1950s and 1960s: Perry Anderson (1938–),[115] Tom Nairn (1932–),[116] E. P. Thompson, Raymond Williams (1921–1988),[117] and Peter Worsley (1924–).[118] Their objective was a thoroughgoing reformulation of Marxist theory that would ground their practice and inform a suitably militant and revolutionary mass movement. They aimed therefore to "challenge the governing ideology of the Labour movement, and in particular its attachment to utilitarianism and paternalism."[119] They rejected Fabianism as too empirical and British communist interpretations of Marx as too dogmatic. For their alternative, they turned for inspiration to the continent, to developments in European Marxism hitherto neglected by British radicals.[120]

In stark contrast to both the Fabians and the communists, international issues were uppermost in the minds of the New Left. The Soviet intervention in Hungary provoked a break with Stalinism and, to an extent, with the USSR as a plausible partner;[121] British conduct in the Suez crisis prompted public demonstrations, the founding of the *Universities and Left Review* (later to merge with Thompson's *New Reasoner* to become the *New Left Review*) and the New Left Club.[122] In response, they developed a socialist critique of international relations in general, and British foreign policy in particular. This critique had three poles. The first concerned the Cold War, which was interpreted as the product of a capitalist reaction to the emergence of the USSR as a world power. The second concerned relations with the remnants of European empire and the decolonized states of the "Third World." The last involved Britain itself, especially the alignment of Britain with the United States and the acquiescence of the Labour Party with that tendency.

The New Left built upon the earlier radical argument, expressed most clearly by the CND, that the Cold War was an arms race fueled by special interests that could only lead to Armageddon. But while good in itself, Perry Anderson argued, this insight was "politically insufficient."[123] More specificity about the interests concerned was needed: the Cold War was not just about the individual arms dealer but the capitalist system within which they worked. Most important of all, the New Left concluded, the Cold War was the product of the hegemonic ideology utilized to justify the perpetuation of capitalism, as much as of the workings of capitalism itself. This argument drew especial inspiration from the work of the Italian Marxist Antonio Gramsci and built upon a new conceptualization of power in late capitalist societies. For Anderson, there were "three main idiosyncrasies of the structure of power" in such societies: "the relative insignificance of bureaucratic or military forms, the exceptionally immediate strikecapacity [sic] of economic forms, and the ultimate, crucial importance of ideological and cultural forms."[124] In this light, the onset and the perpetuation of the Cold War were functions of the manipulation of public opinion by capitalist and imperialist elites, rather than a predetermined clash between classes with differing material interests.

The New Left arguably devoted more and closer attention to imperialism and the Third World. Here they could draw on an established indigenous tradition of radical anti-imperial argument, running back into the nineteenth century, but reaching its highest points in the work of J. A. Hobson, H. N. Brailsford, E. D. Morel, Laski, Woolf, and others, as well as continental European ideas, from Lenin onward.[125] This tradition had attributed imperialism to the nature of capitalism, to the need that it generated for markets for goods and outlets for surplus capital and population. The end of empire, however, posed a serious dilemma for such thinking, for decolonization was decidedly not accompanied by the end of capitalism, as earlier radical thinking had suggested it would. By 1960, it was evident that capitalism in its "highest stage" was not in fact, as Lenin had argued, "moribund."[126] It had outlasted imperialism—or so it seemed.

The New Left concluded that, on this point at least, Lenin and Hobson and the rest had been "wrong."[127] This did not mean, however, that imperialism had disappeared. Rather, it has been transformed, with direct political control replaced by indirect influence over successor regimes, metropolitan banks still holding the purse-strings of postcolonial states, "overseas corporations" able to "exploit the producing country," and the "vicious circle of poverty to which the under-developed countries are bound."[128] Neocolonialism had supplanted colonialism, with capitalism as central to this new system as to the old.

This critique underpinned a number of New Left initiatives. In domestic politics, it provided a platform from which to attack what Tom Nairn called "Labour Imperialism" as well as the more conventional Tory form.[129] In scholarship, it informed a rewriting of international history (and later the emergence of an international theory) which placed the beginnings of contemporary international relations not at the cataclysm of 1914, as realists, liberals, and whigs did, but circa 1885, at the point at which Europeans finally extended their imperial control over the last remaining untouched territory of the globe.[130] The creation of his "world-order founded on conquest and maintained by force" laid the foundations for the power struggles to follow, establishing the "essentially asymmetrical" relationships between "haves" and "have-nots" that were the principal causes of strife in the twentieth century.[131]

Armed with these arguments, the New Left and the student radicals who drew upon their ideas aligned themselves with the Third World against the First.[132] They were bolstered by anti-Americanism, which, like anti-imperialism, also had deep roots in British thought. As the Cold War was "amortized" in the 1960s, as the erstwhile student radical Gareth Stedman Jones put it, and the "storm-centre of international affairs" moved to the Third World, the "USA emerged unmistakably in the role of brutalized world gendarme."[133] In the 1940s, the United States had been seen by many as merely "a sort of loutish and helpful nephew"; in the 1950s, it was viewed as "a huge challenging empire, wilful, challenging Britain, criticizing Britain, lording it over Britain, and claiming to lord it over everyone everywhere."[134] By 1970, the US had been transformed—at least for radicals—into a "super-imperialist" state of unparalleled iniquity.[135]

In response, the New Left and the student radicals declared their solidarity with those willing to resist this imperialism: Third World guerrillas and revolutionaries. "The liberal, 'pluralist' democracy which had been so celebrated by patriotic apologists during the Cold War," wrote Stedman Jones in 1969, "now revealed itself as the military juggernaut responsible for untold death and destruction in Vietnam."[136] The answer to such acts could not be a balance of power, as realists might like, because none was possible between such unequal actors; nor diplomacy or internationalism, neither of which had shown themselves capable in the past of confronting such evils; instead, only violent struggle was proper, justified by the manifest injustices of capitalism and imperialism. It is "only through uninhibited struggle," Stedman Jones argued, "that a genuinely free and democratic society—not an authoritarian state posing as one—can be achieved, and coercion truly abolished."[137]

THE TURN TO SCIENCE

> Soon the liquidation of the British Empire began. The optimistic light of institutional liberalism still shone. It became a virtual necessity that as each country passed from Empire to Commonwealth it should be equipped with an imposing constitution.... And almost all the constitutions so constructed collapsed. Time and again it was demonstrated that the problems of politics could not be solved by formal institutions, however well-intentioned, fair, and honourable they might be.
> ROY E. JONES, *The Functional Analysis of Politics* (1967)[138]

Not all radicals advocated such a dramatic course of action. Many sought instead new understandings of politics, arguing that older approaches, especially the institutionalism favored by liberals and most whigs, had failed to produce the kind of knowledge that was needed to confront the dilemmas of the postwar world. Building on the sociological theories of Schwarzenberger, as well as the earlier work of functionalists like Mitrany, and drawing inspiration often from the United States, they developed a series of novel modes of political analysis. In particular, they utilized psychological theories and formal modeling, focusing their attention, in particular, upon the sources of conflict. At the time—in stark contrast to the climate that came to prevail in Britain in the antipositivistic 1990s and 2000s—the use of scientific modes of generating knowledge did not imply among British thinkers particular political preferences, still less a commitment to "power politics" or American political or theoretical hegemony. Rather, the bulk of those who toyed with positivistic approaches were radical peace or conflict researchers, hardly pawns of a military-industrial-foreign policy complex.[139]

These scholars were few and often far between, beset on almost all sides by adherents to the "classical" ideas and institutions approach, but nonetheless they played their part in shaping the emergent discipline of international relations. They emerged on the margins of British academia, mainly in the new universities created in the early 1960s—the epitome of "a fringe movement," as Michael Nicholson called it.[140] They were driven, in the main, by two beliefs: that inherited ways of thinking about international relations were obsolete and that new ways were needed to inform and improve the practices of international relations.

British scholarship in formal theories of international relations has a far more distinguished record than is commonly acknowledged, largely because it has been obscured in disciplinary histories by more recent interest in the English school and in grounding "postpositivist" theory. Two of the great pioneers of the formal modeling of conflict were British, Lewis Fry Richardson (1881–1953) and Kenneth Boulding (1910–1993), though the latter became a US citizen in 1948. Both came to the subject from other fields—Richardson from physics, and then meteorology, and Boulding from economics—and both were moved to contribute to the development of a science of peace by their religious beliefs, as Quakers. Richardson's effort concerned the compilation of statistical data on conflicts and the attempt to find significant relationships that might cast light on the causes of war and other issues. Belated recognition of this work came in 1959 with the founding of the Richardson Institute for peace research, now at the University of Lancaster, and in 1960 with the posthumous publication of his work on conflict, for which he had not found a publisher during his lifetime. Boulding, by contrast, was a highly prolific author on economics and religion as well as peace, and was a prime mover in the founding of the *Journal of Conflict Resolution* in 1957.

It took some time before a younger generation of scholars moved to build upon the foundations laid by Richardson and Boulding. It also took the expansion of the British university system. The Universities of Nottingham, Southampton, Hull, Exeter, and Leicester came into being between 1948 and 1957, followed by Sussex, Keele, York, East Anglia, Newcastle, Lancaster, Kent, Essex, and Warwick by 1965. With these new institutions came new posts for academics with interests in politics and international relations or even departments, as in the case, for instance, of Lancaster. These new universities also benefited from a series of bequests to support peace and conflict research, such as that of the Quaker Peace Studies Trust, which created the first chair of peace studies at Bradford in 1973. Together these developments encouraged younger scholars to embark upon less orthodox work than that permitted at the LSE or Oxford and permitted older scholars to move from other fields, like psychology or sociology, into fringe areas of the study of international relations such as peace and conflict research. The influx of American scholarship on these subjects, made more readily available by the falling costs of importing books and journals, also had a significant impact.

This impact was not felt immediately, but when it was, it had significant consequences. In 1966, at the tenth meeting of the UK Conference on the University Teaching of International Relations (the "Bailey Conference," informally named after S.H. Bailey) matters came to a head. Michael Banks observed that this conference "virtually buried one dispute" but "inaugurated a new one."[141] The old dispute had been over whether "International Relations" was really a "discipline." On this topic, most were in agreement: the question was simply a distraction to the task of getting on with studying the field. The new dispute stirred far more controversy. It concerned method. The theme of the conference was "Contemporary Theories of International Relations." It split those attending into two groups: those who saw merit in the "behavioural sciences" and those "classicists" who did not. The scientific versus classical debate was not just one between Americans and Britons: there were indigenous advocates on both sides of the argument.

Banks noted at the time that those interested in "behavioural" theory were a "small minority" in Britain, but that they were nonetheless a significant one.[142] They shared the vision of David Easton, Morton Kaplan, and others of a "general theory" not just for international relations, but for all social behavior, and detected that progress was being made toward that goal. They were enthusiastic, too, for the "partial" theories of parts of the various systems under analysis—theories of balance and equilibrium, decision-making, bargaining, functionalism, and integration—which might later be unified into a general theory.[143] They took a deductive approach, but sought to build theories which were potentially falsifiable by empirical evidence to the contrary, and they aspired to be value-neutral, though they often recognized that this was rarely possible.

Banks gave few examples. He mentioned Michael Nicholson's work on the formal modeling of conflict, which built upon the earlier efforts of Lewis Richardson.[144] He might have mentioned John Burton's eccentric attempt to build a "general theory" of international relations mainly with tools derived from social psychology.[145] Frankel's work on decision-making has already been discussed; Roy Jones's efforts on functionalism and foreign policy analysis should also be noted.[146]

These scholars made no excuses for the fact that their work drew upon approaches originating in the United States, nor did they disguise their intention to try to inform and change policy. Unlike the classicists, who argued that a distance be maintained between scholarship and practice, they argued that scholars ought to involve themselves in policymaking. They took what Nicholson later called the "Humanist's Wager," recognizing that it might be possible to uncover general laws about war and peace and betting that the costs involved in such a search would be far outweighed by the benefits, however unlikely the possibility of it succeeding might be.[147] In general, they had little impact on the mainstream, but their work did have significant effects, as we shall see in chapter 9, in new areas of study.

CONCLUSION

> If you want to peer into the future ... if you want to know what the foreign policy of this country will be in twenty or thirty years' time, find out what the Dissenting minority are saying now.
> A. J. P. TAYLOR, *The Troublemakers* (1957)[148]

Radicalism was destined to become one of the dominant—if indeed not the dominant—tradition of thinking about international politics in Britain, especially, but not only, in the universities. In the early 1970s in the new discipline of international relations, structuralism was the first of many radical waves to strike—an approach "closely tied," as Banks later observed, to the "classical ideas of Hegel, Marx and Lenin."[149] Theories of imperialism and dependency were thus introduced into British academic writing on the subject. Scholars of peace research and conflict resolution brought with them other radical beliefs, notably the notion—prominent to much of the writing discussed in this chapter—that war and violence were the products of the distortions placed on social relations by special interests and inequalities of power. Most important of all, the radicals of the 1970s and 1980s insisted not upon scholarly distance from the world, as many liberals and whigs thought proper, but on commitment and engagement.

This was entirely consistent with the core beliefs of the radical tradition. The radicals did not necessarily seek power, still less did they have some kind of lust for power, as Wight thought "revolutionists" did, but they had long been concerned to speak what they conceived as "truth" to power. All the postwar radicals, whatever their differences on particular issues, shared the conviction that those in power ought to be treated with the utmost suspicion and held to account, whether through public protest or publications. All, too, had a somewhat fuzzy sense of what sort of alternative politics they would prefer, and particularly of what sort of foreign policy they favored. Like Taylor's dissenters, they were united in a nagging sense that in an ideal world foreign policy would not be necessary. As a consequence, they devoted little time to setting out exactly what they would have preferred.

These points of continuity must be set against highly significant points of change. The radical tradition became more Marxist as the postwar period wore on, but correspondingly less Soviet in inspiration. Stalin and Hungary broke the allegiance of all but a few radicals to the USSR but stimulated a reinterpretation of Marx and Marxism in response. The other shift was the rise of militancy. The British radical tradition—at least until the post–Cold War period—is marked by a concern for practical political action as well as theoretical discussion, but in the 1960s it became increasingly interested in violence as well as protest. This concern led some radicals in one direction, toward identifying themselves with Third World guerrillas and First World terrorists like the German Red Army Faction (Baader-Meinhof group), and some in the opposite direction, toward peace research and peace science. In chapters 8 and 9, I examine these moves—and others—in more detail.

8. The Revolt against the West

Decolonization and Its Repercussions

> Of all the stages in a great country's history, the aftermath of Empire must be the hardest.
>
> ANTHONY SAMPSON, *Anatomy of Britain* (1962)

The rapid decolonization of the British Empire and the concomitant shift toward deeper involvement in the European Economic Community (EEC), beginning in the late 1950s and running well into the 1970s, saw the most significant changes in the nature of British thinking about international politics. Above all, it saw the near eclipse of liberal internationalism. It saw, too, the rise of radicalism, marked most obviously by sympathy for anticolonialism and for the professed ideals of postcolonial states, especially nonalignment and the redistribution of global wealth and knowledge from North to South. After 1960, under American influence, political realism began to make inroads into ground hitherto held by British whigs, sometimes to the point where they were, in practice, indistinguishable doctrines. Other American ideas—especially systems theory and functionalism—also began to make an appearance, largely in radical rather than realist circles. Much of this new thinking was explicitly conceived as a response to Britain's changed circumstances and to the new dilemmas that had emerged as a consequence.

Despite these changes, however, discussion of the empire and imperialism remained inextricably linked with the condition of the Cold War. Some made this linkage deliberately, as the Tory journalist Douglas Jerrold had done in his attacks on Arnold J. Toynbee back in the early 1950s,[1] aiming to discredit those who sympathized with the anticolonial cause by implying that they also had some sympathy for communism. This practice was indeed encouraged in some official circles in Britain, as we shall see, with at least one element of the Foreign Office keen to influence as best it could the nature of the public debate on decolonization.

This chapter proceeds in four stages. The first looks at the ways in which liberal internationalists responded to decolonization, a process which—arguably more than any other development in twentieth-century international relations—refuted their predictions of future world politics. The second turns to the whigs, especially to the thought of Martin Wight and Hedley Bull, whose contrasting reactions to decolonization are revealing about the malleability of that tradition. The third looks at the work of the radicals, especially of the New Left, and the last examines the thought of their critics, in officialdom and beyond.

INTERNATIONALISM BETRAYED

> Here indeed is a reversal of esteem! All through the sixty centuries of more or less recorded history, imperialism, the extension of political power by one state over another, has been taken for granted as part of the established order.
>
> MARGERY PERHAM, *The Colonial Reckoning* (1962)[2]

Some internationalists, as we have seen, were imperialists by conviction, but most were by default. The latter recognized empires, colonies, and imperialism as Perham did, as part of the natural order of things, to be lamented in a sense, especially when imperial rule was poorly done, but to be celebrated if it could be made to serve a higher purpose.[3] For John Stuart Mill as for Gilbert Murray, while the acquisition of empire was unquestionably a crime, once acquired empires could be made vehicles for doing good, whether that meant enlightening the conquered—as Mill or Murray favored—or converting them to Christianity, as late-nineteenth-century muscular Christians desired.[4] For the majority of liberal internationalists in the early years of the twentieth century, empires had a further significance: they offered a potent means, they thought, of bringing the global political order in line with the emerging economic and technological order.[5]

The end of the British Empire had thus far more significance for most internationalists than for any other concerned Britons. It marked one of the most painful set-backs to their broader visions of world order—a greater blow, perhaps, than those dealt by the collapse of the League of Nations, the imperfections of the UN Charter, or the onset of the Cold War. When future historians look back on the twentieth century, Geoffrey Barraclough argued in 1964, "no theme will prove to be of greater importance than the revolt against the west."[6]

At least, so it was to internationalists. The aging Gilbert Murray's objections to the postwar world have already been noted in earlier chapters, but the depth of his pain at the loss of empire ought in this context to be reiterated. In 1952 he had come to the Churchillian view that the British Empire should never be allowed "to cease or to diminish," seeing it as one of the last hopes for the maintenance of "Christian civilization."[7] For Murray, writing in 1955, any change in that position would mean that "many great regions are likely to be re-barbarised," with the Muslim world, in particular, "united against the West."[8] And as decolonization did progress, contrary to his wishes, he observed that it was leading to "a monstrous amount of petty violence—group terrorism, and ordinary assassination" that displayed no signs of abating.[9]

These concerns split internationalists into two groups. The first lamented the end of empire but wished the postcolonial states well; the second were more ambivalent about both subjects. In her Reith Lectures for 1961, Margery Perham, the doyenne of African studies at Oxford,[10] expressed the first view with some grace. She understood the desire of Africans to restore their "lost sense of autonomy and dignity" and thought it natural; she comprehended, too, the idealism of postcolonial leaders in their domestic and foreign policies.[11] She regretted the harsh tone of most anticolonial rhetoric, which she thought unfair and too judgmental of Britain's power and altruism, but she looked forward to an era in which tempers had cooled and better relations between the metropole and its former colonies could be established.[12] Perham thought it a shame that, just at the moment the "rest of the world is seeking to sublimate nationalism," it should have such an effect in the African colonies, but she ended positively, if slightly patronizingly, calling upon fellow Britons to offer help if asked and calling on Africans to "impress us" in their independence.[13]

Not all were so generous. C. E. Carrington's reaction to the "wind of change," for example, was far more critical. Carrington (1897–1990) was by birth a New Zealander. He saw service in both the First and Second World Wars; between the wars he taught at Haileybury and at Oxford. In 1954 Carrington was appointed to the Abe Bailey chair in Commonwealth Relations at Chatham House, a post he held until 1962. His most significant work was an unfinished study of *The British Overseas* (1st ed. 1950), a synoptic history of the empire cast, as the subtitle put it, as the "exploits of a nation of shopkeepers."[14]

Carrington remained throughout a staunch internationalist and imperialist, and latterly a prominent advocate of the Commonwealth and equally prominent critic of European integration. His inaugural lecture at Chatham House expounded a "New Theory of the Commonwealth" and cast that organization as an essential bulwark against nationalism, which he considered "a political concept with no logical basis" but which posed the greatest danger to the modern world.[15] His later, post-decolonization, writings railed against the European idea and Britain's applications to join the Common Market, both of which he thought follies. European economic union, Carrington argued, was everything a liberal ought to oppose, whereas in its economic relations the Empire–Commonwealth embodied the best principles of Adam Smith, and in its politics, the best cooperative ideals of internationalism.[16]

Carrington did not respond well to the end of the empire. He referred to the process of decolonization as "liquidation," an allusion both to Churchill's famous pledge, made in 1942 and repeated in 1943, that he would not "preside over the liquidation of the British Empire," and to the other darker meanings that "liquidation" had in the contemporary world of totalitarianism.[17] In large part Carrington blamed the Americans—whom he thought "ill-informed, even in the highest circles" about the empire—for bringing about the end of Britain's "exploits" overseas.[18] Above all, however, he blamed the doctrine of "self-determination." This, Carrington thought, was a word and a concept with an "amusing history." Once used by philosophers in the context of discussions about individual free will, it had latterly entered the "jargon of revolutionary socialism" and then, apparently by accident, the argot of Woodrow Wilson.[19] Despite repeated refutations by such authorities as Gilbert Murray, the idea persisted, ultimately finding its way into the UN Charter.[20] Once implanted in the structure of international relations, this "dangerous term" had wreaked havoc. As a direct result of its mere utterance, Carrington argued, "The world had been Balkanized, fragmented into a great and ever-growing number of states, many of them so small and weak that using their nuisance-value in the [General] Assembly is their main contribution to world affairs."[21] Emotion had thus triumphed over reason; "atavistic" nationalism over the "multiplication of international and cosmopolitan links between the advanced countries."[22]

This was a classic statement of the internationalist creed, like Perham's own, but unlike Perham, it was tainted by some considerable bitterness. Decolonization was, for Carrington, a "destructive revolution" that could not but lead to further destruction.[23] Imperialism as a cause had been fatally wounded, "smeared" by the followers of Hobson and Lenin.[24] There was little left for Europeans to do but to endure the "diatribes" of the postcolonial states at the UN and try to rescue what was left of the Commonwealth's experiment in "administrative co-operation."[25]

Internationalists like Perham and Carrington thus clung to the Commonwealth as much because it seemed the least likely vessel for their ideals of international order, as they did because it may have offered a means of sustaining Britain's global influence. By contrast, British realists—of which there were growing numbers by 1960—were happy to dispense with the Commonwealth altogether, leaving only the bitterness that stemmed from the constant questioning of British motives and criticism of its imperial conduct. In his otherwise markedly realist account of the postwar world, *Neither War nor Peace* (1960), Hugh Seton-Watson (1916–1984)[26] nonetheless emphasized again that Britain had long intended for its colonies to determine their own affairs, but that since "good government" was "more important than self-government" it was wrong to accede to nationalist demands as soon as they were made.[27] It is, he thundered, "an unpardonable injustice to dismiss the paternalists as hypocrites, to ignore the many generations who honourably served the peoples of India and Africa, with very little material gain to themselves."[28]

For Seton-Watson, decolonization was little less than a disaster, signaling the ever-worsening nature of international relations in the postwar period.[29] Like the "paternalists," he believed that "Britain has obligations towards colonial people which it is cowardice and treachery to abandon."[30] Even as the wind of change blew, Seton-Watson remained convinced that "the truth is that indifference and scuttle ... played their part" in the withdrawal from empire, "and these are things of which Britain cannot be proud."[31] In his conclusion he lamented that

> what has been happening, in the relations between the West and the Asian and African nations, for the last decades and especially since 1945, is not the creation of new democracies, but the abdication of European nations, and especially of European *élites*, which, demoralized by the two great blood-baths in which Europe has twice done its best to commit suicide, have lost all confidence in themselves. . . . [This is not] a glorious extension of democracy, but a tragic decay of a civilization, similar to the decline of the Roman Empire, and followed by the same result, reversion to barbarism. The Europeans are leaving Africa and have left Asia: their place will be taken, not by the Asian democratic statesman, fine flavour of freedom produced by the best cultural heritages of West and East alike, but by the goat, the monkey and the jungle.[32]

And thus, in every anti-British or anti-white—as he saw it—speech, pamphlet, or General Assembly resolution, Seton-Watson saw the specter of a new, anti-white, racist tyranny to come: "it is uncertain how far these nationalisms will take on an anti-European racialist character. The recent trend in this direction is one of the most horrifying features of world politics."³³ This would be the culmination, Seton-Watson thought, of what was soon to become known as the "revolt against the West."

THE "REVOLT AGAINST THE WEST"

> [T]he common characteristics of the leaders of the colonial revolution in 1945 were a deep resentment against the West, combined with an uncritical acceptance of Western ideas and Western techniques.
> RICHARD CROSSMAN, *Government and the Governed* (1969)³⁴

Reactions to decolonization from other scholars of international relations were more varied. Some objected vehemently to what by 1960 had become known as the "revolt against the West" and made dark warnings about its implications for the maintenance of orderly or "civilized" international politics.³⁵ Some offered a cautious welcome and some simply argued that the end of empire had long been in the making, that it was inevitable, and that it simply had to be accepted, whatever its consequences. All, however, were convinced that this "revolt" was the defining feature of postwar international politics—a challenge far greater and far more lasting than the Cold War.

While he recognized their import, Herbert Butterfield, for one, was quite sanguine about these developments, and his response was entirely characteristic of his wider international thought. In *International Conflict in the Twentieth Century* (1960), he suggested that the contemporary "rebellion against what is regarded as Western imperialism or Western exploitation or Western ascendency" was "somewhat analogous" to the revolt of the "Irish peasantry" against British rule in the latter part of the nineteenth century. "Such a revolt," Butterfield wrote, "was a thing which had long been predicated; and if we resent it too much, this is perhaps because we have not sufficiently given ourselves to the task of imagining what our feelings would have been if we had been born Arabs or Indians."³⁶ Rather than blaming a "handful of wicked men" for the woes of Europeans in Africa and Asia, he argued, we had "better examine our own sins" and try to make amends.³⁷

This went little further, however, than Toynbee had done almost a decade before and like all attempts to walk the middle of the road, threatened only to get Butterfield run over. He was far too ambivalent for the times: balancing his call for Europeans to acknowledge injustices they might have committed with a reticence to call their behavior anything stronger than "so-called imperialism."³⁸ Butterfield extended his "imaginative sympathy" in all directions—to the high ideals of "paternal imperialism" and to those of its revolutionary opponents—but without any clear sense of what ought to be done in response to the "revolt."[39]

In stark contrast, Martin Wight was content to lay blame and to make public lamentations for a liberal international order he now thought under serious threat of collapse. In all of his published work, from the mid-1930s on, Wight had expressed deep fears about the prospects for international politics. Like the internationalists, he thought nationalism the principal cause of the decline of "international society"—a phenomenon fueled by the secularization of the West and the concomitant turn of individual allegiances from Church to State, and exacerbated by the nature of contemporary war.[40] The "revolt against the West" simply confirmed these prejudices, marking for Wight the final stage in that decline.

To some degree, these ideas had underpinned Wight's postwar enthusiasm for the reform of British colonial policy in Africa and a renewed commitment to paternalist imperialism. In *Attitude to Africa,* Wight and his co-authors noted the depredations that had been done to indigenous societies by the impact of the West, observing that without adequate "cultural reserves" or defenses against further depredations, they would for some time be vulnerable to influence from unwelcome outside influences or demagogic leaders. Such a vacuum, they feared, could easily be filled with "the tyranny of some little African Hitler"—or indeed Stalin—and made it essential within the empire that the British "retained powers to see that nascent democracies are not turned into totalitarian systems."[41]

The policies pursued and doctrines espoused by postcolonial states in the 1950s did little to assuage Wight's anxieties. He became, indeed, increasingly worried that the postcolonial states would unravel what was left of an already threadbare international order. The proceedings of the Bandung conference of twenty-nine Asian and African states, most newly independent, in 1955 were particularly concerning. In his LSE lectures on "International Institutions," Wight described the "Bandung Powers" as a "Mazzinian revolutionary league" which had, in effect, succeeded in turning the United Nations into an "organ of the anti-colonial movement, a kind of Holy Alliance in reverse."[42] In "The Power Struggle within the United Nations" (1956), however, he went even further.

At the UN, Wight argued, a new clash between the "haves" and "have-nots" was taking place, one analogous to that which had occurred twenty years before in Europe and was described by Carr in his *Twenty Years' Crisis* (1939). In Carr's book, the "haves" were Britain and France and the "have-nots" Japan, Italy, and Nazi Germany. In the postwar world, the "haves" were the same, but the new "have-nots" were the postcolonial states and their anticolonial nationalist allies in the remnants of European empires. Both sets of "have-nots" had, however, the same basic demand: that the "haves" transfer to them some of their unjustly held resources.

For Wight, however, there were further similarities between those interwar "have-nots" and the new postcolonial nations that had gathered at Bandung in 1955. "Like the Axis powers," he wrote, the new "have-nots" also "tend to authoritarianism, with notable exceptions in India and one or two others."[43] More important, Wight argued, they shared a common "state of mind . . . in which resentment, a sense of inferiority, and self-pity are prime ingredients." He went on: "The Axis powers were driven by resentment of the territorial empires and deep-rooted stable cultures of France, Britain, and America. The Bandung powers are moved correspondingly by the contrast between their poverty and our wealth. . . . At its best this is expressed in the demand for equality, and clothes itself in Wilsonian language of natural rights, liberty, and self-determination. But it would be an error to suppose that this language means the same to those whose historical experience and religious premises are totally different from ours as it does to us. Hitler, too, employed it with consummate effect."[44] In any case, Wight thought that economic inequality was not really the issue. What "Afro-Asians" actually "resent" are "what Bismarck called the *injuria temporum*, the injustices of history" and thus they "demand, sometimes arbitrarily, the rectification of those injustices."[45] This was the essential—or rather, since Wight uses this word, "emotional"—stimulus of anticolonial nationalism.

During the 1950s, then, Wight had moved from being a determined, if qualified, enthusiast for liberal imperialism to a disaffected, vehement critic of decolonization, pessimistic for the prospects of postcolonial states, international society, and, indeed, Britain. In a paper to the Institute of Commonwealth Studies delivered in 1958, he rejected the notion that the Commonwealth would do much to help, still less maintain peace and promote justice between its members. It appeared merely "the last tottering stronghold of the liberal optimism of a bygone age."[46] It was akin to the Holy Roman Empire, as the British Empire was analogous to the Roman, which "as its political disintegration proceeded, engendered a great body of political and legal theory, partly noble, partly fantastic."[47] Perhaps, Wight concluded, the Commonwealth's "lasting significance . . . will be in the sphere where it is politically weakest, in the leveling out of different civilizations and cultures and the affirmation of the unity of mankind," but it needed a new "Power"—not Britain—that had "ability and will to make it effective."[48]

The challenges such a power would face in the new postcolonial world were considerable. In "Brutus in Foreign Policy" (1960), Wight analyzed them in the context of a discussion of Prime Minister Anthony Eden's Suez adventure four years before. He sympathized with Eden, for he had had to deal with a world of "dissolving standards" brought about by rampant nationalism.[49] The challenge Eden faced was far greater than merely the problem of protecting British interests at a time when British power was in eclipse—it was more deeply rooted in the normative structure, as it were, of contemporary international politics. For Wight,

> There is a kind of crisis of international society more fundamental than threats to the balance of power; it is when the principle of international obligation itself deliquesces. Such a crisis has been endemic in international politics ever since 1776, with the slow fermenting of the doctrine that the only valid claim to membership of the society of nations is to have established a State expressing the popular will, and the slow exploration of the corruptions that the popular will is liable to. . . . National self-determination has a gallant ring of freedom and fulfilment, but its methods are assassination and arms-running, insurrection against established governments, confiscation of foreign property, repudiation of agreements, dissolution of moral ties.[50]

The consequences of these changes were clear in both state conduct and in international organizations. The United Nations, for example, had not just become an "organ of anti-colonialism"; it was also ever more derelict, as Wight saw it, in other duties, "consistently" refusing at the same time "to condemn breaches of international agreements." What seemed to matter was merely the satisfaction of "[w]orld sentiment," which "regards colonialism as wrong and revolt against it right," regardless of the means employed.[51]

For Wight, Eden's tragedy was that "in trying to enforce the moral conditions of international life he allowed himself to become unscrupulous" in conniving with the French and Israelis to retake the Suez Canal.[52] But while his means were wrong, his ends were not. Eden had been right, Wight implied, to defend Britain's interests, including those of empire and to try to uphold basic moral standards. His opponents, by contrast, had drawn entirely the wrong conclusions from the episode: "Some of Eden's critics seem to argue that the right policy is to grant independence to the rest of Asia and Africa as quickly as possible, and let the newly enfranchised members of international society settle down to industrialize themselves and practise democracy.... This may be a dream-transformation of the historical experience called Balkanisation, which means a *Kleinstaaterei* of weak States, fiercely divided among themselves by nationalistic feuds, governed by unstable popular autocracies, unaccustomed to international law and diplomatic practice as they are to parliamentary government, and a battle-ground for the surrounding Great Powers."[53] This was the final and perhaps the clearest statement of Wight's view of decolonization, making plain that it represented a serious threat to the fabric of international society, that the "Balkanization" of Asia and Africa would have analogous and equally disastrous consequences as it did in Europe after the First World War, and that its speed was as much a problem as its substance.

Wight returned to his subject only once more, in an essay on "International Legitimacy" (1972) later published in *Systems of States*. Nothing in the content was inconsistent with his earlier opposition to decolonization and what he saw as its consequences, though his tone was more measured. The essay traced the change from the dynastic to the popular principle concerning the legitimate locus of sovereignty. The popular principle, Wight argued, was ideological and dogmatic, insisting that "all that is not popularly based is illegitimate."[54] For him, this was doubly problematic: first because it was hard to reconcile with Wight's theological convictions, which had to give some place to a source of rights beyond the human, and second because empirically it is clear that the opinions of the people are rarely, if ever, consulted in processes of national self-determination.[55] Rather, as Wight put it: "The principle *cujus regio ejus religio* is restored in a secular form. The élite who hold state power decide the political allegiance of all within their frontiers; the recusant individual may (if he is fortunate) be permitted to emigrate."[56]

Not all took such a pessimistic view. For Hedley Bull, decolonization was an inevitability to be managed, not, as it was for Wight, a misfortune to be lamented. Moreover—and again in contrast to Wight—Bull thought national self-determination to be something almost natural: it was a tendency to which all developing peoples will eventually lean. He heaped scorn, therefore, on any attempts to obscure or ignore that fact, attacking especially what he called the "Commonwealth myth" and pointing instead—slightly mockingly—to the British Empire's long history of "continuous disintegration."[57] Nation-states, he implied, were the natural ends to which all empires eventually tended. The Commonwealth, Bull thought, was merely a "symbol ... to prolong the spirit long after life has departed the body."[58] It was more important to Britain than to anyone else, partly because it preserves an element of British prestige, partly because it offers a "moral reply to the critics of imperialism," who can be told that "the principle of Commonwealth was immanent in the Empire," and partly because it dulls the "sense of historical defeat" that was decolonization.[59]

Unlike Wight, who feared its "power politics," Bull favored "a plurality of sovereign states" over the alternative models of international order.[60] The state could, he believed, have a "positive role" to play in "world affairs."[61] The danger lay not in national self-determination itself, but in the values and beliefs that animated leaders and peoples in its aftermath.

Thus decolonization did not trouble Bull per se, as it did Carrington or Wight, nor was he especially worried about the prospects of "Balkanization." But this did not mean that he was entirely happy about these processes. Adam Watson later observed that Bull was quite "uneasy about the relationship of the newly independent non-white world to Western values and standards of civilization." Watson went on: "To many Westerners of the 1960s and 1970s, the decolonization movement and the adoption of universally valid standards of human rights, democracy, the position of women in society, the protection of the environment and so on, went hand in hand. Hedley personally favoured these values.... But ... the world was moving towards a society of some 200 substantially independent and therefore culturally very diverse states."[62] Much of Bull's later work tried therefore to address the consequences of this change.

Bull's unease about the results of decolonization—as opposed to its fact, as it were—is readily apparent in *The Anarchical Society* (1977), particularly in his account of the normative structure of international society. *The Anarchical Society* is rightly famous for arguing that there is a tension between the maintenance of order and the pursuit of justice in international politics, but central to the second half of the book is a discussion of the contemporary instance of that tension—that which exists between a Western order and non-Western notions of justice.[63] In the laws of war, Bull noted, the traditional restriction of just war to self-defense was under challenge by doctrines advocating wars of national liberation.[64] More troubling, he found, were "Third World" arguments in favor of subordinating international order to justice for individuals, whether by wholesale reform of the states-system by "world-order activism," by regionalism, or by revolution.[65] Each threatened the "consensus about common interests and values that provides the foundation for common rules and institutions" that exists among practitioners of international politics, as well as being a "corrupting" influence on the academic study of international relations.[66]

Bull found refuge from these various storms in quite a different way from the internationalists or indeed Butterfield and Wight: namely, in statism. In his essay on the "State's Positive Role," published the same year as *The Anarchical Society*, he observed that for most of the last century, if not longer, Westerners have been prone to "disparage" the state. "A number of factors," Bull argued, "account for this." One was the dominance of liberalism and internationalism over the Western mind, but there were others: "Loyalties that compete with loyalty to the state—allegiances to class or ethnic group or race or religious sect—can be openly proclaimed and cultivated in western societies and often cannot be elsewhere. Moreover, it is only in the West that it has been possible to assume that if the barriers separating states were abolished, it would be our way of life and not some other than would be universally enthroned."[67] Westerners, he suggested, might soon change their mind when we shared the "vulnerability" that non-Western societies had long felt when our ideas, customs, and conceptions of the good life had been foisted on them, unasked.[68] What was needed, in that context, was not an effort to abolish the state that the internationalists had long sought, but rather a concerted attempt to find "some modus vivendi . . . between these [i.e., our values] and the very different values and institutions in other parts of the world with which they will have to co-exist."[69]

While Wight thought international society under threat from "Balkanization" and dissolving standards and while Bull worried about the erosion of its cultural underpinnings, Adam Watson (1914–2007)[70] perceived a quite different relationship between it and the postcolonial states. In part, this was because Watson had experienced the estrangement between the European states and their former possessions at first hand, as head of the Foreign Office's Africa department in the late 1950s, as minister for African affairs at the Paris embassy, and finally, in the early 1960s, as ambassador to the newly independent Mali, Senegal, Mauritania, and Togo. He drew two lessons from his diplomatic work: first, that the postcolonial states were nowhere near as independent as they might claim; and second, that if theorists allow themselves to be too "Westphalian" in their attitudes, they will neglect the real nature of relations between the former imperial metropoles and their erstwhile colonies. Together, these allowed Watson to build an argument about decolonization that might serve as a salve to those wounded by the end of empire.

It was in this context that the idea of "international society" held a very particular appeal for Watson. Rather than seeing it in terminal decline, as Wight did, Watson conceived it in far more positive terms.

He saw the concept of "international society" as an antidote to what he called "anarchophilia."[71] For Watson, there were three kinds of "anarchophiliacs." The first were anticolonialists, who saw state sovereignty as the ultimate object of their national self-determination and as a bulwark against external interference. The second were the political realists, who conceived all international relations in worlds in which there were many different states as being power-political in nature. The third were the disaffected internationalists and imperialists, for whom "anarchy" meant more than just the absence of an authoritative, law-enforcing power in international relations, but which meant also something more than what we conventionally understand by anarchy, as chaos and disorder. This was the kind of "anarchophilia" or perhaps "anarchophobia" found in Wight's pessimistic account of a world fractured by nationalism, where Western values and interests have been eclipsed, standards have "dissolved," and rules broken. Watson's account of "international society" was intended to address both of these sets of beliefs, in part to convince his audiences that the effects of decolonization were not as dramatic as they might seem, and in part to suggest that there were indeed important continuities between the colonial and postcolonial international orders that held out hope for Britain. We will return to this agenda in a moment.

Tracing the early development of Watson's views is difficult, partly because his private papers are not yet available and partly because his earliest published writings were reprints of speeches made in an official capacity. His "Problems of Adjustment in the Middle East" (1952), for instance, is a straightforward piece of public diplomacy. It was designed in essence to persuade American audiences of the virtuousness of Britain's intentions, arguing that Britain had altered from its "imperialistic course" in that region and encouraging the United States to aid British efforts in dealing with the "grim reality of the power vacuum" that might emerge there, "right on the Soviet Union's frontier."[72]

Watson later recalled that the Suez crisis, four years later, persuaded him that such extensive intervention in that region and others was now impossible for Britain, that a continued "imperialistic course" was in any case futile, and that complete decolonization was inevitable.[73] Instead, he set himself the task of analyzing the end of empire and its implications, publishing two books while still in the diplomatic service: *Emergent Africa* (1965), published under the pseudonym "Scipio," and *The Nature and Problems of the Third World* (1968).

In *Emergent Africa*, Watson sketched a generic outline of African postcolonial states, with their small "detribalized and Westernized elites," the single parties that brought them to power, and the expectations of their citizens.[74] Like Carrington and Wight, Watson portrayed African anti-colonialism as essentially sentimental and unrealistic—"picturesque and emotionally satisfying"—contrasting it with the far more realistic views of their former colonial rulers.[75] It was the instrument, he argued, of a Westernized elite that had little in common with the ordinary African. Moreover, it was not actually all that dangerous, and nor—by extension—was the Westernized elite itself. "[R]adical though their ideas may be," Watson argued, this elite "tend to become a force for stability once their party machine is in control of government."[76] True, they tended to establish one-party states, but in reality their values were intrinsically "managerial" rather than revolutionary in their mindsets.[77]

Of course, this was not to suggest that there were not some problems. The popularity of Marxist ideas in postcolonial states did pose, for Watson, a significant challenge that needed to be addressed by the West. He thought it critical to emphasize, in response to such claims, the positive work done under imperial rule to aid and develop the colonies, not just the negative aspects of imperialism. In the colonies, Watson argued, "[t]he assumption that colonial rule held back technical progress was fostered by certain Marxists with their analytical theory of imperialism as the final and most exploitative phase of capitalism. It was also encouraged by progressive Western liberals with their more generous desire to establish human equality and dignity. Both held that colonialism was the essential cause of the misfortunes and the relative backwardness of tropical Africa . . . In fact . . . the colonial system did distort the progress of tropical Africa towards modern statehood. . . . But colonial rule has at the same time been the main agency of this progress."[78] It was necessary, too, Watson argued, to rebut the allegation that the relations of the newly independent states with their former rulers was somehow "neo-colonial." Although "popularized" by communist "propaganda machines," such ideas merely reflect "certain fears, rather than objective realities."[79]

Watson positioned himself between this communist extreme and what he called the "conservative" imperialist alternative, arguing that the first few years of postcolonial government had vindicated the view that "rapid devolution of power" was possible.[80] He argued that decolonization had not, in fact, led to the disasters Carrington and the other prophets of doom had predicted; rather, it had worked reasonably well and had thus been justified. What Watson called the "official" or "moderate" view had been vindicated.[81] In postcolonial Africa, there was "comparative stability," "internal order and authority," and a "relative rarity of armed aggression or subversion directed by one new African state against another."[82] The West, therefore, need not worry: the fate of Africans might not be in democratically elected hands, but at least there was a core of "politically quite competent" individuals running most of the new states.[83] And "[i]n any case," Watson argued, somewhat cynically, "tropical Africa produces little, if anything, that the West really needs."[84] His message was clear: Africans are "no longer the wards of the West," and thus "the West is not responsible for what they decide to do."[85]

These themes were reprised three years later in *The Nature and Problems of the Third World*. There Watson argued that although the "expansion of Europe"—this euphemism for imperialism appears throughout—was driven largely by a desire for "gain" and "profits," its "withdrawal" was due to a sense that it was "morally wrong."[86] While it was now *"meaningless* to say that the extension of Europe or its withdrawal was a good or bad thing," he considered that the "great benefits" brought to the other peoples of the world were "more lasting than the damage."[87] Watson thus found it hard to understand the new anti-imperialism that had arisen both in the West and the Third World—another "sentiment" or "emotional complex" in which "absurd and passionate exaggerations distort a limited reality."[88] As before, he offered reassurance to worried Westerners: "I do not think the developed nations of the world need be too disturbed by this understandable, if largely unjust resentment. Most governments of the Third World show a gratifying awareness of where their material interests lie."[89]

Two lines of argument were thus developed in Watson's two books on decolonization. The first was that although Western imperialism had been moved by greed, the West deserved credit for its realization that its actions had been morally wrong, with self-determination conceived as a one-sided and altruistic act of atonement by the West, rather than a panicked response to a valid moral claim on the part of colonial peoples. The second was that decolonization did not substantially change the nature of relations between the West and the rest.

Watson developed this latter theme in his later work, utilizing the idea of "international society" as a means of emphasizing the ties that continued to bind, rather than those that were broken by national self-determination and the attainment of sovereignty. In the 1960s, he recalled, he began to "see the new international order that emerged from wholesale decolonization not only in Westphalian terms"—conceiving the new international relations in rather different terms, in other words, to disaffected, antistatist internationalists. Instead, Watson perceived an order comprising of "a core of economically and politically developed states, surrounded by an ever more numerous periphery of weak and inexperienced states."[90] Decolonization had produced, in other words, an order better understood in terms of "'hegemony" and "dependence," ideas Watson developed in *The Evolution of International Society* (1992), *The Limits of Independence* (1997), and in *Hegemony and History* (2007).

Watson's mature argument was that far from being an "anarchy" or even an "anarchical society" of states, contemporary international politics was better understood as an unbalanced order comprising a "loose informal concert of the strongest powers" led by the United States and a multitude of weak, mostly postcolonial states.[91] There were, he argued, limits on independence, especially in the global South. In the event, the "revolt against the West" had not amounted to anything like what Wight or Bull had thought it might. Rather, it was the norms, interests, and objectives of the hegemonic powers—the promotion of peace, prosperity, and "standards of civilization," including democracy, human rights, and environmental protection—that had prevailed. Watson recognized, of course, that these hegemonic demands were sometimes resisted, in word if not in deed, by the weaker states, but he argued that their "[a]nti-hegemonial rhetoric and the glorification of independence are often an alibi or cover-story [for] complying with hegemonial demands."[92] "Multiple independencies seemed to us legitimate and desirable" in the 1960s, Watson noted later, but in practical terms they were never realized.[93] The end of empire, despite all the fears of internationalists, whigs, and even realists, had been little more than sound and fury, signifying nothing, and disguising the more important continuities.

THE RADICAL REPOST

> It is no ideological assertion, but a simple generalization rooted in empirical observation, that the prime content of colonial political rule was economic exploitation.
> PETER WORSLEY, *The Third World* (1964)[94]

It is somewhat ironic that Watson, an apologist for the act and the manner of decolonization, ended up arguing much the same as the Establishment's radical critics, namely, that decolonization had actually changed very little in the relations between the West and its former colonial possessions. That European imperialism had been succeeded by Western— that is, American as well as Western European—"neo-imperialism" was and remains a core article of faith for radicals. It permitted them, as we have seen in chapter 7, to confront the dilemma to their beliefs posed by the fact that decolonization had occurred without the parallel revolution in the colonial metropoles that Marxian theories had predicted. Like Watson's arguments about the essential continuities between imperial and postcolonial relations between Britain and its former possessions, it was essentially consolatory: designed to give comfort in the face of what might appear, at first glance, to be defeat.

The radical argument about empire, namely that it was above all a system for the economic exploitation of the colonies, made great inroads in the British academic and public spheres in the 1960s. Here, as elsewhere in British debates over international relations, historians played a critical role. In the interwar and immediate postwar years, the historiography of empire had tended to concentrate on the political, telling a whiggish story about the building of institutions that culminated in the creation of a Commonwealth of free and equal nations. C. E. Carrington, Lionel Curtis, W. H. Hancock, Nicholas Mansergh, and many others subscribed to this view.[95] While this view had long been challenged by those anti-imperialist radicals inspired by Hobson's or Lenin's economic critique of the empire, like Laski or Woolf, it was not until the postwar period that British historians offered a substantive counterargument to the whig orthodoxy. This came in 1953 with the publication of John Gallagher and Ronald Robinson's article "The Imperialism of Free Trade," which sparked a comprehensive revision of the causes, as it were, of empire.

Gallagher and Robinson argued against the notion, put forward most obviously by Hobson and Lenin, that there was a difference between "old" and "new imperialism," asserting instead that there were fundamental continuities between the mid-Victorian empire and the late Victorian and Edwardian version.[96] To do this, they also had to contest one of the key assumptions of the whig orthodoxy, which conventionally considered as parts of the empire only those territories formally annexed or otherwise acknowledged to be subject to British political control. This kind of "legalistic" thinking, Gallagher and Robinson argued, overlooked those areas of "informal empire" in which Britain held sway de facto, if not—or not yet—de jure.[97] There was, they asserted, an "inconsistency between fact and the orthodox interpretation" which required a throughgoing revision of imperial history, one that took proper account of "informal as well as formal expansion, and must allow for the continuity of the process."[98]

Gallagher and Robinson defined imperialism as "a sufficient political function of [the] process of integrating new regions into the expanding economy"—a rather different concept of empire to those held by the whigs.[99] Formal control over territories was extended, they argued, only when the existing "polities of these new regions fail to provide satisfactory conditions for commercial or strategic integration."[100] In this light, the continuities between the "old" and "new" imperialisms were far more significant than the disjunctions, not least because the rapid late-nineteenth-century expansion of the formal empire could not have occurred without the mid-century economic expansion of informal empire that preceded it. And this argument came with a highly important coda. If empires could pass from informal to formal imperialisms, Gallagher and Robinson implied, surely they could pass from formal to informal imperialisms just as easily. Indeed, they suggested that India had already passed to what they called the "third" stage of empire and that British West Africa (and presumably the rest of the empire) may soon follow.[101]

Gallagher and Robinson elaborated their argument in *Africa and the Victorians* (1961), which again provoked considerable controversy, especially among Marxists and radicals.[102] They were roundly attacked by members of the New Left, most notably V. G. Kiernan, for their supposed misinterpretation of Hobson and Lenin and later by other Marxist-inspired writers for being overly Eurocentric in focus.[103] Their wider contribution to this radical tradition should not, however, be ignored, for in Gallagher and Robinson's notions of "informal" empire and the "imperialism of free trade" lay a weapon of great utility for anti-imperialists in the postimperial era.

Few radicals greeted the end of empire with unalloyed enthusiasm, for they suspected—as Gallagher and Robinson implied—that little would change in the essentials of the relationship between Britain and its former colonies. True, some veteran anticolonialists within the Labour movement, like John Strachey (1901–1963),[104] did display considerable satisfaction at decolonization, casting it as a vindication of the Attlee government's wisdom and far-sightedness in beginning the process.[105] For Strachey, at least, decolonization heralded a new world in which capital—indeed American capital—might be put to the use of development of the Third World, rather than operate to facilitate its political subjugation in a new informal empire. He called therefore for a "publically controlled and directed export of capital"—a new Marshall Plan—that might raise living standards throughout the world, not just the West.[106]

On the Left, however, Strachey's views were increasingly subject to challenge. The New Left, in particular, argued that decolonization was not, in fact, as significant as the internationalists, whigs, and more conventional radicals had claimed. If imperialism was "the extension of the power of a class, of an economic and social system, from one country to another," Michael Barrett Brown argued in a review of Strachey's *End of Empire* in the *New Left Review*, then the continued existence of that class implied that "imperialism still remains," just in different form.[107] "It is," he maintained, "that circle of poverty to which the under-developed territories are bound. This pattern or relationship between the 'haves' and 'have-nots' is held in place by certain historical distortions which still obtain: the terms of trade, the distorted single-crop or single-mineral dependence of their economies, the entrenched position of feudal and comprador governments which hold back development."[108] A new informal imperialism had indeed replaced the old formal empire.

For the New Left, the only proper response to this predicament was to align themselves with Third World resistance to neocolonialism. In the late 1950s and early 1960s, this meant support for the Bandung principles of nonalignment or neutralism.[109] This stance had the added advantage, critical after Stalin and after 1956, of giving the appearance of positioning oneself equidistant between the superpowers. "Positive neutralism" was, for Worsley, "a new kind revolutionary theory in which the major conflict is seen as one between the hungry 'proletarian nations' and affluent Euro-America, capitalist or communist."[110] Where the internationalists and whigs expressed deep regret at what they thought the resentful and unreasonable moralism of the "have-nots," denouncing it as an invitation to disorder, some radicals reveled in it. For Worsley, neutralism marked the emergence of a new way of thinking that went beyond liberalism and even socialism: "Today, new extensions of humanity's conception of a truly human life are being created out of the "self-interest" of the deprived emergent peoples. They are not only reviving old values, they are also creating new conceptions of internationalism, neutralism, independence and peaceful relationships. And new concepts of personality, respect, and social obligation, too."[111] Given these changes, it was inevitable, as well as desirable, that the demands of the neutralists be met—meaning, in practice, "the distribution of aid via the UN."[112]

This kind of thinking, as we have seen, deeply troubled the internationalists and whigs, not because they did not perceive a need for aid to the "Third World," but because they thought relative poverty, for all its evils, did not justify dictatorship, repression, and guerrilla warfare. In the end, the increasing prevalence of political violence posed dilemmas, too, for the proponents of nonalignment. By the late 1960s, in response, many of those attracted to the policy by its espousal of pacifism, like the Australian John Burton, whose *International Relations: A General Theory* (1965) was actually more paean of praise to nonalignment than a systematic theoretical treatise, quietly dropped their earlier enthusiasms for the policy.[113] Instead, they moved to distinguish their preference for nonviolence and to outline innovative modes of conflict resolution based, as we shall see in the next chapter, more on Western rather than Third World thinking.

Other radicals, by contrast, came to embrace the violence, conceiving it as a legitimate rejoinder to past colonial humiliations and present neo-imperialist oppression, as Franz Fanon and others did.[114] This was a novel move: many British radicals of the past had opposed imperialism and made public arguments against it, but very few had openly justified and supported the use of armed force by anticolonial movements against the British or other European empires. Their pacifism—or at least "pacificism"—was generally consistent and evenhanded, applying to both sides. The new militant radicals, however, rejected pacifism and criticized nonviolence, like those of the CND, for mistaking "a tactic for a principle."[115] Anti-Western violence was justified, they argued, because it was a "reaction to the unremitting violence of US imperialism."[116] It demanded the demonstration of solidarity by Western radicals with anti-imperialists worldwide, regardless of their tactics. The "revolt against the West" should be welcomed, the radicals argued, rather than lamented.

This stance is significant for two reasons. First, these attitudes came over time to exercise considerable influence within the academic disciplines of politics and international relations as it coalesced during the 1970s. In part, this occurred because these beliefs were borne into the field by radicals-turned-academics, individuals like Gareth Stedman Jones and Fred Halliday, who were later to hold prestigious chairs at Cambridge and the LSE, respectively. Second, and perhaps more important, the radicals subjected to thoroughgoing "critique" all of their inherited knowledge of politics and international relations, as well as the relation of that knowledge to practice. To a degree, this enabled a self-conscious discipline of international relations to emerge; to a greater extent, it laid the foundations for the rise of "theory" in the British variant of the discipline from the late 1980s on.

CONCLUSION

> It bears repeating that for an empire which declined from thirteen million square miles and nearly 500 million inhabitants in 1914 to a handful of rocky outposts ... fifty years later ... the absence of any serious or sustained debate on the direction of imperial policy and the consequences of imperial decline is somewhat surprising.
>
> J. G. DARWIN, "The Fear of Falling" (1986)[117]

Historians, as we saw in the previous chapter, have long argued that decolonization had little "impact" on the British. In part, they suggest, this was due to straightforward indifference, especially among the public; in part, too, it was a function of successful "stage-management" by politicians, who successfully "cosseted" the electorate in "illusion."[118] None of this should be taken to suggest, however, that there was no discussion of the end of empire at all. Among those professionally bound to take an interest—students of politics and international relations—and those activists with moral or political commitments to the subject, there was an extensive discussion about decolonization. Moreover, it had a considerable influence over the course of British thinking not just about Britain or its foreign policy, but about the nature of contemporary world politics.

Above all, decolonization dealt the final blow to internationalism, exposing its internal divisions—between imperialists and anti-imperialists, between liberals and radicals—and demonstrating the weaknesses of its preferred vision of international order. It provided a devastating display of the power of nationalism, which internationalists had long and erroneously predicted would wither away once the economic and strategic unification of the world was revealed. The dominance the new nations quickly established at the UN, especially in the General Assembly, which they used to such effect to prosecute a campaign of criticism against the West, showed up the inherent flaws of internationalist institutions.

Together these changes strengthened the hands of realists and radicals. The first merely pointed to the consequences of decolonization as evidence—if evidence was needed—of the perennial truth of their beliefs; the second found, in the new nations, allies whom they could call upon, at least rhetorically, for support in their demands that the West change its ways. But these changes also had one further effect. The internationalists had long argued that war was obsolete in contemporary international relations and that its study, apart from being morally questionable, was thus of little use. Decolonization, in the midst of the Cold War, suggested otherwise. In response, British scholars began in the 1950s—as the next chapter explores—to cast off some of their inherited internationalist inhibitions about war and peace and to look again at the means by which they might best be pursued.

9. War and Peace

> The newer generation—some middle-aged in the 1960s—which reached adult age in the later war and early post-war years, grew into a world accustomed to violence and the exercise of physical force among the nations.
> E. F. PENROSE, "Britain's Place in the Changing Structure of International Relations" (1970)

The 1960s saw the development of two new ways of thinking and writing about international relations in Britain: strategic studies and peace research. Both built upon existing traditions of thought about international relations. Both drew upon or reacted against prior work in these fields done elsewhere in the world, principally in the United States, and both were generously supported with funds from the United States and elsewhere. In terms of both approach and style, strategic studies inherited much from the whig tradition but it also borrowed from the influential and energetic school of civilian strategists on the other side of the Atlantic. Peace research was more heterodox, bringing in new methods and concepts from abroad and blending them with established ideas from the internationalist and radical traditions. Both subfields benefited from the immigration of people as well as the import of ideas. Australians, in particular, played crucial roles in their development: Hedley Bull (1932–1985) loomed large in British strategic studies in the 1960s,[1] while John Burton (1915–2010) assumed a similar profile in peace and conflict research.

Although the approaches, methods, and preferences of strategic studies and peace research differed—sometimes dramatically—both are best understood as responses to the immediate dilemmas posed by total war, nuclear weapons, and missile technologies, as well as to the underlying dilemmas posed by the nature of twentieth century international relations. Like earlier generations of thinkers about these subjects, they detected failings in contemporary practices of international relations and were convinced that a systematic body of knowledge could help improve them. The difference between these earlier generations and that of the 1960s and early 1970s lay in the kinds of knowledge they sought. For the earlier, established ideas or extensions of established ideas could generally, though not always, suffice; for the later, wholly new knowledge was required to address wholly new dilemmas. There was no longer any point, Burton argued, in trying to restate "old arguments" to fit the "changed circumstances of the day," for "the re-statement required is so different that less confusion in thought might be created by new statements."[2]

The desire for new knowledge is readily apparent in the peace research of the period and especially evident in their enthusiasm for novel approaches and insights. Peace research was the only area in which positivistic approaches—behaviorialism, systems theories, and various kinds of statistical analysis—were used in Britain to any significant extent. For Burton, at least, these methods were the means by which "scientists" like himself could move beyond the traditional power-oriented concerns like alliances or the mechanisms of collective security and instead concentrate on the "hidden or suppressed" "operations or processes of relations between States" that really shape the contemporary world.[3] They also offered a way to move beyond what he called the "philosophic" and "interdisciplinary" phase of the study of international relations, with its generalist "frontiersmen," into one in which the "discipline" of "International Relations" was properly constituted as a "science" with its "own teachers."[4]

The desire for new knowledge is less obvious—but no less present—in British strategic studies. Although not always immediately apparent, in large part because British strategists tended to define themselves and their approaches by contrasting them to what they argued to be excessively newfangled American ideas, the strategists were nonetheless concerned to build a new—or at least to organize afresh—body of useful knowledge. In the immediate aftermath of the Second World War, with the atomic bombings uppermost in their minds, some American thinkers had argued that a new science of strategy was required and—in a deliberate echo of Clemenceau—that the development of such a science was too important to be left to the generals.[5] Bernard Brodie, for example, insisted that the study of strategy could no longer consist of the rote learning of venerable maxims or "enduring principles." In a total or even a nuclear war, such an old-fashioned and dogmatic approach was simply too risky, since "the magnitude of disaster which might result from military error today bears no relation to situations of the past."[6]

Like Brodie, all the thinkers considered here worked in the shadow of total war, in the shadow of a "good war" that many thought had been fought badly, both in moral and strategic terms, and in the shadow of another potentially more cataclysmic war that might well be prosecuted in an even less justifiable and effective way. Each of these factors shaped their thought. First, despite its horrors, the Second World War reconciled many intellectuals to the notion that war could sometimes be justifiable, persuading them that strict pacifism was not the best response to the dilemmas of contemporary international relations.[7] This, as I will argue, marked an important shift from the prevailing tenor of interwar thinking. Second, the war, and especially the manner of its ending, demonstrated that radical changes had taken place in the nature of modern warfare that demanded equally dramatic changes in the ways in which it was thought about, as well as the ways in which it was fought. Third, the war and its aftermath, together with the threat of the Cold War turning hot, all demanded that the moral implications of any theorizing about war be confronted and addressed.

This insistence on keeping the moral dimension in view was a particular feature—a feature much vaunted by British thinkers—of British approaches to both strategic studies and peace research. The strategists, in particular, eschewed the idea of a "science" of strategy, seeking more systematic analytical thinking on the subject without compromising what they implied to be their moral integrity. The peace researchers, perhaps because they were surer of their moral footings, did sometimes dabble in science, but only in the service of their higher ends. This chapter examines—in two parts—the ways in which both sets of thinkers reconciled these competing imperatives. It traces, too, the growing importance of foreign influences—positive and negative—on British thinking about war and peace, and indeed international relations more generally, in the 1960s and early 1970s. Finally, it explores the latent and sometimes overt antagonism between the strategists and the peace researchers as they vied to dominate scholarly discussion of those subjects.

POLITICS AND STRATEGY

> [T]he historian and the political scientist cannot discuss war
> in terms of good or evil, normality or abnormality, health or
> disease. For them it is simply the use of violence by states for
> the enforcement, the protection or the extension of their political
> power. . . . The desire for, acquisition, and exercise of power is the
> raw material of politics, national and international, and violence
> may sometimes prove an effective means to secure or retain it.
> MICHAEL HOWARD, "Military Power and International Order" (1964)[8]

In the 1930s and 1940s, British strategic thinking was dominated by two tarnished titans: J. F. C. Fuller (1878–1966)[9] and Basil Liddell Hart (1895–

1970).[10] Although both were remarkably prescient about the nature of mechanized warfare, both managed to secure for themselves somewhat tainted reputations: Fuller because he was "unashamedly authoritarian and anti-democratic" and had flirted with Mosley's fascists in the late 1930s, and Liddell Hart because he was so vocal in advocating a negotiated peace with Germany in 1940 and then in attempting to defend the honor of the *Wehrmacht* after 1945.[11] In the postwar years, neither disguised their belief that the domination of central Europe by the Soviet Union was an evil that might have been prevented had the Allies heeded their advice and sought a negotiated peace with Germany. Questionable sympathies and unfashionable opinions thus barred Fuller and Liddell Hart from academic posts and some outlets in the media, making it difficult for either to establish something akin to an "English school" of strategic studies.

For Fuller and Liddell Hart, moreover, "strategy" meant the art of coordinating military operations to win wars rather than the broader meaning—of orchestrating all the means that a state has at its disposal, including violence, to secure its national interests—it had for later strategists. Fuller's work thus concentrated on the best means by which contemporary technologies could be utilized to overcome the apparent superiority of defensive over offensive forces on the modern battlefield, which entailed the use of a highly mobile mechanized army, closely coordinated with sea- and airpower.[12] Liddell Hart ranged a little further, appreciating that military triumph alone was often insufficient to win wars, but his main concern was with the battlefield. Indeed, Liddell Hart was profoundly disturbed by the ideas of "total wars" of "nations-in-arms," desiring instead a return to limited wars fought by small armies of professionals.[13]

For all their insight, the work of Fuller and Liddell Hart was therefore ill-suited to their times. This helped to stymie the emergence of strategic studies in Britain, though other factors were also at play. On the one hand, there was a lack of any formal institutional structures for the study of war or strategy; on the other, the field was overlooked, as it were, by the study of international relations, on the one side, and by military history, on the other. Interwar specialists in international relations, as we have seen, often took war to be an unmitigated evil and could not countenance the notion that it could be the subject of scholarly analysis. The military historians had few such concerns, but concentrated instead on the narrower tasks of recounting the stories of past battles or penning regimental histories.

As a consequence, the few places where strategic studies might have taken root in the interwar period tended to prove barren. The Chichele Chair in the History of War had been founded at Oxford in 1909, albeit as a chair in military history until 1946, but while its first holder, Spenser Wilkinson (1853–1937),[14] did concern himself with matters of strategy, his successors were more reluctant.[15] That reticence seems to have been matched by the electors, who chose in 1946 to place Cyril Falls rather than Liddell Hart in the chair. A former soldier with wide "historical and literary interests," Falls was again no strategist; rather, he was a military historian with particular interests in the Elizabethan era. He held the chair until 1953, when he was succeeded by Norman Gibbs (1910–1990), the longest serving Chichele Professor to date, who retired in 1977.[16]

Strategic studies fared little better elsewhere. A chair in military studies was also created at King's College, London, in 1927.[17] The first holder was Major-General Sir Frederick Maurice (1871–1951),[18] but he served in the post for only four years (1929–1933). When Maurice left he was not replaced, though the department that the professor was meant to run remained in being. It took until the early 1950s, however, before positive efforts were made properly to found "war studies" at King's. In 1953, the historian and former soldier Michael Howard was appointed a reader and took on that task. In 1963 he was made professor of war studies and formal successor to Maurice.[19]

It was largely through the efforts of Gibbs at Oxford and Howard at King's that strategic studies gained academic respectability in Britain during the 1950s and especially in the 1960s. Howard was especially energetic in the early stages, both in building his department and constructing what would now be considered a research network of scholars and other parties with interests in the field.[20] In 1955, for example, Howard commissioned a series of public and BBC radio lectures on "War and Society" to which Martin Wight, Richard Titmuss, and P. M. S. Blackett, among others, made contributions.[21] In these early stages, Howard was aided and abetted by Charles Webster, professor of international history at the LSE, whose history of British strategic bombing in the Second World War, co-authored with Noble Frankland and finally published in 1961, was a major contribution to the nascent field of strategic studies.[22]

In the first decade after 1945, Chatham House provided the principal focal point for these and other thinkers to debate strategic issues, hosting working groups and commissioning lectures from academics, politicians, and civil servants, as well as serving and former soldiers.[23] One such working group on nuclear weapons—which included Blackett, Rear Admiral Sir Anthony Buzzard, Healey, and Howard—led to the pamphlet *On Limiting Nuclear War* and, more substantively, to a proposal to create a new body, the Institute for Strategic Studies (ISS).[24] Led by Alastair Buchan, formerly the defense correspondent of *The Observer*, the ISS finally came into being in 1958—though not without some official resistance. Liddell Hart was accused by an unnamed functionary of the Ministry of Defence of doing a "dangerous and unpatriotic thing" in supporting the ISS, on the classic Civil Service grounds that "[o]nly the present people in the Ministry of Defence and the War Office had the up-to-date knowledge to form a judgment and guide policy."[25] In 1962, such views were defied once more by the efforts made to turn the moribund Royal United Services Institute (RUSI) into a similar kind of independent think tank.[26]

In the 1960s, however, it was the ISS that provided the main forum for the emergence of a new group of civilian strategists, albeit civilians often with military experience, like Howard, who had won the Military Cross in Italy in the Second World War, or Frankland, awarded the Distinguished Flying Cross (DFC) while serving in Bomber Command. Until well into the 1970s the house journal of the ISS, *Survival*, provided a window on the latest foreign strategic thinking, reprinting condensed versions of articles published elsewhere, especially in the United States, but also in the USSR and continental Europe. American influences—both positive and negative—were critical to the ISS's wider endeavor. The most obvious positive influence was American money, which flowed in large quantities to the British strategists, as it did to Butterfield's international theorists in the British Committee.[27] The initial funding of the ISS came, at Healey's request, in the form of a $150,000 grant from the Ford Foundation, and more followed in later years.[28] In the early 1960s the foundation also paid for Buchan and Howard to tour the United States visiting universities and think tanks and meeting their American counterparts,[29] just as Rockefeller had supported Butterfield and Wight to make similar trips in the early and mid-1950s.[30] Thereafter, American funds continued to be crucial to the endeavors of the strategists—the Ford Foundation gave more money to ISS when the first grant ran out, for instance, and the Carnegie Endowment for International Peace supported the work that led to Alastair Buchan and Philip Windsor's *Arms and Stability in Europe* (1963).[31]

While the British strategists—like the theorists—were impressed by American largesse, and by some American scholars, they were not so keen on what they perceived to be the mainstream of American thinking. Brodie had thought that strategy was too important to be left to the generals; the British strategists—and, by extension, the Australians—thought it too important to be left to the Americans. This was especially true where nuclear weapons were concerned. British thinkers had, in general, responded badly to the American debate over the utility of nuclear weapons prompted by the acquisition of the bomb and by the parallel debate about preventive war against the USSR, especially in the early 1950s.[32] John Foster Dulles's embrace of "massive retaliation" (in 1954) and the Soviet launch of Sputnik (in 1957) did not improve British moods. The consternation caused by Dulles is well captured by Esmond Wright's observation, in a review of a biography of the then secretary of state, that he was "a clever man, but one of the least lovable figures in modern history."[33] Massive retaliation was no more liked: it was "too drastic and inflexible" to achieve any strategic objective, observed Rear Admiral Buzzard in a discussion of the topic at Chatham House.[34]

In the 1950s, British writing on strategy tended thus to concentrate on nuclear weapons and tended, on the whole, to disapprove of their use or argue for them to be scrapped.[35] Moreover, it tended not to be published by scholars working in universities.[36] Those works that contemplated the actual use of nuclear weapons were written by the generals—Sir John Slessor's *The Great Deterrent* (1957) being the most prominent example.[37] The bulk expressed serious doubts. The veteran internationalist Philip Noel-Baker, in *The Arms Race* (1958), urged what he had long argued: that arms races make wars more likely and that only a "grand design" for disarmament would suffice. This, Noel-Baker declared, was not "starry-eyed idealism"; it was "plain realistic common sense."[38] In *Power Politics in the Nuclear Age* (1962), Sir Stephen King-Hall—late of the Navy, rather than Slessor's RAF—concurred, arguing that an occupied Britain would always be preferable to an obliterated Britain, no matter the nature of the occupier. He also recommended disarmament.[39] These latter arguments helped underpin and sustain the antinuclear mass movement in Britain, especially the CND, founded in 1957.[40]

Among scholars and civilian strategists, however, these arguments provoked a significant reaction. Its tone and approach were prefigured in Hedley Bull's famous coruscating review of Noel-Baker's *The Arms Race*. The theoretical basis for Bull's critique was an unmistakably[41]—and American—understanding of international politics: echoing (but not citing) John Herz, he pointed to the centrality of the "security dilemma" in explaining the behavior of states in international society; alluding to Hans Morgenthau, he insisted on the "primacy of politics" over law or morality in international relations.[42] The assumptions on which Noel-

Baker's "dated" argument rested, Bull argued, simply could not withstand the power of these postwar realist insights.[43] We now know, he asserted, that complete disarmament is a useless chimera and that arms races are not the principal causes of war: the acknowledgment of systematic anarchy and simple pluralism have put paid to such old-fashioned and idealistic notions. Moreover, we now know that only military power will "bring recalcitrant states to order"—and that it is "millennialist" to think, as Bull thought Noel-Baker did, that "moral, diplomatic or economic sanctions" could fulfill that function.[44]

Bull set out his own position on disarmament in *The Control of the Arms Race* (1961). The book was formed from a series of papers he wrote for the newly founded ISS. Like Bull's earlier review, it was strongly influenced by American writing in the field. In 1957–58 Bull had spent a year in the United States on a Rockefeller fellowship, partly (it seems) to avoid his having to do military service in the UK.[45] There he met Thomas Schelling and Henry Kissinger at Harvard, Herman Kahn at the Hudson Institute, Paul Nitze and Robert Osgood at Johns Hopkins, and Morton Kaplan at Chicago. Later, at the ISS seminars on arms control that led to his book, he met Albert Wohlstetter, acknowledged in the preface to *Control of the Arms Race*.

Schelling's account of strategic violence, what he called the "diplomacy of violence" in international relations made the most lasting impression on Bull, as Robert Ayson has rightly argued[46]—and vice versa, as Schelling's admiring review of *Control of the Arms Race* in *Survival* clearly shows.[47] That Bull described "Schelling's illuminating observations about violence and international politics" as having the status of "unprovable and untestable judgments" was a criticism only in so far as it speaks to Schelling's optimism about his ability to prove and to test his observations, but it was not in the sense that Bull recognized his own observations were also "unprovable and untestable" by science.[48] This should not be taken to imply that Bull thought Schelling uninteresting, still less that he thought him wrong. He praised the latter's "shrewd political judgment" and there is no doubt that he meant it; Bull was attacking the medium, not the message.[49]

Between Bull and the Americans there were many points of common cause. Like the Americans, Bull thought it necessary to "think the unthinkable," as Herman Kahn had put it,[50] and to put aside one's aesthetic or moral revulsion to modern war or even nuclear holocaust, if only to fight Kahn on his own terms.[51] Indeed, in stark contrast to the bulk of earlier British writers on the subject Bull eschewed any discussion of the morality of war, arguing in *Control of the Arms Race* that there was "no way of finally settling this or any other moral issue," since the "only moral criteria we are able to employ are parochial ones."[52] Here Bull betrayed his debt to the philosophical realism of his former teacher, the empiricist John Anderson, and, at the same time, the beliefs that allowed him to be better disposed to "value-free" social science on the American model.[53] Moreover, for Bull, "strategy" was "one thing" and "morals are another"— it was perfectly possible to think strategically and to be as "sensitive to moral considerations" as any "other intelligent and educated persons in the West."[54]

This might sound commonsensical to later ears, but Bull's argument did mark a departure from the positions held by older generations of British thinkers for whom such a dispassionate treatment of war was nearly unconscionable. This stark contrast is clear, for example, in the very different tones and conclusions of Wight's unpublished talk "War and Peace" (1963) and Bull's "War and International Order" (1972) or his chapter on war in *The Anarchical Society* (1977). The former begins by asking whether the advent of nuclear weapons has indeed transformed international politics, as John Herz had recently argued,[55] but quickly moves to a discussion of the proper moral response to the challenge they pose, after the fashion of the CND.[56] Bull's approach is very different, concentrating as it does on the functions of war within international society, as well as the unwarranted optimism of those who yearn for its abolition. His starting point, as he put it in "Strategic Studies and Its Critics," was the "fact of military force" which resulted from the "capacity for organized violence . . . inherent in the nature of man and his environment."[57]

The strategic studies that Bull did so much to foster were "traditionalist" in the sense of being attentive to "history" and suspicious of "science," but they were novel in their shift of focus from the moral to the empirical. They retained the concern with ideas and institutions, as well as a whiggish account of Britain's strategic predicament, but approached them with modernist empiricism rather than the philosophical idealism dominant among the internationalists. Alastair Buchan's *War in Modern Society* (1966) illustrates this well. The book is an "introduction to the history of ideas about war and its control, and in part to the history of developments, especially in technology, and in such forms of international association to prevent war as alliances"—it fits, in other words, with the broader concern with "ideas and institutions."[58] But the approach is different: it is dispassionate and skeptical rather than committed, and no argument is made that the history of these ideas and institutions shows any significant progress or improvement over time. Like Bull, Buchan found affinities between his way of thinking and those of the American classical realists—the book draws heavily on Kenneth Waltz's *Man, the State and War* (1959), Inis Claude's *Power and International Relations* (1962), and Samuel Huntington's *Changing Patterns of Military Politics* (1962)—and distanced himself from moralistic "idealists."[59] And like Bull, too, Buchan was suspicious of scientific modes of political thinking—he was, as he noted in a later book, "a historian" who had merely "attempted to educate myself as a political scientist," blessed with "only a concerned layman's knowledge of economics and finance, sociology and technology."[60]

None of this is to say that British strategic studies were unsuccessful or unimportant. Quite the opposite is true. If publication in prominent American journals is taken as a measure of success, the British strategists did very well. Buchan's work appeared regularly in *Foreign Affairs* in the first half of the 1960s[61] (in the second half, the frequency of publications by Britons declined dramatically, but picked up again in the early 1970s), as did Michael Howard's. Bull's writings were prominent in outlets like *World Politics* and the very first issue of *International Security*,[62] while Laurence Martin's studies may be found in the *American Political Science Review*, *Political Science Quarterly*, and the *Journal of Politics*.[63] Their books, likewise, were published, reviewed, and discussed on both sides of the Atlantic.

If access to politicians is adopted as a similar measure, much the same picture can be drawn. For all Bull's insistence on scholarly objectivity and distance from policymaking,[64] it must be emphasized that he was one of the few British academics to hold, for a time, a position within the civil service, as director of the Arms Control and Disarmament Research Unit in the Foreign Office from 1965 to 1967. His acceptance of that post presumably reflected his belief, expressed in 1968, that the "standard and tone of strategic debate" within government might be raised by academic involvement in "developing" what he called "strategic ideologies."[65] Robert O'Neill suggests that Bull's experience of "bureaucratic life" demonstrated—as it did for the historians at Versailles some fifty years earlier—how difficult it was to influence policymaking, but he seems still to have believed that the effort was worth making.[66]

The ambiguities of Bull's thinking here may reflect broader and deeper doubts about the whole enterprise of strategic studies, shared by others in the field. Contemporary strategic thinking represented, for Bull, only the "first, faltering steps" rather than a last word.[67] Howard demonstrated equal modesty in questioning the relevance of what he called "traditional strategy"—in essence, Clausewitzian thinking about the use of force by states—and its neglect of that "sinister development" of violence employed by nonstate actors.[68] But the greatest source of misgiving was the Vietnam War, which obsessed British strategists—and many others— toward the end of the 1960s.[69] That war signaled, for them, a preoccupation with military power completely out of balance with the values the United States sought to defend, and a concomitant neglect of diplomacy.[70]

Bull's turn away from strategic studies to international theory may indeed mark, as O'Neill suggested, some recognition of these challenges; certainly his anxious meditations of a chaotic "neo-medieval" future implied a belief that true "anarchy," as Howard described it, might have been just around the corner.[71] Such worries also contributed to one of the marked obsessions of British strategic thinking in the late 1960s and 1970s, namely its concern with unconventional war. Guerrilla warfare had, of course, fascinated British strategists from the turn of the century on, if not before, resulting in classic studies (still read today) like C.E. Callwell's *Small Wars* (1896) or T.E. Lawrence's *Seven Pillars of Wisdom* (1922).[72] The exploits of the Special Operations Executive (SOE) in the Second World War maintained British interest, fed by the works of Fitzroy Maclean, among others,[73] as did the anticolonial struggles in postwar Kenya and Malaya.

The nascent British "strategic community" counted among them many former guerrillas or students of their craft. Monty Woodhouse, the erstwhile director of Chatham House (1952–1955) who had fought with the partisans in Greece and helped engineer the 1953 coup in Iran, was an assiduous reviewer of books on guerrilla war for *International Affairs* and other outlets. Robert Thompson and Richard Clutterbuck, among others, made more substantive contributions.[74] The most prominent, however, was the Australian-born Brian Crozier, author of *The Rebels* (1960), *The Struggle for the Third World* (1966), and *A Theory of Conflict* (1974).[75] An unabashed Cold Warrior, Crozier had worked with the Foreign Office's Information Research Department (IRD) and the Congress for Cultural Freedom (CCF); his studies of contemporary guerrilla war tended thus to emphasize its revolutionary qualities and its purported ties to Moscow.[76] It was marked, too, by a deep hostility to the new modes of studying "peace and conflict" that emerged in the 1960s, and which prompted Crozier to create the Institute for the Study of Conflict (ICS), in London, in 1970.

Just as the IISS offered a congenial home for the civilian strategists, the ICS provided a forum for all those concerned with unconventional war with objections to the pacifist and positivist conflict studies examined more closely in the next section. This included scholars like the impeccably liberal Paul Wilkinson, author of the ICS pamphlet *Terrorism vs. Liberal Democracy: The Problems of Response* (1976),[77] as well as the far more conservative Crozier. Their work was, of course, highly controversial in the context of the 1970s, attracting significant salvos from radicals and peace researchers alike.[78]

Crozier's work marked the wilder fringes of what was otherwise a welltilled and established field of strategic studies, one which was already exercising a significant influence over related areas. When Roger Morgan came to reflect on the study of international politics in 1972, indeed, he observed that one of the most significant recent developments was the "increasing interdependence" of strategic studies and international relations proper. A merger seemed in the offing, indicated by Bull's attempts to bring the insights of strategy to international relations, Buchan's translation from the IISS to Oxford's Montague Burton chair (in 1972), and Laurence Martin's move from the Wilson Chair in Aberystwyth to war studies at King's.[79] He also noticed some other changes: a loss of confidence in the "quantifiers," on the one hand, matched by a proliferation of futurological thinking on the other. On the whole, Morgan detected a welcome shift away from "abstract models" to the "real world."[80] This shift was not, however, welcomed by all concerned, especially among the growing band of critics of strategic studies in peace and conflict research.

PEACE AND CONFLICT

> The study of International Relations is now moving out of the philosophical phase of the fifties into a period of consolidation. Terminology and clarity of concepts, tested against actual conditions, are the preoccupation of the sixties.
> JOHN BURTON, *Systems, States, Diplomacy and Rules* (1968)[81]

Many accusations can and have been leveled at peace and conflict research, but disinterest in the "real world"—at least in the early stages of its development—cannot be one of them. Like strategic studies, the origins of British peace and conflict research lie in reactions to American promptings, both positive and negative. There were, of course, other influences, not least extra-European philosophies of pacifism and nonviolence,[82] as well as work done in continental Europe, especially in Scandinavia.[83] In contrast to the strategists, however, the peace and conflict researchers were more welcoming to the new methods of studying international politics that had emerged in the United States from the 1920s on. Science, in a number of different forms, was embraced as a means to the peace researchers' ends; indeed, it is almost exclusively among peace and conflict researchers that one can find any openly committed and enthusiastic British positivists.[84]

The peace researchers were moved—and continue to be moved—by the lethality and brutality of modern war, but also by the tendency of conventional ways of thinking about international relations to render such behavior "normal" and thus acceptable. They were particularly vexed by realism, which they conceived in much broader terms than it was usually understood either by American self-professed realists or their British critics of the late 1940s and 1950s. For the peace researchers—in contrast to the internationalists or the whigs, but like the radicals—realism was the "orthodoxy," as Burton put it: it was the dominant mode of thought and practice in international relations.[85] It consisted of fallacious assumptions about human nature, especially concerning a "natural" tendency toward aggression, and the state, not least that sovereignty entailed anarchy and thus war. It presented, therefore, a theory of power politics in which war was considered an "instrument of policy" and an appropriate response to the assertiveness, real or latent, of others. Against realism, the peace researchers took two approaches. The first was to attempt to build up a nearly insurmountable body of empirical data that might be subjected to various modes of analysis in order to invalidate realist principles and policies. The second was to co-opt in the fight against realism the findings of other disciplines, notably sociology and psychology, to the study of international conflict.[86]

The first approach is clearest in the work of Lewis F. Richardson, notably in his *Statistics of Deadly Quarrels* (1960). For Richardson, students and practitioners of international relations simply lacked the empirical evidence from which to make the generalizations that they all too frequently made. His objects, therefore, were to gather as much data on "deadly quarrels" as might be found and to subject it to statistical analysis. He devoted the last thirteen years of his life to this endeavor, from 1940 until his death in 1953, driven by his Quakerism and his conviction that because "Mankind is surely more complicated than lifeless matter," there must be more to discover about politics than ordinary "journalistic" political writing revealed.[87] Thus he employed mathematics "inductively to summarize facts and deductively to trace the consequences of hypotheses" in order to establish "persistent quantitative relations."[88]

In so doing, Richardson was punctilious in laying out his assumptions, acutely aware that even those who "take a pride in their adherence to facts" and "despise theories" make certain presuppositions, albeit "unspoken."[89] He was especially conscious of the problems inherent in defining "war" in general and in identifying particular violent episodes in history as "wars." He eschewed therefore political and legal definitions, choosing instead to concentrate his attention on "deadly quarrels" indicated by the incidence of violent deaths, between 1820 and 1945. These data were thus analyzed with the aim of establishing relationships between the magnitudes of conflicts and their frequency. Richardson observed that territorial contiguity between potential belligerents—which provided what he termed "geographical opportunities for fighting"—was a common element in the majority of quarrels, perhaps explaining the high number of civil wars he found and suggesting, moreover, that when it came to international wars, the more borders a polity had the more likely it was to be involved in many conflicts.[90]

Lastly, Richardson sought to detect what he called "pacifiers"—factors that prevented "deadly quarrels" when they might otherwise have broken out. He hypothesized that intermarriage between groups, common language, common religion, and common enemies might play such a role, as might the presence of a common government. The latter was the clearest—and perhaps the least surprising—conclusion, seemingly confirming what political theorists had long argued was the case. Richardson also suggested that sport could distract potential belligerents from fighting but discounted the claims of deterrence theorists, on the one hand, and enthusiasts for collective security, on the other, that the possession of obvious and significant armed strength is sufficient to ward off conflict.[91]

Richardson also committed much effort to the examination of arms races, this time building a series of models of different scenarios to test with the data he collected, and to "war moods," perceptions of conflict among populations.[92] His work on these topics arguably proved the most influential among British scholars.[93] Especially at the new universities, and notably at Lancaster, these two endeavors were pursued with some vigor. Richardson's work on arms races was extended and elaborated by Paul Smoker (1938–1998), a mathematician and physicist, and member of the CND, who helped create the Peace Research Centre at Lancaster.[94] A highly prolific scholar, Smoker utilized Richardson's work to critique contemporary international relations far more directly than his mentor, arguing, for example, that postwar alliance formation had merely brought about more insecurity and instability, but that "submissiveness" born of fear of nuclear war would soon bring about a "peace race" that would prevent further rearmament.[95] His later work integrated the insights of systems theory and functionalism derived from Talcott Parsons, as well as Galtung's thought on structural violence.[96]

This heterodox approach was common among peace researchers, driven by their desire to find means to fulfill their political objectives to experiment with many and varied means.[97] Thus Peter Cooper (University of Manchester) explored the development of the idea and understanding of war in children by means of structured interviews and psychological theory, while Alan Coddrington (York, later Queen Mary, University of London) used first content analysis of newspapers to assess the policies they advocated in conflicts and then game theory to assess strategic reasoning.[98] The first holder of a chair in peace studies in Britain, at the University of Bradford, in 1973, was Adam Curle—another Quaker—who had a background in social psychology and thus promoted "education for liberation" as well as peace.[99] By contrast, the highly rigorous Michael Nicholson (Lancaster) applied formal theory to the analysis of interdependence, building a bargaining model of conflict.[100] Together with P. A. Reynolds (also Lancaster), Michael Banks (LSE), and Roy Jones (Cardiff), Nicholson was also instrumental in applying ideas drawn from the systems theories of the American scholars David Easton and Karl Deutsch to the study of international conflict.[101]

In their attempts to utilize and integrate new theories in the study of peace and conflict, all of these efforts were surpassed, at least in terms of breadth of interest and sheer volume of publication, by the work of the Australian John Burton. A former diplomat educated at LSE, Burton had worked as a research fellow at the Australian National University (ANU) in the early 1960s before returning to Britain. He joined Schwarzenberger at University College, London, in 1963, and stayed there until his elevation to a chair at the University of Kent in 1978, moving from the Centre for the Analysis of Conflict he helped create at the former to the Institute for the Analysis of Conflict at the latter. His first book, *The Alternative* (1954), was an attack on Australian foreign policy; his second, written at ANU, was *Peace Theory* (1962).[102]

Burton's thinking was unorthodox. He rejected—as has been noted—"realism," as well as what he considered the conventional verities of the study of international relations. He did this partly on the grounds that traditionalists were too historical in their approach and that, being thus, they made fallacious assumptions about human beings and the state, and partly because traditional international relations, as he saw it, was incapable of addressing change by any other means but war. Peace research, by contrast, had for Burton a "dynamic quality":

> It is concerned with disarmament, not as a history but from political and technical viewpoints; it is concerned with new states, not as an interesting consequence of the decline of imperialisms but as a source of an alternative system of relationships in which major power relations are confined; it is interested in negotiation, not as a national instrument but as a subject for study from a psychological, mechanical, or domestic point of view; it is interested in regional and functional arrangements, not as part of an international structure but to see whether conflicts are more easily resolved through them . . . [103]

As this passage shows, Burton was a considerable rhetorician. His theory, however, was more questionable.

Far more than his peers, Burton displayed magpie-like qualities in his theoretical endeavors. He called his *Peace Theory* "behavioristic"—which befuddled some American readers[104]—and his *International Relations* (1965) a "general theory," which confused many more. In the latter, Burton argued that the "altered world environment"—by which he meant the advent of nuclear weapons, the "democratization of foreign policy," decolonization, and the rise of neutralism and nonalignment—was beginning to limit the freedom of action hitherto available to great powers, necessitating that they act in different ways.[105] Where once they could exercise power to shape events, now they needed to use influence; where there had been a society of states, now there was a community, with moral leadership in the hands of the nonaligned. In sum, Burton wished to see Western states accommodate themselves to "change" by "negotiation" and "adjustment," reconsidering "the value of alliances to peace and security, the wisdom of . . . not recognizing States on the grounds of their ideology or policies . . . and generally the pay-off thought previously to be obtained from policies that have been regarded as traditional policies of power politics."[106]

For the early Burton, as Joseph Frankel noted in a review, the "major cause of conflict [lay] in the traditional models of power politics and in ignorance of alternatives."[107] Thus it looked to contemporaries—and looks now—as the vaguer and less effectual forms of interwar internationalism repackaged.[108] From *Systems, States, Diplomacy and Rules* (1968) on, the differences with that earlier mode of thinking became much clearer, as Burton seized upon the latest American approaches to make his case. Having once described his thought as behavioristic, he now turned for inspiration to the systems theory of David Easton and the cybernetics of Karl Deutsch.[109] Thus Burton overcame the traditional representation of international relations as the relations of states with "hard exteriors," the "interactions or contacts" of which could be seen as analogous to those of "billiard-balls"—either separate and discrete or bouncing off one another.[110] Instead, he argued, international relations was better conceived as a "world society" comprising a number of "systems" or sets of relationships, with channels of communication between them. The study of international relations, in other words, required the student to examine not just what state elites did or said to other state elites, but all the various interactions at all the levels at which there are cross-border interactions. States themselves, on this model, ought to be "regarded as the resultant of the interacting behaviour of systems" rather than given and fixed elements of a wider system.[111]

Burton's theoretical effort concerned far more than merely the analysis of conflict: his ultimate aim, like that of later enthusiasts for conflict resolution,[112] was a thorough reshaping of the study of international relations as a whole. In this, he did not succeed, for while peace research and conflict resolution have prospered as niche subdisciplines, their wider claims have been casualties of the turn against "value-oriented" or "problem-solving" theory that occurred in Britain in the late 1970s and especially in the 1980s. That Burton and others did succeed in creating a space for their subdiscipline, however, is a significant achievement, given the deep-seated hostility of historically and philosophically minded traditionalists to their methods and modernist empiricists to their overt political commitments.

CONCLUSION

> A study of the development of strategic thought, of weapons-systems, or even of the use of war as an instrument of national policy since 1919 would cover only one aspect of our topic. The soldier was one actor in a drama which involved also the guerrilla fighter, the policeman, the torturer, the terrorist, and the assassin.
> MICHAEL HOWARD, "Changes in the Use of Force, 1919–1969"[113]

Together strategic studies and peace research transformed the study of international relations in Britain from a field concerned with the ideas and institutions to one far broader in its concerns. The strategists did remain wedded to "traditionalism," though quite what that meant underwent a significant transformation; the peace researchers, by contrast, went far further, experimenting with theories and methods the earlier generation thought pointless, ugly, or downright immoral. Together, if largely unwittingly and uncooperatively, these two groups transformed the academic study of international relations. It is no accident that it was the strategists and peace researchers from Bull to Banks that were at the forefront of efforts, in the late 1960s and early 1970s, to place that field on firmer theoretical foundations: their work was marked by a rigor unprecedented in British international thought and by its openness to external influences.

The strategists and peace researchers were not, of course, alone in these efforts. Their work was paralleled by significant British contributions to international political economy, notably by Susan Strange; in foreign policy analysis, by Joseph Frankel and others;[114] and in area studies, including Soviet studies.[115] It is indeed highly significant that it was Buchan and Strange—a strategist and a political economist—who were the motivating forces behind the creation of the British International Studies Association, the first disciplinary association for the field, rather than more traditionalist champions of "international relations" like Geoffrey Goodwin. The next, final chapter traces the confluence of these various streams of thinking into the nascent British discipline of international relations, as well as their influence on wider British thinking about international politics and Britain's role in the world.

10. Conclusion
British Intellectuals and the Retreat from Power

> Scholarship necessarily involves conceptualization, categorization, and explanation, and assumes transmission of the knowledge gained to others.... It deteriorates into scholasticism when its practitioners shift from attempts to address common questions from different perspectives to competition among different "schools"; in which each multiplies definitions and explanations, develops its own deliberately obscure terminology, and concentrates much of its efforts on attacking the methods and terminology of competing groups.
>
> WILLIAM WALLACE, "Truth and Power, Monks and Technocrats" (1996)

This book tries to tell the story of the evolution of British thinking about world politics in the postwar period in terms of what was inherited from the past and what was changed—or stayed the same—when intellectuals were confronted with new dilemmas. I have argued and attempted to demonstrate that traditions are vital analytical tools in explaining that evolution and that they can be thought about in ways that do not reify them into structures, imprisoning individual thinkers. It is not my intention to drag the British discipline of international relations back to the "inter-paradigm debate" of the 1980s, which tended to overemphasize the distinctions between different inherited traditions and between British scholarship and its American cousin. Like Wallace, I am convinced that such debate does little to improve the quality of work done in the field or to help address any pressing problems of world politics.

Instead, this book has emphasized three points. The first is that traditions, because they are inherited and transmitted by individuals, are mutable. The realist, liberal, internationalist, whig, and radical traditions were all restated, reinvented, and modified by their inheritors. Carr's realism and Frankel's, for example, bear little relation to each other. One is Marxist in inspiration and progressivist in intention; the other stems from a different continental tradition, reshaped by American terminology and concepts, and purports to academic neutrality. The second point is that none of these traditions were the exclusive preserve of one group or another. They are best regarded as a common inheritance, and different scholars drew upon them in different ways. The last is that practice—not just scholarly "discourse"—influenced the ways in which these traditions were developed by successive generations of thinkers, inside and outside universities.

These kinds of processes can be traced in other contexts. What distinguishes the British one, however, is that as British intellectuals reinterpreted their traditional knowledge about world politics during the postwar period, they moved further and further away from making any pronouncements on how they might be conducted. This movement, this retreat from power, is unusual, if not unique. Whereas American or French intellectuals retained a concern with influencing their countries' foreign policies,[1] British students of international relations largely abandoned the cause. In part, as we shall see, this was due to the rise of particular norms of academic conduct which insisted that scholars guard their "neutrality" above all else. In part, too, it was the product of contingent and peculiarly British factors, not the least of which being the insistence of the civil service that its own expertise is sufficient to guide policy and that academic research can add little to their deliberations.

This concluding chapter outlines these developments in an effort to explain why, despite the many books and articles on world politics produced by British intellectuals in the postwar years, so few had anything tangible to say about how Britain ought to conduct its foreign policy. It does so also in order to account for the parameters of the British discipline of IR as it developed after 1975.

THE EMERGENCE OF A DISCIPLINE

> [I]nquiry into international relations is a different activity from running the foreign policy of a country and necessarily clashes with it.
>
> HEDLEY BULL, "International Relations as an Academic Pursuit" (1972)[2]

> The point about a science or indeed any discussion of human affairs is not whether it is aesthetically pleasing, but whether it is correct and useful.
>
> MICHAEL NICHOLSON, "The Enigma of Martin Wight" (1981)[3]

The first issue of the *British Journal of International Studies*—first published in April 1975 and later to become the *Review of International*

Studies—opened with a retrospective essay by one of the stalwart pioneers of the postwar study of international relations, Philip Reynolds. Characteristically, for British thinkers, much of the piece consisted of an extended denial that the "field" the new journal served ought to be thought anything like a "discipline." The term "international studies," Reynolds insisted, had been chosen for the new journal and for the title of the British International Studies Association for a reason: "international politics" and "international relations" were too narrow and too limiting.[4] In deference to the field's interdisciplinary origins in Britain, the door had to be left ajar for international historians, lawyers, and economists to contribute. For Reynolds, this continued attachment to interdisciplinarity did not imply any disrespect to those who had sought to create a "discipline" of international relations or to furnish it with an autonomous theoretical base. Nor was the fact that these scholars were predominantly American and predominantly behavioralist in method an obstacle to "international studies"; indeed, Reynolds detected signs that the "post-behavourial revolution" of the past decade might bring the British "traditionalists" and the American "scientists" "back together."[5]

One issue, however, was left untouched. Reynolds said little about relations between British scholars and British practitioners of foreign policy. This omission was odd. For a decade or more a substantive debate had been conducted in Britain as to the virtues of "policy relevance" and the respective obligations of academics to scholarship and practice. It had begun, as did so many debates in postwar Britain, in response to developments in America.[6] As it went on, two concerns became especially prominent: money and power. British scholars worried that the considerable sums of research funding available, especially from American private foundations like Ford or Rockefeller, might tempt scholars to distort the work to suit their paymasters; likewise, they were anxious that the lure of political influence might entice academics to write what they thought politicians wanted them to write, rather than what they should.[7] These concerns united traditionalist liberals and whigs with some of their radical cousins, who rallied to calls for "objectivity" (if empiricists) or intellectual "independence" (if more Idealistically inclined).[8]

A substantial minority of scholars did not, however, share these views. When in 1981 Roy Jones and Michael Nicholson launched their pincer attack on the "English school" it was, in part, an assault on their apparent insistence that academic work on international politics eschew both political commitment and policy relevance. They objected deeply to the refusal of the "English school" to lower themselves, as Jones put it—with heavy sarcasm—to "vulgar agonizing over so-called world problems of poverty, commodity prices, monetary reform and such."[9] It was one thing to dismiss "world-scale reformism" and the violence that it would probably entail if was to be realized, Jones acknowledged, but to insist upon the wholesale separation of scholarship from "issues of policy" was quite another.[10] First, it implied a wholesale rejection of two centuries of social science devoted to "rigorous" and "analytical thinking" explicitly designed to contribute to "human betterment." Second, it reduced "the study of international relations to a wholly second order activity, utterly dependent on what politicians do for its material."[11]

Jones and Nicholson laid the blame for these attitudes at the doors of Manning and, to a greater extent, Wight. "No passion," Jones argued, "singes Wight's pages. Indeed the commitment to international society is so mild . . . that the unmistakable impression is conveyed that what happens to us sinners here below matters very little."[12] Nicholson rightly observed that at first glance this disinterest in worldly matters stood in contradiction to Wight's Christian pacifism, which ought to imply a thoroughly practical mission.[13] He concluded that the explanation for this apparent contradiction was that Wight's pacifism was a product of a thoroughgoing pessimism about the condition of the contemporary world as well as of his religious beliefs, and that Wight had resolved that the best means that he could cleave to his convictions was not to try to act in the world, but to retreat into his particular conception of scholarship and pursue political "quietism."[14] Not for nothing did Wight allude repeatedly to Socrates' discussion of the plight of the philosopher in the lawless city, who "like a human being who has fallen in with wild beasts and is neither willing to join them in injustice nor sufficient as one man to resist all the savage animals," and thus stays still, "content if somehow he himself can live his life here pure of injustice and unholy deeds."[15] This was Wight's own view, a function of his acute dissatisfaction with the contemporary world.

For Nicholson, this was an extreme and unusual position—one that he could understand but not agree with[16]—and hardly a position on which to ground an understanding of the proper tasks of an academic discipline. Surely, he argued, the world is not so predetermined as to be unchangeable. And surely, too, its workings are not completely "random" and thus are comprehensible to some degree. Wight arguably admitted this himself, when he wrote that "war is inevitable but particular wars can be avoided."[17] Yet Wight and his followers, Nicholson argued, had done little to discover how such things might be achieved; instead, they seemed to think that the "point of studying international relations" was not to "improve the human condition" but to "stand as passive spectators deploring the appalling standards of play."[18] Other pacifists, like Kenneth Boulding, had taken a different tack. Though "not . . . necessarily optimistic," Boulding had decided that what Nicholson called the "Humanist's Wager" was worth taking; gambling that the possible losses to be had from the failure of an attempt to pursue knowledge that might bring peace were far outweighed by the possible gains.[19]

Neither Jones's nor Nicholson's arguments were well received, but the response they prompted was telling. Defending Wight, Alan James advanced four lines of argument. The first two were *ad hominem*: entirely correctly, he noted that Wight had repeatedly addressed contemporary "moral and political dilemmas" in his teaching and his (largely unpublished) writings, and, with equal accuracy, James judged that Wight thought pacifism had too little purchase in the contemporary, postwar world to pursue it with any more vigor than he had in the 1930s and early 1940s.[20]

James's other two arguments, however, said more about the state of the study of international relations in Britain in the early 1980s than they did about Wight. First, he posed a rhetorical question: is there "no place" in the field for a "scholar, the man dedicated to finding out how the world works because he is fascinated by it" or a teacher who wishes "just to pass on to others the understanding one has gained."[21] Second, James queried the propriety of social scientists bringing "moral judgment" into their scholarship. Moral judgments, he argued, "are not called for in his capacity as a social scientist," for an "academic's moral judgement, like that of the butcher, baker and candle-stick maker, is based on his own belief system, *the choice of which is, ultimately, entirely arbitrary*" [my emphasis].[22]

James's article was a restatement, in other words, of modernist empiricist orthodoxy—an orthodoxy from which Wight, and indeed Manning, dissented with vigor, but one which they were ultimately powerless to resist. As we have seen, this orthodoxy posited the "scholar" as a disinterested observer whose object is to sift the facts of a matter from evidence and arrange them in a truthful representation of that matter. It held that facts and values can, if the scholar is sufficiently well trained, be separated, and that the values of the scholar must be left at the door, as it were, before work begins. It implied, moreover, what T. D. Weldon had famously argued, namely that all values were inexorably subjective— our judgments of the merits of democracy, justice, or war being akin to preferences for different flavors of ice cream.[23] Taken together, these elements of modernist empiricism presented a picture of academic endeavor in international relations that was indeed, as Jones suggested, a "second order activity," with the aim of "understanding" what occurred out there in the world and transmitting that understanding to others. This was scholarship for its own sake and strictly for no other.

There were, however, problems with all of this, which contemporary peace and conflict researchers—also dissenters from the modernist empiricist orthodoxy—and later post-positivist theorists well recognized.[24] But while the latter concentrated on the philosophical failings of the orthodoxy, the peace and conflict researchers were more concerned with its implications for practice. The private academic world and the public world, they argued, were not as hermetically sealed as the modernist empiricists thought. To say that "the values of the scholar of International Relations are of no greater interest than anyone else's," Nicholson argued, "is an evasion" of the fact that one's private actions have public consequences, some admittedly negligible and others more significant.[25] It was moreover hypocritical, since modernist empiricists—whether in area studies or even in international relations theory—had in fact been influential in practice. They wrote books, articles for academic and not-so-academic journals or newspapers, and they attended study groups or discussions at Chatham House, IISS, or the Foreign Office, and even, at times, in Washington. Perhaps most important of all, they taught students who became politicians, diplomats, humanitarians of one sort or another, and indeed citizens.

The peace and conflict researchers had one further complaint. It was bad enough, they argued, that orthodox scholars professed no direct interest in influencing policy in theory and then sought to do exactly that in practice—worse still, when they did try to influence what was done in the outside world they had been unsuccessful. As Michael Banks noted in 1989, one of the striking features of postwar international politics was the failure of international relations specialists to influence their conduct. The formative ideas, he argued, came from elsewhere, from inherited diplomatic practices or from knowledge generated in other disciplines: "The United Nations was an amalgam of collective security theory with balance of power and a limited degree of functionalism; the Bretton Woods plan was devised by economists; the Marshall Plan and the later modernization efforts at economic aid and technical co-operation to close the North-South development gap came from outside our field; the human rights conventions were inspired by lawyers; the growth of the European Communities were partially underpinned by David Mitrany's work of fifty years ago; the various summit conferences have been modeled on the theory and practice of the nineteenth century Concert."[26] This was not completely fair, of course, for Banks's argument depended on how narrowly one defined the field of IR, but nor was it completely inaccurate, for reasons that this concluding chapter examines.

As Britain retreated from its world role, so the majority of British intellectuals retreated from the practice of international relations. By 1975, by the time that the "discipline" of international relations had finally coalesced, this retreat was almost complete. Whereas internationalism in the 1950s and radicalism in the 1960s had sought to address policymakers and to offer the findings of their studies for policymaking, by the early 1970s only the two small bands of strategists and peace researchers continued to do so, plus the occasional specialist in political economy, like Susan Strange. Even in those fields, doubts can be detected as to the efficacy of their efforts—in Michael Howard's worries over the continued relevance of traditional strategy, for example, or in the shift of John Burton's pedagogic focus from "decision-makers" to popular "advocacy."[27] In the 1980s, it became fashionable to argue that this retreat from power was the fault of the policymakers, who "shunned" the academic community, rendering "policy-relevance" irrelevant and making the term itself a "rather a dirty word."[28]

This argument did not go unchallenged, but it did help to explain, for many academics in the new discipline of international relations, why their work did not have the "impact" that it might, as well as having the not-completely fortuitous consequence of providing further justification for the orthodox view of the proper duties of the "scholar."

THEORY IN PRACTICE

> There is . . . something about the whole business of Foreign Affairs, which must unsettle the brains of those who live with it. It is a profession where coherent schools of thought are useless; where there have never been sure harbours or even recognized waterways. Diplomats search desperately for a current or tide of any kind . . . and, all the time, at the back of their minds, is the lurking feeling that what they are doing may not be of any importance at all; that the course of history will not be altered one jot by their endeavours.
>
> HUGH THOMAS, *The World's Game* (1957)[29]

Such was the view of the disillusioned British diplomat of the postwar years. Hugh Thomas had been a young high-flyer in the Foreign Office, but offended by Britain's conduct in the Suez crisis, he resigned and penned a gently satirical novel about the diplomats he had known.[30] His former colleagues, Thomas concluded, were "able men" "condemned to serve a directionless and waterlogged machine" and were thus driven, sooner or later, "either into the quicksands of frivolity or the wastelands of cynicism; perhaps into both."[31] Diplomacy was just an endless game in which principle and even abstract thought had no place; the Foreign Office was a "junkshop of out-of-date architecture and furnishings."[32]

It is all too tempting to accept this view and to conclude that ideas, especially academic ideas, had and have little influence on British foreign policy or diplomacy—that they are driven, instead, by calculations of interest and by sheer expediency. The unusually closed nature of the Foreign Office to external influences tends to reinforce that conclusion. In stark contrast to the American foreign policymaking process, which can and often does involve inputs from academics and intellectuals, some of whom might hold posts in the White House or State Department, especially in the National Security Council, British foreign policy in the postwar period was made with hardly any formal contact with such individuals. There was no British George Kennan or Henry Kissinger, moving back and forth between scholarship and policymaking. Hedley Bull's brief and apparently unhappy stint at the Foreign Office in the late 1960s does not compare to the intimate involvement in high-level decision making of such individuals.

There were, of course, other kinds of informal contacts between these two worlds. Above all, academics had some influence over their former pupils in the civil or diplomatic services, both in shaping their intellectual development as undergraduates and in maintaining longer-term relationships as occasional mentors, advisors, or friends. Herbert Butterfield's correspondence with his former pupil, the intelligence officer, diplomat, and scholar Adam Watson illustrates this well. Watson frequently reported to Butterfield on aspects of Foreign Office thinking and even of foreign policy, and the latter offered his advice in return. In May 1949, for instance, Watson asked Butterfield what he thought of the idea of a Foreign Office unit designed to counter Soviet propaganda—what became the semicovert Information Research Department (IRD). The historian responded positively, arguing that "if we get only one-sided evidence about Russia from free journalism, you in the Foreign Office would be foolish not to supplement this."[33]

Such relationships were common in postwar Britain, especially between tutors and former undergraduates at Oxford and Cambridge, who formed tightly knit social and intellectual networks. These networks are significant both in terms of providing means by which academics might advise, cajole, or just convey knowledge of areas of which they had expertise, and in terms of their extent and coverage. The overwhelming majority of thinkers discussed in this book read for a degree at Oxford or Cambridge, often in history or classics; only a few prominent postwar intellectuals and scholars of international relations were graduates of other universities or studied politics or international relations degrees. They moved, in other words, in circles in which the whiggish conceptions of politics were dominant, where "ideas and institutions" were the key foci of political thought, and these were the beliefs they conveyed to those of the students destined for politics, civil service, or diplomacy.

Chatham House and later the IISS offered important forums for the continuance of dialogue between dons and practitioners, but there were others, some institutionalized and some not. For his part, Butterfield utilized the British Committee on the Theory of International Politics to cultivate contacts in government, like William Armstrong (1915–1980),[34] sometime permanent secretary to the Treasury and cabinet secretary; Donald McLachlan (1898–1971),[35] foreign correspondent for *The Economist* and later *The Daily Telegraph;* and Michael Palliser (1922–)[36] and Robert Wade-Gery (1929–),[37] both of the Foreign Office, all of whom were invited to meetings. Then there were political clubs, party organizations, and interest groups. This ranged from small gatherings like the Liberal Foreign Affairs Group, which met in the mid-1950s, and of which Martin Wight was a member, along with Jo Grimond, the Liberal leader from 1956 to 1967, to major bodies like the Campaign for Nuclear Disarmament, which allowed intellectuals direct access to likeminded politicians.[38]

Whether such contacts had any recognizable impact on this or that aspect of British foreign policy is difficult to assess and beyond the scope of this book. It is, however, possible to locate particular beliefs and traditions in the speeches, memoirs, and other writings of politicians and diplomats. Until well into the 1960s, the bulk of these were whiggish ideas, leavened with aspects of internationalism, and this is true on both sides of the political divide.

The most monumental expression of a whig conception of Britain's role in the world can be found, of course, in Winston Churchill's history of *The Second World War* (1948), as well as in his speeches.[39] There Churchill drove the *via media* between Germanic *Realpolitik* and excessive moralism, emphasizing the "constitutional" aspect of international society over one understood purely in terms of power and interest. His Britain had continental commitments and imperial ones, both conceived as duties rather than purely as interests.[40] These whiggish themes remained powerful under Clement Attlee and on through the 1950s.[41] They were reprised in Anthony Eden's memoirs, as Martin Wight recognized, but by that point—circa 1960—they were beginning to look a little worn.[42]

Particularly threadbare was the notion that Britain could exercise a decisive influence over international relations. It was still just possible to argue in 1954, as Oliver Franks (1905–1992) argued in his Reith Lectures for that year, that "Britain is going to continue to be what she has been, a Great Power."[43] After 1956, as we have seen, it was not. It is commonplace to observe that this reversal prompted something of a revolution in British thinking about its role in the world. No longer, it is argued, could Britain see itself at the center of the three interlocking circles of the United States, Europe, and the Commonwealth—what Franks called "the three circles of our life and power."[44] After Suez, so the argument runs, Britain was forced to choose between them.[45]

This argument is rightly influential, but it occludes continuities of thought that arguably made the decisions British policymakers had to take somewhat easier. At the core of whig thinking already lay an intellectual "continental commitment." This was the conviction that Britain should involve itself in the maintenance of European liberties and security that provided the justification for Churchill's opposition to appeasement in the late 1930s and which grounded his advocacy of European unity a decade later.[46] It underpinned a series of calls for stronger ties with Europe from the Right of British politics, which had the deeper attachment to whiggish conceptions of international relations, from Lord Vansittart's call for "Anglo-French integration" (in 1947) to Edward Heath's promotion of the cause as the acme of "realism" in foreign policy.[47]

This broad whig commitment to British involvement in Europe was reinforced, of course, by other factors. Much has been made—not least by Heath himself[48]—of the shift in attitudes in the Foreign Office that occurred toward the end of the 1950s as the generation born in the interwar years, some with experience of military service during the Second World War, began to displace the older generation. In 1961, Max Beloff could still observe that "the concept of Britain merging its identity into some form of European union, as a desirable object in itself, was not seriously entertained in any influential quarter," but such judgments were soon to be rendered obsolete.[49] The old guard with the foreign policymaking establishment retained residual commitments to empire and internationalism; the new thought little of imperial matters, were more European in outlook, and favored pragmatic and piecemeal functionalist or technocratic solutions to international problems along the lines proposed by Jean Monnet and Robert Schuman.[50]

Hugo Young, for instance, highlights the role of John Robinson, in background a classic British diplomat of his age, educated at Westminster and Christ Church, Oxford, where he read "Greats" (classics), but a man whose appraisal of Britain's relations with Europe was radically different from that of his predecessors. He was the author of a famous memorandum, "The Next Steps," circulated in the Foreign Office in February 1963, in the aftermath of de Gaulle's veto of Britain's first application for entry into the EEC. Young notes that the analysis of the memorandum was "cold-eyed," marked by "conspiratorial realism," and that its tone was striking: "confident, assertive and effortlessly Machiavellian."[51] Robinson's elders were, as Young puts it, "[t]rained in Anglo-Americanism, pickled in the heritage of Commonwealth"; his peers, however, who included Michael Butler, Con O'Neill, and Michael Palliser among others, were more European in orientation.[52]

The integrationists had to overcome the opposition not just of die-hard imperialists and Commonwealth romantics, but also radical opinion, which was in the postwar period generally anti-European. The Labour left had opposed the European project from the 1940s onward on the grounds that it would hamper Britain's ability to build a socialist welfare state—a view expressed in the National Executive Council's pamphlet *European Unity* (1950), which set out the ground for Labour's rejection of the Schuman Plan to create the first supranational authority for Europe, the European Coal and Steel Community, founded without British support in 1951.[53] The long-running resistance mounted by radicals to the European project was, however, the only area in which they had significant success in influencing British foreign policy. Their other concerns—nuclear disarmament, disengagement from the American alliance, an embrace of nonalignment, and Third Worldism—were all stymied.

Instead, much to the radicals' chagrin, the British Left tended to take a line that blended elements of "realism" with elements of internationalism. Denis Healey's thought, discussed in earlier chapters, offers classic examples of this kind of compromise. Hugh Gaitskell's *The Challenge of Co-Existence* (1957), a series of lectures given at Harvard, is equally representative.[54] The book opens with a qualified defense of the United Nations system, urging that people not overestimate its powers or its capacities, as well as the urge for British leadership. It affirmed, too, the need for British commitment to NATO in the face of the "threat" of communist "aggression."⁵⁵ As to the future of the "uncommitted areas"—what Gaitskell called the emerging postcolonial states—he urged the best policy was to emphasize the merits of parliamentary democracy and the benefits of "progressive colonial policies."⁵⁶

Though indicative of mainstream Labour thinking, these views are also somewhat unremarkable: they are iterations of consensus beliefs about the proper conduct of international relations and Britain's place in the world with which few would have disagreed. Their influence, moreover, was limited. They framed foreign policymaking rather than prescribed its direction, which, throughout the postwar period, was often reactive, sometimes uncoordinated with other areas of government or strands of policy, and normally conducted with little immediate reference to outside expert advice, from scholars of international relations or others. Beloff complained of these problems in 1961, contrasting the practice of sending promising civil servants out for a year's research at Nuffield or training at a staff college with the Foreign Office's unwillingness to make "comparable use of whatever expertise in foreign affairs may be presumed to exist outside the government service."⁵⁷ This, he thought, might be changing, but only in so far as greater informal use was being made of Chatham House and the Institute for Strategic Studies.

Later recommendations to make more formal arrangements for the involvement of academic and other outside experts in policymaking also had little effect. Both the Plowden Report of 1964 and the Duncan Report of 1969 concentrated more on the reform of the internal structures of the Foreign Office, related departments—especially the Colonial and Commonwealth Offices, merged into one in 1966 and then into the Foreign and Commonwealth Office in 1968—as well as overseas missions.⁵⁸ The latter report, in particular, militated against any sustained attempt at grand strategizing about foreign policy, insisting as it did that British diplomats concentrate their efforts on the promotion of British exports and the amelioration of Britain's perennial balance of payments problems.⁵⁹ The report itself took special aim at that "style" of thinking about British foreign policy which conceives Britain as having any significant role in influencing global events—much to the annoyance of those critics who thought the report's "objectives" simply "narrow, selfish, [and] materialist."⁶⁰

For defenders of the Duncan Report, such complaints were merely the product of a deep-rooted but now irrelevant "barely post-imperial, worldwide missionary instinct" inherent in British thinking about international relations.[61] There is, as we have seen, some truth to this contention—certainly such high-minded sentiments were not uncommon among British intellectuals in the postwar period. But there was a further complaint about the report that bears some attention. For Michael Donelan, the report erred because it failed properly to grasp the nature of politics itself. He went on: "In this failure, the Duncan Report mirrors the attitudes of the present day. There has perhaps never been a time when politics were so prominent and yet when the acutest minds were so impatient of them or so defensive about them in favour of technical and supposedly more realistic pursuits such as economics or commerce or military strategy."[62] Ever the Idealist, Donelan argued that what were needed were "political ideas" rather than an exclusive concentration on economic well-being. In particular, he thought Britain needed "a diplomatic service equipped to think . . . generally of what political, military and economic structures might be desirable in the southern part of the world and to debate them with southern countries in concert with her European associates and the United States."[63] Here again is Britain in a global role for which it was arguably no longer suited; here again some intellectual decolonization seems necessary.

It is notable that no professor from a British department of international relations was invited to serve on the Plowden or Duncan Committees, nor indeed on the Berrill Committee which reviewed Britain's diplomatic representation again, in 1977.[64] It may be notable too that only seven graduates with degrees in international relations out of a total of 223 gained entry into the administrative stream of the Diplomatic Service between 1964 and 1975.[65] Mutual "disdain"—James Cable's term—had by the 1960s become a feature of the relations between academics in that field and practitioners. To some extent, this cannot be thought anything other than justified, for British scholars had singularly failed in the postwar period to build the kind of body of knowledge about international relations that might speak to policymaking, let alone shape it, and the British foreign policymaking and diplomatic apparatuses remained too closed to permit such influences to prevail.[66]

Neither scholars nor practitioners dealt well with the dilemmas of decline, partly for these reasons. By 1975 Britain was a much better place for most of its inhabitants, as George Bernstein and others have argued, than it had been in 1945—better in terms of quality and access to education, healthcare services, and housing, if not perhaps in infrastructure or productivity.[67] British intellectuals struggled nonetheless to make sense of Britain's international relations and to articulate a foreign policy that might meet the challenges it faced. They struggled because of their inheritance—because neither internationalism nor whiggism, the two dominant schools, were appropriate to the new circumstances—and they struggled because of the modernist empiricist conception of the professional duties of scholars they developed in the postwar years. As Britain retreated from power, so too did British thinkers.

This development was not predetermined, but it was a function of their intellectual inheritance, one which tended to prize historical knowledge over a grasp of contemporary issues, and emphasized the need to distance oneself from events and practitioners. Together, they conspired to make it difficult for British intellectuals properly to confront and respond to the dilemmas they and their country faced in the postwar years.

Notes

CHAPTER 1

EPIGRAPH: Philip Larkin, *Collected Poems* (London: Marvell Press and Faber & Faber, 2003), 141.

1. See David Reynolds, *From World War to Cold War: Churchill, Roosevelt, and the International History of the 1940s* (Oxford: Oxford University Press, 2006), especially 309–330.
2. F. S. Northedge, *Descent from Power: British Foreign Policy, 1945-73* (London: George Allen & Unwin, 1974), 362.
3. For a brief and partisan account of the literature on decline and for a response, see Alan Sked, *An Intelligent Person's Guide to Post-War Britain* (London: Duckworth, 1997). For a more measured, outsider's view, see George L. Bernstein, *The Myth of Decline: The Rise of Britain since 1945* (London: Pimlico, 2004), 1–26.
4. On "declinism," see Bernstein, *Myth of Decline*, 1; as well as Richard English and Michael Kenny, "Public Intellectuals and the Question of British Decline," *British Journal of Politics and International Relations* 3:3 (2001), 259–283. The peak of the first wave of "declinism" is marked by a series of famous works, including Anthony Sampson, *Anatomy of Britain* (London: Hodder & Stoughton, 1962); Arthur Koestler (ed.), *Suicide of a Nation?* (London: Vintage, 1994), first published by *Encounter* in 1963; and Anthony Hartley, *State of England* (London: Hutchinson, 1963). A second wave came in the 1970s, with works like Correlli Barnett's *The Collapse of British Power* (London: Eyre Methuen, 1972) and Martin J. Wiener's *English Culture and the Decline of the Industrial Spirit* (Cambridge: Cambridge University Press, 1981).
5. I use "world politics" quite deliberately and I treat "international relations" as synonymous quite self-consciously. Almost all the thinkers discussed in this book were interested in the political relations between states and nonstate actors in the world, not their economic or social relations. "World politics," as an expression, captures this focus well.

6. Max Beloff, *The Future of British Foreign Policy* (London: Secker & Warburg, 1969), 1.

7. For a wider discussion of the notion of the *Primat der Aussenpolitik*, see Brendan Simms, "The Return of the Primacy of Foreign Policy," *German History* 21:3 (2002), 275–291; and for a demonstration of the power of this approach to explain British politics and international relations in the eighteenth century, see Simms's *Three Victories and a Defeat: The Rise and Fall of the First British Empire* (Harmondsworth: Penguin, 2007).

8. Northedge observed in 1974: "Every pundit, of every school of thought, has tried his hand at diagnosing, prescribing cures for and working out the prognosis of the British malaise since the war." (*Descent from Power*, 359).

9. Ibid.

10. See, for example, David Reynolds, *Britannia Overruled: British Policy and World Power in the Twentieth Century* (London: Longman, 1991).

11. Here I follow Michael Kenny's suggestion that to be considered established, an academic discipline ought to have a professional association, an academic journal, and a "specialist ethos" ("The Case for Disciplinary History: Political Studies in the 1950s and 1960s," *British Journal of Politics and International Relations* 6:4 [2004], 565–583). According to these criteria, international relations did not coalesce into a discipline in Britain until the mid-1970s, with the creation of the British International Studies Association (1974) and the first publication of the *British Journal* (now the *Review*) *of International Studies* (1975), although the founding of the journals *International Relations* (1960) and *Millennium: Journal of International Studies* (1971) mark significant milestones on the road to the "discipline." The case of *International Affairs*—which is anyway not a purely scholarly journal—is a special one, since it, like its sponsor, the policy institute Chatham House, was created to further public rather than academic knowledge of world politics.

12. Until 1964–65, Chris Brown notes, the only "major" departments teaching IR were at LSE and Aberystwyth ("The Development of International Relations Theory in Britain: Traditions, Contemporary Perspectives, and Trajectories," *International Studies* 46:1–2 [2009], 225).

13. Steve Smith, "The Discipline of International Relations: Still an American Social Science?," *British Journal of Politics and International Relations* 2:3 (2000), 398.

14. Robert Adcock and Mark Bevir, "Political Science," in Roger E. Backhouse and Phillipe Fontaine (eds.), *The History of the Social Sciences since 1945* (Cambridge: Cambridge University Press, 2010), 90.

15. Mark Bevir and R. A. W. Rhodes, *Governance Stories* (London & New York: Routledge, 2005), 37.

16. Jack Hayward, "British Approaches to Politics: The Dawn of a Self-Deprecating Discipline," in Jack Hayward, Brian Barry, and Archie Brown (eds.), *The British Study of Politics in the Twentieth Century* (Oxford: Oxford University Press for the British Academy, 1999), 31.

17. Mark Bevir, "Prisoners of Professionalism: On the Construction and Responsibility of Political Studies," *Public Administration* 79:2 (2001), 471.

18. Hayward, "British Approaches to Politics"; and Brian Barry, "The Study of Politics as a Vocation," in Hayward, Barry and Brown (eds.), *British Study of Politics*, 467.

19. See Christopher Hill, "The Study of International Relations in the United Kingdom," in Hugh C. Dyer and Leon Magasarian (eds.), *The Study of International Relations: The State of the Art* (New York: St Martin's Press & Millennium, 1989), 265–274.

20. See, for example, Smith, "International Relations," 374–402.

21. Brown, "Development of International Relations Theory in Britain," 222.

22. Hedley Bull, "International Theory: The Case for the Classical Approach," *World Politics* 18:3 (1966), 361–377.

23. See Tim Dunne, "A British School of International Relations," in Hayward, Barry, and Brown (eds.), *British Study of Politics*, 394–424; and his *Inventing International Society: A History of the English School* (Basingstoke: Macmillan, 1998).

24. Steve Smith, "Positivism and Beyond," in Ken Booth, Steve Smith, and Marysia Zalewski (eds.), *International Theory: Positivism and Beyond* (Cambridge: Cambridge University Press, 1996), 11.

25. For discussions of this relationship, see D. S. A. Bell, "International Relations: The Dawn of a Historiographical Turn?," *British Journal of Politics and International Relations* 3:1 (2001), 115–126; as well as Dunne, *Inventing International Society*, 1; and Brian C. Schmidt, *The Political Discourse of Anarchy: A Disciplinary History of International Relations* (Albany, NY: State University of New York Press, 1998), 5–7. For other examples of postpositivist intellectual history, see Seán Molloy, *The Hidden History of Realism: A Genealogy of Power Politics* (New York: Palgrave, 2006); or Hartmut Behr, *A History of International Political Theory: Ontologies of the International* (Basingstoke: Palgrave, 2009).

26. This point is made well by William A. Callahan in his "Nationalising International Society: Race, Class and the English School," *Global Society* 18:4 (2004), 305–323.

27. Bevir, "Prisoners of Professionalism," 479.

28. Beloff, *Future of British Foreign Policy*, 21. Beloff returned to this theme in "The Politics of Oxford 'Politics': An Undelivered Valedictory Lecture," *Political Studies* 23:2–3 (1975), 129–139.

29. Bernard Crick, *The American Science of Politics: Its Origins and Conditions* (London: Routledge & Kegan Paul, 1959), 244.

30. Many works have recently appeared on Morgenthau, but on his early life see especially Christoph Frei, *Hans J. Morgenthau: A Life* (Baton Rouge: Louisiana State University Press, 2001); and for his impact on American thinking, see Campbell Craig, *Glimmer of a New Leviathan: Total War in the Realism of Niebuhr, Morgenthau and Waltz* (New York: Columbia University Press, 2003), chapter 3.

31. On the British Committee, see Dunne, *Inventing International Society;* and Brunello Vigezzi, *The British Committee on the Theory of International Politics (1954–1985): The Rediscovery of History,* trans. Ian Harvey (Milano: Edizioni Unicopli, 2005). On the work of the Rockefeller Foundation and its attempt to shape the nature of postwar political and international studies, see Nicholas Guilhot, "The Realist Gambit: Postwar American Political Science and the Birth of IR Theory," *International Political Sociology* 2 (2008), 281–304.

32. On Wight's views, see Ian Hall, *The International Thought of Martin Wight* (New York: Palgrave, 2006), 92–93.

33. Bernard Crick, "The British Way of Political Studies" (1980), in his *Thoughts and Politics* (Edinburgh: Edinburgh University Press, 1990), 35.

34. These questions were posed in Roger Morgan, "The Study of International Politics," in his edited *The Study of International Affairs: Essays in Honour of Kenneth Younger* (London: Oxford University Press for the Royal Institute of International Affairs, 1972), 271.

35. Beloff, "The Politics of Oxford 'Politics,'" 132.

36. For the American numbers, see David M. Ricci, *The Tragedy of Political Science: Politics, Scholarship, and Democracy* (New Haven & London: Yale University Press, 1984), 133. For the British, see Norman Chester, "Political Studies in Britain: Recollections and Comments," *Political Studies* 23:2–3 (special issue) (1975), 31.

37. In the first membership list published in *Political Studies* 1:3 (1953), 260, containing 136 names in total, only 12 specialists in international relations at 3 institutions can be identified: I. G. John and P. Reynolds at Aberystwyth; A. Cobban, G. L. Goodwin, C. A. W. Manning, G. H. N Seton-Watson, and Sir Charles Webster at London, and M. Beloff, J. L. Brierly, R. B. McCallum, H. G. Nicholas, and M. Perham at Oxford.

38. In the United States, by contrast, the postwar years witnessed an extraordinary expansion of scholarly work, some within the confines of "political science" and much outside it. The creation of the International Studies Association (ISA) in 1959 signaled a move on the part of some to define a separate disciplinary identity.

39. See, for example, the response to Manning's contribution to the UNESCO study of the teaching of international relations from Herbert Butterfield, professor of history at Cambridge, who thought it "too immediate and direct in its utilitarian direction" and thus too prone to produce "dabblers in a journalistic type of thinking." Rigorous training in the "precise technique" of diplomatic history was to be preferred (Butterfield, "How Far and Should the Subject of International Relations be Included in the Curriculum for Undergraduate Students of History?," Butterfield MS 130/2, 1, Cambridge University Library). Manning's response is contained in his "International Relations: An Academic Discipline," in Geoffrey Goodwin (ed.), *The University Teaching of International Relations* (London: Blackwell, 1951), 11–26.

40. It is notable that of the four "identikit portraits" of British intellectuals described by Stefan Collini, one is the historian. The others are the "poet

and critic"; the "journalist, essayist, and novelist"; and the radical philosopher (*Absent Minds: Intellectuals in Britain* [Oxford: Oxford University Press, 2006], 120).

41. As Michael Nicholson observed, "If there was a hegemony in the United Kingdom [in the field of international relations], surely it was that of historians, as a jaundiced observer might still think" ("What's the Use of International Relations?," *Review of International Studies* 26 (2000), 194).

42. C. S. Nicholls, *The History of St Antony's College Oxford, 1950–2000* (Basingstoke: Macmillan, 2000), 77. Nicholls, tellingly, devotes fewer than three pages to the study of international relations at the college. Beloff, in his "The Politics of Oxford 'Politics'" (especially 133–138), alludes to some of the problems faced by those who wished, like him, to see the study of international relations more developed at Oxford. Montague Burton's chair, it should be noted, is based at Balliol, not St Antony's, College.

43. Her *Oxford Dictionary of National Biography* entry, written by one of her successors, notes that she had a "very restricted view" of international relations as "recent European diplomatic history" and that all the works she included on the philosophy, politics, and economics (PPE) bibliography for the subject concerned the interwar period. See Adam Roberts, "Morley, Agnes Headlam- (1902–1986)," *Oxford Dictionary of National Biography*, online.

44. Take, for instance, the work of Alan Booth, adviser to the World Council of Churches (WCC) and a member of the International Institute for Strategic Studies. His "message" may be found in his *Christians and Power Politics* (London: SCM, 1961).

45. See Donald Soper, *Christian Politics* (London: Epworth, 1977); and V. A. Demant, *Our Culture: Its Christian Roots and Present Crisis* (London: SPCK, 1947).

46. See, for example, Larkin's "Homage to a Government"; or Graham Greene's *The Quiet American* (London: Heinemann, 1956).

47. Toynbee to Lord Allen of Hurtwood, 11 May 1938, copy in Liddell Hart MS, King's College, London, 1/698/9-11.

CHAPTER 2

EPIGRAPH: Mark Bevir, *The Logic of the History of Ideas* (Cambridge: Cambridge University Press, 1999), 201.

1. For an overview, see Duncan Bell, "Writing the World: Disciplinary History and Beyond," *International Affairs* 85:1 (2009), 3–22.

2. See, for example, Schmidt, *Political Discourse of Anarchy*; or Behr, *History of International Political Theory*; as well as Jonathan Haslam, *No Virtue Like Necessity: Realist Thought in International Relations since Machiavelli* (New Haven & Oxford: Yale University Press, 2002).

3. See Anthony Pagden's *Lords of All the World: Ideologies of Empire in Spain, Britain and France, c. 1500–1800* (New Haven & Oxford: Yale Univer-

sity Press, 1998); or David Armitage, *The Ideological Origins of the British Empire* (Cambridge: Cambridge University Press, 2000).

4. David Armitage, "The Fifty Years' Rift: Intellectual History and International Relations," *Modern Intellectual History* 1:1 (2004), 97–109. It is nonetheless highly significant that the first issue of this flagship journal included such an article.

5. Martin Wight, *International Theory: The Three Traditions*, ed. Gabriele Wight and Brian Porter (London: Leicester University Press, 1991).

6. For a representative complaint, see Tim Dunne, "Mythology or Methodology? Traditions in International Theory," *Review of International Studies* 19:3 (1993), 305–318.

7. For a brief critical account of the development of Cambridge School contextualism, see Petri Koikkalainen, "Contextualist Dilemmas: Methodology of the History of Political Theory in Two Stages," *History of European Ideas* 37:3 (2011), 315–324; and for a discussion of its uses in the history of international thought, see Bell, "International Relations: The Dawn of a Historiographical Turn?"

8. Ido Oren, for example, employs an approach derived from Karl Mannheim's sociology of knowledge in his *Our Enemies and US: America's Rivalries and the Making of Political Science* (Ithaca, NY: Cornell University Press, 2003).

9. F. Melian Stawell, *The Growth of International Thought* (London: Thornton Butterworth, 1929), 246.

10. D.P. Heatley, *Diplomacy and the Study of International Relations* (Oxford: Clarendon, 1919).

11. Stawell, *Growth of International Thought*, 7.

12. Ibid., 7.

13. For a fuller discussion of this development, see Ian Hall, "Power Politics and Appeasement: Political Realism in British International Thought, c. 1935–1955," *British Journal of Politics and International Relations* 8:2 (2006), 178–182.

14. E.H. Carr, *The Twenty Years' Crisis, 1919–1938: An Introduction to the Study of International Relations*, 1st ed. (London: Macmillan, 1939).

15. Ibid., chapter 5.

16. See, for instance, John Herz, *Political Realism and Political Idealism: A Study in Theories and Realities* (Chicago: University of Chicago Press, 1951).

17. Georg Schwarzenberger, *Power Politics: A Study of International Society*, 2nd ed. (New York: Frederick A. Praeger, 1951), 5; Wight, *International Theory*, 267.

18. This exercise is prefigured in Wight's three-cornered dialogue describing the balance of power in 1939—see his "The Balance of Power," in Arnold J. Toynbee and F.T. Ashton-Gwatkin (eds.), *Survey of International Affairs, 1939–1946: The World in March 1939* (London: Oxford University Press and Royal Institute of International Affairs, 1953), 508–532.

19. Wight, *International Theory*, 252–254.

20. Chris Brown, "IR Theory in Britain: the New Black?," *Review of International Studies* 32:4 (2006), 680.

21. See especially Martin Wight's "Western Values in International Relations," in Butterfield and Wight (eds.) *Diplomatic Investigations: Essays on the Theory of International Politics* (London: Allen & Unwin, 1966), 89–131; and the lectures collected in *Four Seminal Thinkers in International Theory: Machiavelli, Grotius, Kant & Mazzini*, ed. Gabriele Wight and Brian Porter (Oxford: Oxford University Press, 2005). On Lovejoy and Wight's treatment of the history of international thought, see Hall, *International Thought of Martin Wight*, 153–154.

22. See Hedley Bull, "Martin Wight and the Theory of International Relations," *British Journal of International Studies* 2 (1976), 101–116; and Robert H. Jackson, *Classical and Modern Thought on International Relations* (New York: Palgrave, 2005); as well as the essays in Michael Donelan's edited *The Reason of States: A Study in International Political Theory* (London: Allen & Unwin, 1978). For a snapshot of contemporary thinking about traditions in the school, see Richard Little, "The English School's Contribution to the Study of International Relations," *European Journal of International Relations* 6:3 (2000), 395–422.

23. See, inter alia, Stefano Guzzini, *Realism in International Relations and International Political Economy: The Continuing Story of a Death Foretold* (London and New York: Routledge, 1998); and Michael C. Williams, *The Realist Tradition and the Limits of International Relations* (Cambridge: Cambridge University Press, 2005).

24. See especially Thomas Kuhn, *The Structure of Scientific Revolutions*, 3rd ed. (Chicago & London: University of Chicago Press, 1996 [1962]).

25. There was a brief flurry of interest in "paradigms" in Britain in the second half of the 1980s, stimulated by works such as Michael Banks's "The Inter-Paradigm Debate," in Margot Light and A.J.R. Groom (eds.), *International Relations: A Handbook of Current Theory* (London: Frances Pinter, 1985), 7-26.

26. See, for example, Jeffrey W. Legro and Andrew Moravcsik, "Is Anybody Still a Realist?," *International Security* 24:4 (1999), 5–55.

27. See K.J. Holsti, *The Dividing Discipline: Hegemony and Diversity in International Relations Theory* (Boston: Allen & Unwin, 1985).

28. See, for example, Duncan Bell, *The Idea of Greater Britain: Empire and the Future of World Order, 1860–1900* (Princeton, NJ: Princeton University Press, 2007).

29. See Molloy, *The Hidden History of Realism*.

30. John G. Gunnell, *Imagining the American Polity: Political Science and the Discourse of Democracy* (University Park, PA.: The Pennsylvania State University Press, 2004); Schmidt, *Political Discourse of Anarchy*.

31. Ibid.

32. See, for instance, Peter Wilson, "The Myth of the 'First Great Debate'," *Review of International Studies* 24:5 (1998), 1–16.

33. Renée Jeffery, "The Invention of Tradition: The 'Traditions Tradition' and the History of Ideas in International Relations," *Millennium: Journal of International Studies* 34:1 (2005), 57–84.

34. See, for example, Tim Dunne, Milja Kurki, and Steve Smith (eds.), *International Relations Theories: Discipline and Diversity* (Oxford: Oxford University Press, 2006).

35. See Bevir, *Logic of the History of Ideas*, especially 200–218.

36. In philosophical terms, as Bevir argues, the "concept of tradition captures an ontological fact or argument: that is, human beings necessarily have their being in a social context which influences them" ("On Tradition," *Humanitas* 13:2 [2000], 36). Human beings do not establish their beliefs either through pure reason or pure experience of the world. Instead, they are taught names of things, concepts, and theories about how things work by others—by their parents, their peers, their teachers, and so on. In this way, they inherit traditions.

37. Michael Oakeshott, "Introduction to *Leviathan*," in his *Rationalism in Politics and Other Essays* (Indianapolis, IN: Liberty Fund, 1991), 227.

38. What follows draws heavily on Bevir's *Logic of the History of Ideas* and his "On Tradition."

39. Bevir, *Logic of the History of Ideas*, 201, 203.

40. On this problem, see Dunne, "Mythology or Methodology"; and Jeffery, "The Invention of Tradition."

41. This phrase comes from the introduction to Quentin Skinner's *Visions of Politics, Volume I: Regarding Method* (Cambridge: Cambridge University Press, 2002), 8–26.

42. This kind of activity was rife in the debate that followed the publication of Legro and Moravcsik's "Is Anybody Still a Realist?' in 1999. See the correspondence from various authors published under the title "Brother, Can You Spare a Paradigm? (Or Was Anybody Ever a Realist?)," *International Security* 25:1 (2000), 165–193.

43. On this issue, see especially Bevir, "On Tradition."

44. Bevir, *Logic of the History of Ideas*, 213.

45. Arnold J. Toynbee, *Civilization on Trial* (New York: Oxford University Press, 1948), 7–8.

46. Stanley Hoffmann, "An American Social Science: International Relations," *Daedalus* 106:3 (1977), 41–60. The common claim that the British discipline emerged in response to the horrors of the First World War is another example of this kind of argument.

47. Schmidt, *Political Discourse of Anarchy*, 38.

48. The determinist sociology of knowledge in Haslam's *No Virtue Like Necessity*, for example, comes from Mannheim via Carr.

49. See especially Karl Mannheim's *Ideology and Utopia: An Introduction to the Sociology of Knowledge*, trans. Louis Wirth (New York: Harvest, 1936).

50. Carr, *Twenty Years' Crisis*, 1st ed., 87.

51. Hoffmann, "An American Social Science."
52. For a different view, see Oren on what he perceives to be the "general marginality of oppositional ideology" (*Our Enemies and US*, 18).
53. Hall, "Power Politics and Appeasement."
54. Bevir, *Logic of the History of Ideas*, 29.
55. Schmidt, *Political Discourse of Anarchy*, 38.
56. Bevir, *Logic of the History of Ideas*, 222.
57. Ibid., 235.
58. On Toynbee, see W. H. McNeill's *Arnold J. Toynbee: A Life* (New York: Oxford University Press, 1989).
59. Beloff, "The Politics of Oxford 'Politics,'" 131.
60. On "diachronic" and "synchronic" explanations, see Bevir, *Logic of the History of Ideas*, chapters 5, 6.
61. Bevir, "On Tradition," 36.
62. Ibid., 48.
63. Ibid., 49.
64. Temple's ideas may be found in *Christianity and Social Order* (Harmondsworth: Penguin, 1942); and Dawson's in *The Making of Europe: An Introduction to the History of European Unity* (London: Sheed & Ward, 1932).
65. The classic treatment of this subject is Eric Hobsbawm and Terence Ranger (eds.), *The Invention of Tradition* (Cambridge: Cambridge University Press, 1992).
66. Bruce Frohnen, "Tradition, Habit, and Social Interaction: A Response to Mark Bevir," *Humanitas* 14:1 (2001), especially 114–115.
67. For a painstaking study of the inner workings of the British Committee, see Vigezzi, *The British Committee on the Theory of International Politics*.
68. See Ian Hall, "Challenge and Response: The Lasting Engagement of Arnold J. Toynbee and Martin Wight," *International Relations* 17:3 (2003), 389–404; as well as my "Power Politics and Appeasement" and "'A Shallow Piece of Naughtiness': George Orwell on Political Realism," *Millennium: Journal of International Studies* 36:2 (2007), 191–125.
69. Northedge, *Descent from Power*, 360.

CHAPTER 3

EPIGRAPHS: A. J. P. Taylor, "Second Thoughts," in his *The Origins of the Second World War* (Harmondsworth: Penguin, 1964), 27; George Orwell, "Who Are the War Criminals?" (review of Cassius, *The Trial of Mussolini*, *Tribune*, 22 October 1943), in Peter Davidson (ed.) *The Complete Works of George Orwell*, vol. 40 (London: Secker & Warburg, 1998), item 2328, 292–293.

1. Political realism is notoriously hard to define and realists themselves frequently disagree about its core elements. Realist theorists of international relations emphasize the role of power, anarchy, and the state in world politics, and are commonly conservative and pessimistic, though realism cannot

be reduced to either conservatism or pessimism. IR realism need not imply, moreover, any commitment to philosophical realism. Indeed, many IR realists are philosophical idealists of one kind or another. On realism in general, see R.N. Berki, *On Political Realism* (London: Dent, 1981); and on IR realism, see Jack Donnelly, *Realism and International Relations* (Cambridge: Cambridge University Press, 2000).

2. For a balanced contemporary discussion of the reception of the realist tradition in Britain, see Herbert Butterfield, *The Statecraft of Machiavelli* (London: G. Bell and Sons, 1960 [1940]), especially 135–166.

3. Carr was educated at Merchant Taylor's, London, and Trinity College, Cambridge, after which he joined the Foreign Office, where he worked until taking up the Woodrow Wilson chair at Aberystwyth in 1936. On Carr's postwar peregrinations, see Jonathan Haslam, *The Vices of Integrity: E.H. Carr, 1892-1982* (London: Verso, 1999), 119–154; and on Carr and international relations, see Michael Cox (ed.), *E.H. Carr: A Critical Appraisal* (Basingstoke: Palgrave, 2000); as well as Charles Jones, *E.H. Carr and International Relations: A Duty to Lie* (Cambridge: Cambridge University Press, 1998).

4. Lewis Namier, for example, periodically described himself as a "realist" (see Ian Hall, "The Realist as Moralist: Sir Lewis Namier's International Thought," in Ian Hall and Lisa Hill [eds.], *British International Thinkers from Hobbes to Namier* [New York: Palgrave, 2009], 229–246), while Butterfield, Schwarzenberger, and Wight are described as "realists" in Hedley Bull, "The Theory of International Politics, 1919–1939," in Brian Porter (ed.), *The Aberystwyth Papers: International Politics, 1919–1969* (London: Oxford University Press, 1972), 37–38. See also Jonathan Haslam's comment that "After Carr's seminal contribution, and despite Butterfield's meetings, Britain struggled to produce a thinker of any originality in the realist tradition" (*No Virtue Like Necessity*, 210).

5. Taylor was educated at Bootham School, York, and Oriel College, Oxford. He taught at the University of Manchester, under Namier, from 1930 to 1938, then returned to Oxford, to Magdalen College.

6. Doubts about the nature of Carr's realism have been voiced for some time. Hans J. Morgenthau, for example, described Carr as a "utopian of power" ("The Political Science of E.H. Carr," *World Politics* 1:1 [1948], 134).

7. For a discussion of these associations, see Hall, "Power Politics and Appeasement."

8. George Orwell provided a useful contemporary assessment of this group in his "The Intellectual Revolt: Pessimists," *Manchester Evening News*, 24 January 1946, in *Complete Works* 18, item 2875, 58. Among the pessimists he named were F.A. Voigt, Michael Roberts, Malcolm Muggeridge, Friedrich Hayek, Michael Polanyi, and the Bertrand Russell of *Power: A New Social Analysis* (1938). To this group could be added Herbert Butterfield and Martin Wight.

9. Peter Lyon surveyed teachers of international relations and asked about the texts they used in 1963. He found that American books dominated the

reading lists and that British books were rare. See "Texts and the Study of International Relations," *Political Studies* 13:1 (1965), 79–84.

10. Ken Booth, *Security and Self: Reflections of a Fallen Realist* (Toronto: YCISS Occasional Paper 26, October 1994), 7.

11. Wight to Fulton, 8 December 1960, Wight MS 233 7/9.

12. Murray to Carr, 5 December 1936, Murray MS 227/136–137, Bodleian Library, Oxford.

13. British writers before the First World War do not seem to have sought a direct English translation for *Realpolitik*, preferring to use the original German or to use "Machiavellianism." See, for example, Goldsworthy Lowes Dickinson's *The European Anarchy* (London: G. Allen & Sons, 1916), 9, 40; as well as J. A. Hobson's discussion of that "calculating, greedy type of Machiavellianism, entitled 'real-politik' in Germany . . . which remodelled the whole art of diplomacy and erected national aggrandizement without pity or scruple as the conscious motive form of foreign policy." See *Imperialism: A Study* (Ann Arbor: University of Michigan Press, 1965 [1902]), 12–13.

14. Alfred Zimmern, *Spiritual Values and World Affairs* (Oxford: Clarendon, 1939), 63.

15. Neville Thompson, *The Anti-Appeasers: Conservative Opposition to Appeasement in the 1930s* (Oxford: Clarendon, 1971), 29–30.

16. E. H. Carr, "Mr Chamberlain's Struggle for Peace: The Realistic Quest for Peace," *Times Literary Supplement* 1948, 3 April 1939, 322.

17. Ibid.

18. E. H. Carr, *Britain: A Study in Foreign Policy* (London: Longman, 1939), 166–167.

19. On the cuts made to the second edition of *The Twenty Years' Crisis*, see Martin Wight, "The Realist's Utopia," *The Observer*, 21 July 1946, 3.

20. Carr, *Twenty Years' Crisis*, 1st ed., 14.

21. Carr's realism has been much debated. See, inter alia, Morgenthau, "Political Science of E. H. Carr"; Whittle Johnson, "E. H. Carr's Theory of International Relations: A Critique," *Journal of Politics* 39 (1967), 861–884; Graham Evans, "E. H. Carr and International Relations," *British Journal of International Studies* 1 (1975), 77–97; W. T. R. Fox, "E. H. Carr and Political Realism: Vision and Revision," *Review of International Studies* 11 (1985), 1–16; Paul Howe, "The Utopian Realism of E. H. Carr," *Review of International Studies* 20 (1994), 277–297; and Ken Booth, "Security in Anarchy: Utopian Realism in Theory and Practice," *International Affairs* 67 (1991), 527–546.

22. Carr, *Twenty Years' Crisis*, 1st ed., 14.

23. E. H. Carr, "Is Machiavelli a Modern?," *The Spectator* 5844 (1940), 868.

24. Carr, *Twenty Years' Crisis*, 1st ed., 87.

25. Ibid., 96.

26. Ibid., 304.

27. Ibid., 306.

28. This argument is made most clearly in Carr's *Conditions of Peace* (London: Macmillan, 1942).

29. Bertrand Russell, *Power: A New Social Analysis* (London: Allen & Unwin, 1971 [1938]), 175–176.

30. M. Bryant (ed.) *The Complete Colonel Blimp* (London: Bellow, 1991), 55. Similar views were expressed by Arnold J. Toynbee in his *Survey of International Affairs 1937* (London: Oxford University Press, 1938), 24; and by R. W. Seton-Watson, in *Britain and the Dictators* (Cambridge: Cambridge University Press, 1938), 433. Seton-Watson was educated at Winchester and New College, Oxford; Berlin; and the Sorbonne, and later dedicated his life to the history of the Austro-Hungarian Empire and its successor states. From 1922 until 1945 he was the Masaryk Professor of Central European History at King's College, London, then Professor of Czechoslovak studies at Oxford. See Wickham Steed (revised by R. J. W. Evans), "Watson, Robert William Seton- (1879–1951)," *Oxford Dictionary of National Biography*, online.

31. "Cato" [Frank Howard, Frank Owen, and Michael Foot], *Guilty Men* (Harmondsworth: Penguin, 1998 [1940]), 43.

32. See the discussion of appeasement in Hans J. Morgenthau, *Politics among Nations: The Struggle for Power and Peace*, brief edition, ed. K. W. Thompson (New York: McGraw Hill, 1993), 6.

33. George Orwell, "Review of *The Trial of Mussolini* by 'Cassius'" (1943), in *Orwell and Politics*, ed. Peter Davison (Harmondsworth: Penguin, 2001), 208.

34. Orwell, "Review of *The Machiavellians* by James Burnham" (1944), in *Orwell and Politics*, ed. Davison, 224.

35. Ibid., 226.

36. Orwell, "Review of *The Trial of Mussolini* by 'Cassius'," 209. I have argued elsewhere that Orwell's *Nineteen Eighty-Four* can also be read as a critique of the wild claims of political realists (Hall, "A Shallow Piece of Naughtiness'").

37. Herbert Butterfield, Letter on "The Lie about Munich," *Cambridge Review* 63:1544 (1942), 215.

38. Herbert Butterfield, *The Statecraft of Machiavelli* (London: G. Bell & Sons, 1960 [1940]), 120.

39. Ibid., 115.

40. Laski was educated at Manchester Grammar School and New College, Oxford, becoming a journalist, then editor of the *Harvard Law Review*, and then taking a lectureship at the LSE. He became Graham Wallas Professor of Political Science at the LSE in 1926, a post he held until his death.

41. Harold Laski, *Where Do We Go from Here? An Essay in Interpretation* (Harmondsworth: Penguin, 1941).

42. Ibid., 30.

43. Ibid., 69, 78.

44. Nicholas Spykman, *America's Strategy in World Politics: The United States and the Balance of Power* (Harcourt, Brace & Co., New York, 1942); Walter Lippmann, *U.S. Foreign Policy: Shield of the Republic* (Boston: Little, Brown & Co., 1943); Reinhold Niebuhr, *The Children of Light and the Children*

of Darkness (New York: Scribner's, 1944); Hans J. Morgenthau, *Scientific Man versus Power Politics* (Chicago: University of Chicago Press, 1946); *Politics among Nations: The Struggle for Power and Peace*, 1st ed. (New York: Alfred A. Knopf, 1948); *In Defense of the National Interest: A Critical Examination of American Foreign Policy* (New York: Alfred Knopf, 1951); and George Kennan, *American Diplomacy, 1900–1950* (Chicago: University of Chicago Press, 1950).

45. Lippmann, *U.S. Foreign Policy*, 101.

46. Morgenthau, *Politics among Nations: The Struggle for Power and Peace*, 3rd ed. (New York: Alfred A. Knopf, 1956), 64.

47. Saul Rose, review of Hans J. Morgenthau and Kenneth W. Thompson (eds.), *Principles and Problems of International Politics*, *International Affairs* 27:3 (1951), 406–407; A. F. Ensor, review of Morgenthau, *Politics among Nations*, *International Affairs* 25:2 (1949), 192.

48. C. H. Desch, review of Morgenthau, *Scientific Man versus Power Politics*, *International Affairs* 23:3 (1947), 378.

49. David Mitrany, review of Niebuhr, *The Children of Light and the Children of Darkness*, *International Affairs* 21:4 (1945), 524; George Catlin, review of Kennan, *American Diplomacy, 1900–1950*, *International Affairs* 28:3 (1952), 400–401.

50. L. B. Namier, *Diplomatic Prelude, 1938–1939* (London: Macmillan, 1948), xi.

51. J. W. Wheeler-Bennett, *Munich: Prologue to Tragedy* (London: Macmillan, 1948), 437, 181, 320.

52. Namier, *Diplomatic Prelude*, 330.

53. L. B. Namier, *In the Nazi Era* (London: Macmillan, 1952), 169; and *Europe in Decay* (London: Macmillan, 1950), 166.

54. Winston S. Churchill, *The Second World War: The Gathering Storm* (London: Reprint Society, 1951), x.

55. Wheeler-Bennett, *Munich*, 7–8.

56. Namier was educated at Lwów University, Lausanne, the LSE, and Balliol College, Oxford. Turned down for a fellowship at All Souls, Namier went into business and worked for the Zionist movement until being offered a chair at the University of Manchester in 1931, which he held until 1953. For a more detailed examination of Namier's realism, as well as the similarities and contrasts between his work and Carr's, see Hall, "Realist as Moralist."

57. L. B. Namier, *Conflicts: Studies in Contemporary History* (London: Macmillan, 1942), 28.

58. Namier, "Memoirs of a Realist," in *In the Nazi Era*, 168–181.

59. Namier, *Diplomatic Prelude*, 145, 141.

60. Martin Wight, "International Institutions" (1952–3), Wight MSS 121, 19d. Friedrich Hayek, *The Road to Serfdom* (London: G. Routledge & Sons, 1944), 135–163.

61. Wight, "Germany," in A. J. Toynbee and F. T. Ashton-Gwatkin (eds.), *Survey of International Affairs 1939–1946: The World in March 1939* (London:

Oxford University Press and Royal Institute of International Affairs, 1952), 317.

62. Ibid., 319–320.

63. See Hall, "The Art and Practice of a Diplomatic Historian: Sir Charles Webster, 1886–1961," *International Politics* 42 (2005), 470–490.

64. G.L. Arnold, "Realpolitik," *Cambridge Journal* 2:7 (April 1949), 415.

65. Wight, *Power Politics*, Looking Forward Pamphlet no. 8 (London: Royal Institute of International Affairs, 1946), 65–66.

66. Ibid., 68.

67. Berki, *On Political Realism*, 3.

68. Goodwin, "Teaching of International Relations in Universities in the United Kingdom," in his edited *The University Teaching of International Relations*, 110.

69. Gilbert Murray, *From League to United Nations* (London: Oxford University Press, 1948), 7.

70. Carr's influence over "war-time thought about peacemaking" is discussed also in David Thomson, E. Meyer, and Asa Briggs, *Patterns of Peacemaking* (London: Kegan Paul, 1945), 180. These commentators were more sanguine than Murray about the effects of Carr's realism, seeing it as a "reaction" with little positive in the way of proposals (181).

71. Arnold J. Toynbee, *Civilization on Trial* (New York: Oxford University Press, 1948), 135.

72. Wight, "Arnold Toynbee at 80," talk for Radio Baden-Baden, September 1969, Wight MS 47, 1.

73. Wight, "World War III," Wight MS 19.

74. Wight to Oldham, 27 June 1946, Wight MS 12.

75. See Hall, *International Thought of Martin Wight*.

76. Quoted in ibid., 149.

77. Lauterpacht was, like Namier, of Galician Jewish origin. He was educated at the University of Vienna and in 1923 entered the LSE as a research student. He was made reader in public international law at the University of London in 1932. His international thought is examined in Renée Jeffery, "Hersch Lauterpacht, the Realist Challenges and the 'Grotian Tradition' in 20th Century International Relations," *European Journal of International Relations* 12 (2006), 223–250.

78. Mannheim was born in Hungary, educated at the University of Budapest, and taught at both Heidelberg and Goethe University of Frankfurt-am-Main. A Jew, he was forced from his post in 1933, whereupon he moved to Britain. He taught at the LSE and at the University of London Institute. See Geoff Whitty, "Mannheim, Karl [Károly] (1893–1947)," *Oxford Dictionary of National Biography*, online.

79. On the influence of these thinkers and of continental theories on British political and international thought in the late 1930s and early 1940, see especially David Thomson, "British Studies of International Relations 1918–

1948," in UNESCO's *Contemporary Political Science: A Survey of Methods, Research and Teaching* (Paris: UNESCO, 1950), 582–593.

80. For a brief summary of Schwarzenberger's career, see the biographical note in Bin Cheng and E. D. Brown (eds.), *Contemporary Problems in International Law: Essays in Honour of Georg Schwarzenberger* (London: Stevens & Sons, 1988), xi–xii.

81. The *Year Book* was founded in 1947 and ceased publication in 1984.

82. Georg Schwarzenberger, "The Study of International Relations," *Year Book of World Affairs* 3 (1949), 5.

83. Ibid., 7.

84. Manning, *Nature of International Society*, 36, 79, 81.

85. Schwarzenberger, "Study of International Relations," 1.

86. Ibid., 4.

87. Ibid., 5.

88. Ibid.

89. Schwarzenberger, *Power Politics: A Study of International Society*, 2nd ed. (London: Stevens, 1951), 8.

90. Schwarzenberger, "Study of International Relations," 7.

91. Schwarzenberger, *Power Politics*, 8, 10.

92. For Schwarzenberger, the nature of "society" was best captured in the work of Hobbes or Spinoza, and "community" in Roman Stoicism, the Sermon on the Mount, and the thought of Confucius ("The Study of International Relations," 8–12). See also Schwarzenberger, *Power Politics*, 12.

93. Schwarzenberger, *Power Politics*, 12.

94. Ibid., 13.

95. Wight's assessment of "power politics" is closely bound to his religious views, notably to his conviction that the calamities of the twentieth century were a consequence of apostasy. See Hall, *International Thought of Martin Wight*, 21–42.

96. Schwarzenberger, "International Law and Society," *Year Book of International Law* 1 (1947), 159–177.

97. Schwarzenberger, *Power Politics*, part 2.

98. Ibid., 706.

99. Ibid., 716–720.

100. A. J. P. Taylor, *The Struggle for Mastery in Europe, 1848–1918* (Oxford: Oxford University Press, 1971 [1954]), xix. Taylor's international theory, such as it is, is dissected by F. H. Hinsley in *Power and the Pursuit of Peace: Theory and Practice in the History of Relations between States* (Cambridge: Cambridge University Press, 1967 [1963]), 323–334; and, in more detail, by Paul Schroeder in "A. J. P. Taylor's International System," *International History Review* 23:1 (2001), 2–27.

101. Greene, *The Quiet American*, 163.

102. Ibid., 158.

103. Isaiah Berlin, "Realism in Politics," *The Listener* 17 December 1954, 774.

104. A. L. Rowse, *All Souls and Appeasement: A Contribution to Contemporary History* (London: Macmillan, 1961), 83.

105. C. M. Woodhouse, *The New Concert of Nations* (London: Bodley Head, 1964), 19.

106. Cornelia Navari, "English Machiavellianism," in her edited *British Politics and the Spirit of the Age* (Keele: Keele University Press, 1996), 132–133.

107. C. R. Attlee, *Purpose and Policy: Selected Speeches*, ed. Roy Jenkins (London: Hutchinson, 1947), 140–141.

108. Quoted in Rhiannon Vickers, *The Labour Party and the World, Volume 1: The Evolution of Labour's Foreign Policy, 1900–1951* (Manchester: Manchester University Press, 2003), 169.

109. For one of the earliest and best expressions of the Third Force idea, see Richard Crossman, Michael Foot, and Ian Mikardo, *Keep Left* (London: New Statesman and Nation, 1947).

110. Denis Healey, "Power Politics and the Labour Party," in R. H. S. Crossman (ed.), *New Fabian Essays* (London: Turnstile Press, 1952), 161. Healey's realism was shaped, according to his memoirs, by his reading of "Hans Morgenthau and William Fox, and by Christian pessimists like Reinhold Niebuhr and Herbert Butterfield" (*The Time of My Life* [London: Michael Joseph, 1989], 99). His essay in *New Fabian Essays* also demonstrates the influence of Karl Mannheim's *Ideology and Utopia*.

111. Healey, "Power Politics and the Labour Party," 174.

112. Ibid., 166.

113. Ibid., 178–179.

114. See, for example, Wight's sympathetic review of Kenneth W. Thompson, *Political Realism and the Crisis of World Politics*, *International Affairs* 37:3 (1961), 344.

115. See Bull, "Theory of International Politics," 33–37.

116. For an attempt to distinguish again between idealism and appeasement, see Cornelia Navari, *Beyond Appeasement: Interpreting Inter War Peace Movements in World Politics* (Ithaca, NY, & London: Cornell University Press, 1999).

117. Lyon, "Texts and the Study of International Relations," 81.

118. It is rarely acknowledged, but Schwarzenberger's influence was felt even within their school. It was Schwarzenberger—not Manning or Wight—who first sketched out a distinction between what Bull later called "pluralist" and "solidarist" concepts of international society. See Schwarzenberger, "International Law and Society," *Year Book of World Affairs* 1 (1947), 159. The similarity between Bull's understanding of this distinction and Schwarzenberger's is noted by Alderson and Hurrell in "Bull's Conception of International Society," in their edited *Hedley Bull on International Society* (Basingstoke: Palgrave, 2000), 17n18.

119. See Joseph Frankel, *International Relations*, 2nd ed. (London: Oxford University Press, 1969 [1964]), 1–25.

120. Compare Frankel, *International Relations*, 92–116, to Schwarzen-

berger, *Power Politics*, 162–169. Frankel's early work on foreign policy analysis is summarized in "Towards a Decision-Making Model in Foreign Policy," *Political Studies* 7:1 (1959), 1–11; in "Rational Decision-Making in Foreign Policy," *Year Book of World Affairs* 14 (1960), 40–66; and in *The Making of Foreign Policy: An Analysis of Decision-Making* (London: Oxford University Press, 1963).

CHAPTER 4

EPIGRAPH: Lionel Curtis, *World War: Its Cause and Cure*, 2nd ed. (London: Oxford University Press, 1945).

1. George Dangerfield, *The Strange Death of Liberal England* (Stanford, CA: Stanford University Press, 1997 [1935]).

2. There is no comprehensive study of interwar liberal thought, though the literature on the subject is growing. Martin Ceadel's contribution is the most significant. See his *Pacifism in Britain, 1914–1945: The Defining of a Faith* (Oxford: Clarendon, 1980); *Semi-Detached Idealists: The British Peace Movement and International Relations, 1854–1945* (Oxford: Oxford University Press, 2000); and *Living the Great Illusion: Sir Norman Angell, 1872–1967* (Oxford: Oxford University Press, 2009). Casper Sylvest's *British Liberal Internationalism, 1880–1930: Making Progress?* (Manchester: Manchester University Press, 2009) takes the story to the halfway point, while David Long and Peter Wilson's edited *Thinkers of the Twenty Years' Crisis: Inter-War Idealism Reassessed* (Oxford: Clarendon Press, 1996) remains a key reference work.

3. For a representative account, see Alfred Zimmern, *The League of Nations and the Rule of Law, 1918–1935* (London: Oxford University Press, 1936).

4. For a fine contemporary summary of the liberal position and its relation to internationalism, see Gilbert Murray's Ramsey Muir lecture, *Advance under Fire* (London: Victor Gollancz, 1951).

5. For a brief discussion, see Michael Howard, *War and the Liberal Conscience*, new ed. (London: C. Hurst & Co., 2008), 83–100.

6. Arnold J. Toynbee, "After Munich: The World Outlook," *International Affairs* 18:1 (1939), 1–28.

7. See, for example, Leonard Woolf, "Utopia and Reality," *Political Quarterly* 11:2 (1940), 167–182. For variations on the internationalist theme, see Lionel Curtis, "World Order," *International Affairs* 18:3 (1939), 301–320; Viscount Cecil, *A Great Experiment* (London: Jonathan Cape, 1941); Harold Laski, *Where Do We Go from Here? An Essay in Interpretation* (Harmondsworth: Penguin, 1941); Hersch Lauterpacht, "The Resurrection of the League," *Political Quarterly* 12:2 (1941), 121–133; and Curtis, *World War*.

8. Following Luke Ashworth, David Long, and Peter Wilson I do not treat "idealism" as a tradition. Ashworth has rightly argued that "idealism" is not an appropriate term to describe a very disparate group of writers or a helpful one, as it tends to get "confused with the more specific use of the

term in political theory" ("Where Are the Idealists in Interwar International Relations?," *Review of International Studies* 32 [2006], 293). See also David Long, "J. A. Hobson and Idealism in International Relations," *Review of International Studies* 17:3 (1991), 285–304; and Peter Wilson, *The International Theory of Leonard Woolf: A Study in Twentieth-Century Idealism* (New York: Palgrave, 2003), 11–22.

9. This argument has a long pedigree, described best by Bell, *Idea of Greater Britain*. For an interwar expression of the argument, see Arnold J. Toynbee, *Economics and Politics in International Life* (Nottingham: University College, 1930).

10. For an overview of these projects in interwar internationalism, see especially Long and Wilson (ed.), *Thinkers of the Twenty Years' Crisis*.

11. Hayek (1899–1992) was educated at the University of Vienna but took up a post at the LSE in 1931 at the invitation of Lionel Robbins, remaining there until he left for Chicago in 1950. He is exceptional among British liberal internationalists (he became a British subject in 1938) in insisting on the restoration of an internationalist order rather than the construction of a new one modifying old liberal principles to fit contemporary demands. See *Road to Serfdom*, 163–176.

12. On paradigm shifts, see Thomas S. Kuhn's *The Structure of Scientific Revolutions*, 3rd ed. (Chicago: University of Chicago Press, 1996 [1962]); and on paradigm shifts in international theory, see K.J. Holsti, *The Dividing Discipline: Hegemony and Diversity in International Theory* (Boston: Allen & Unwin, 1985).

13. See, for example, Gilbert Murray's horror at the League's losing the "support of so many of its old friends," including Carr, Charles Manning, and Alfred Zimmern (Murray to Lord Robert Cecil, 25 May 1938, Murray MS 232/202).

14. Curtis, *World War*, 272.

15. On this issue, see Noël O'Sullivan, *European Political Thought since 1945* (Basingstoke: Palgrave, 2004), 20–21.

16. On the origins of the ideas and institutions approach, see Robert Adcock and Mark Bevir, "The Remaking of Political Theory," in Robert Adcock, Mark Bevir, and Shannon C. Stimson (eds.), *Modern Political Science: Anglo-American Exchanges since 1880* (Princeton, NJ: Princeton University Press, 2007) , 209–233; and on its enduring influence on British political studies, see Bernard Crick, "The British Way," *Government and Opposition* 15:3–4 (1980), 297–207.

17. Murray to Russell, 29 June 1948, Murray MS 166/77.

18. Brierly was educated at Charterhouse and Brasenose College, Oxford, and was Chichele Professor of International Law and Diplomacy at Oxford and Fellow of All Souls (1922–1947) and thereafter Montague Burton Professor at Edinburgh (1948–1951). He served on the UN International Law Commission from 1948 to 1951. His most prominent works are *The Law of*

Nations: An Introduction to the International Law of Peace (Oxford: Clarendon, 1924), and *The Outlook for International Law* (Oxford: Clarendon, 1944).

19. Cecil was the son of Prime Minister Lord Salisbury and was educated at Eton and Christ Church, Oxford. He served in the war cabinet during the First World War and represented South Africa at the League of Nations Assembly in the early 1920s. He played a critical role in the League of Nations Union in the interwar years, giving "respectability" to Conservative internationalism (Martin Ceadel, "Cecil, [Edgar Algernon] Robert Gascoyne-, Viscount Cecil of Chelwood, 1864–1958," *Oxford Dictionary of National Biography*, online).

20. Curtis was educated at Haileybury and New College, Oxford, and became a central figure in the so-called Milner Kindergarten, the Round Table, Chatham House, and later in the federalist movement. See especially Deborah Lavin, *From Empire to Commonwealth: A Biography of Lionel Curtis* (Oxford: Clarendon, 1995).

21. Lauterpacht was born in Poland, emigrated to Britain in 1923, became reader in international law at the University of London in 1935, held the Whewell Chair at Cambridge from 1938 to 1955, and sat on the UN International Law Commission 1951 to 1955. On his life and work, see Jeffery, "Hersch Lauterpacht, the Realist Challenge and the 'Grotian Tradition'."

22. Murray, an Australian, was educated at Merchant Taylor's and St John's College, Oxford, became professor of Greek at Glasgow and then Regius Professor of Greek at Oxford (1908–1936). He was a leading figure in the League of Nations Union and later served as president of that movement's successor organization, the United Nations Association. See Duncan Wilson, *Gilbert Murray OM, 1866–1957* (Oxford: Oxford University Press, 1987) and Christopher Stray (ed.), *Gilbert Murray Reassessed: Hellenium, Theatre and International Politics* (Oxford: Oxford University Press, 2007).

23. Webster was educated at Merchant Taylor's, Crosby, and King's College, Cambridge, and became an historian and internationalist who attended both the Versailles and the San Francisco Conferences on behalf of the British government. His life and work are discussed in Hall, "Art and Practice of a Diplomatic Historian."

24. Zimmern was educated at Winchester and New College, Oxford, and was like Murray a classicist as well as an internationalist. He became the first Woodrow Wilson Professor of International Politics at Aberystwyth in 1919, held the chair for two years, and later became the first Montague Burton Professor in 1930. He held that post until his retirement in 1944. He spent much of the remainder of his life in the United States. See D.J. Markwell, "Sir Alfred Zimmern Revisited: Fifty Years On," *Review of International Studies* 12 (1986), 279–292; and Paul Rich, "Alfred Zimmern's Cautious Idealism: The League of Nations, International Education and the Commonwealth," in Long and Wilson (eds.), *Thinkers of the Twenty Years' Crisis*.

25. A South African, Manning trained as a lawyer at South Africa Col-

lege, Cape Town, and Brasenose College, Oxford. He worked for the League of Nations in 1922–23 and held a fellowship at New College, Oxford, in 1930. He became Cassel Professor of International Relations (later Montague Burton Professor) at the London School of Economics in 1930, a post he held until 1962. See Alan James, "Manning, Charles Anthony Woodward, 1894–1978," *Oxford Dictionary of National Biography,* online.

26. Noel-Baker was a Quaker and politician, though he worked for the League of Nations during the early 1920s and was Cassel Professor at the LSE from 1924 until 1930. He served as an MP, first for Coventry (1929–1935) and then Derby (1936–1970), pursued internationalist causes, published *The Arms Race* in 1958, and won a Nobel Peace Prize for his pains.

27. Toynbee was educated at Winchester and New College, Oxford, and became a classicist and historian. He held a fellowship at Balliol before the First World War, attended the Versailles Conference after wartime service in government, and later became Stevenson Professor of History at the University of London and director of studies at Chatham House. See McNeill, *Toynbee.*

28. Woolf served in Ceylon in his early life, but he returned to Britain to become what would now be called a "public intellectual." He was the author of many books advocating internationalism. See especially Peter Wilson, *The International Theory of Leonard Woolf: A Study in Twentieth-Century Idealism* (New York: Palgrave, 2003).

29. McNeill, *Toynbee,* 222, 225.

30. See Richard Cockett, *David Astor and The Observer* (London: André Deutsch, 1991).

31. Geoffrey L. Goodwin, *Britain and the United Nations* (London: Oxford University Press, 1957).

32. For a biography, see Penry Williams, "Herbert George Nicholas," *Proceedings of the British Academy* 105 (2000), 503–510.

33. Luard was educated at several schools and then King's College, Cambridge, after which he joined the foreign service. He resigned during the Suez crisis, and later held a number of fellowships at St Antony's as well as serving as an MP for Oxford. See Adam Roberts, "Luard, (David) Evan Trant, 1926–1991," *Oxford Dictionary of National Biography,* online.

34. Woodhouse was educated at Winchester and New College, Oxford, and fought with the Special Operations Executive in the Second World War. He later spent some time with the Secret Intelligence Service (SIS) before becoming the director of Chatham House and a Conservative MP for Oxford. He wrote a number of books on Greece, as well as *British Foreign Policy since the Second World War* (London: Hutcheson, 1961) and *The New Concert of Nations* (London: Bodley Head, 1964).

35. Younger was educated at Winchester and New College, Oxford, then practiced law, fought in the Second World War, and became—in 1945—the Labour MP for Grimsby. He left Parliament in 1959 to take up his post at Chatham House. Among other publications, he edited with T. E. M. McKitterick a volume of *Fabian International Essays* (London: Hogarth, 1957). See

also Jo Grimond, "Younger, Sir Kenneth Gilmour (1908–1976)," *Oxford Dictionary of National Biography*, online.

36. Buchan, the son of the novelist John Buchan, was educated at Eton and Christ Church, Oxford. He served in the Army in the Second World War and was assistant editor of *The Economist* (1948–51), then Washington correspondent of *The Observer* (1951–58). He was the director of IISS from 1958 until 1969, when he joined the Imperial Defence College, and succeeded Headlam-Morley in the Montague Burton chair at Oxford in 1972. See Michael Howard, "Buchan, Alastair Francis, 1918–76," *Oxford Dictionary of National Biography*, online.

37. Strange was educated at the Royal School, Bath, and the LSE. She worked briefly for *The Economist* and then replaced Martin Wight as *The Observer*'s American and UN correspondent. She joined Schwarzenberger's group at University College, London, in 1949. She worked at Chatham House from 1965 to 1976 and succeeded Goodwin in the Montague Burton chair at the LSE in 1978.

38. Alastair Buchan, *The Spare Chancellor: The Life of Walter Bagehot* (London: Chatto & Windus, 1959).

39. See the membership list for the group, dated January 1952, in Wight MS 228.

40. Charles Manning, *The Nature of International Society* (London: G. Bell & Sons for the London School of Economics, 1962), x.

41. Norman Angell, *The Unseen Assassins* (London: Hamish Hamilton, 1932).

42. Ibid., 22–23.

43. For a discussion, see Jeanne Morefield, "The Never-Satisfied Idealism of Goldsworthy Lowes Dickinson," in Hall and Hill (eds.), *British International Thinkers*, 209–228.

44. Alfred E. Zimmern, *The Study of International Relations* (Oxford: Clarendon, 1931), 6.

45. Leonard Woolf, *International Government* (London: The Fabian Society and George Allen & Unwin, 1916); Zimmern, *The League of Nations and the Rule of Law, 1918–1935* (London: Macmillan, 1936).

46. See, for example, Harold Laski's discussion of the League of Nations in his *A Grammar of Politics*, 3rd ed. (London: George Allen & Unwin, 1934), 587.

47. Wight, "What is International Relations?," Wight MS 101, 7; Butterfield, "How Far and Should the Subject of International Relations Be Included in the Curriculum for Undergraduate Students of History?," Butterfield MS 130/1, 1, 3.

48. On the anti-utopianism of the LSE scholars, see Hidemi Suganami, "The Structure of British Institutionalism: An Anatomy of British International Relations," *International Relations* 7:5 (1983), 2367–2370.

49. Geoffrey Goodwin, "Teaching of International Relations in the Universities in the United Kingdom," in his edited *The University Teaching of*

International Relations (Oxford: Blackwell, 1951), 110, emphasis in original. Goodwin was then a lecturer at the LSE; he later was a reader (1958–62) and succeeded Charles Manning in the Montague Burton Chair in 1962.

50. Ibid., 110–111.

51. Ibid., 118.

52. Ibid., 126.

53. C. A. W. Manning, "Varieties of Worldly Wisdom," *World Politics* 9:2 (1957), 150.

54. On Manning's "social maps," see his *Nature of International* Society, 1–10.

55. Roy E. Jones, "The English School: A Case for Closure," *Review of International Studies* 7:1 (1981), 1–13; for a more sympathetic view, see Peter Wilson, "Manning's Quasi-Masterpiece: The Nature of International Society Revisited," *The Round Table* 93:377 (2004), 755–769; and David Long, "C. A. W. Manning and the Discipline of International Relations," *The Round Table* 94:378 (2005), 77–96.

56. Manning, *Nature of International Society*, x.

57. On the impact of philosophical Idealism on political studies in Britain, see Den Otter, "The Origins of a Historical Political Science," in Adcock, Bevir, and Stimson (eds.), *Modern Political Science*, 52–58, as well as Jeanne Morefield, *Covenants without Swords: Idealist Liberalism and the Spirit of Empire* (Princeton, NJ: Princeton University Press, 2004).

58. Manning, *Nature of International Society*, 6.

59. Ibid., 11.

60. Ibid., 27.

61. Hidemi Suganami, "C. A. W. Manning and the Study of International Relations," *Review of International Studies* 27 (2001), 91–107.

62. In his *Nature of International Society*, Manning refers to an eclectic list: Aristotle, John Austin, Albert Camus, Dante, Karl Marx (but not G. W. F. Hegel), G. E. Moore, Blaise Pascal, Plato, and Jean-Paul Sartre.

63. Jones, "The English School," 3.

64. C. A. W. Manning, "The Legal Framework in a World of Change," in Porter (ed.), *Aberystwyth Papers*, 303.

65. Wight was probably referring here to G. M. Gathorne-Hardy's much-updated text *A Short History of International Affairs, 1920–1939*, 4th ed. (London: Oxford University Press, 1950).

66. Wight, "History and the Study of International Relations," no date but probably 1950–52, Wight MS 112, 7.

67. On Strauss's epic theory, see John Gunnell, "The Myth of the Tradition," *American Political Science Review* 72:1 (1978), 122–134.

68. Wight, "Why Is There No International Theory?," in Butterfield and Wight (eds.), *Diplomatic Investigations*, 20.

69. These two approaches are discussed in more detail in Hall, *International Thought of Martin Wight*, 141–156.

70. Hedley Bull, *The Anarchical Society: A Study of Order in World Politics*

(Basingstoke: Macmillan, 1977); Brian Porter, "Patterns of Thought and Practice: Martin Wight's 'International Theory,'" in Michael Donelan (ed.), *The Reason of States: A Study in International Political Theory* (London: George Allen & Unwin, 1978), 64–74; Michael Donelan, *Elements of International Political Theory* (Oxford: Clarendon, 1990).

71. Peter Lyon, *Neutralism* (Leicester: Leicester University Press, 1963); R.J. Vincent, *Nonintervention and International Order* (Princeton, NJ: Princeton University Press, 1974);

72. These essays are contained in Wight's *Systems of States*, ed. Hedley Bull (Leicester: Leicester University Press/LSE, 1977).

73. Michael Donelan, *The Ideas of American Foreign Policy* (London: Chapman & Hall, 1963), 7.

74. For one valiant attempt to do just that, see N.J. Rengger, "Serpents and Doves in Classical International Theory," *Millennium: Journal of International Studies* 17:2 (1988), 215–225.

75. D. Mackinnon, "Natural Law," in Butterfield and Wight (eds.) *Diplomatic Investigations*, 74–88; and Charles Reynolds, *Theory and Explanation in International Politics* (London: Martin Robertson, 1973).

76. Reynolds, *Theory and Explanation*, 331. In the preface, Reynolds described his book as having "a rationalist head, a positivist body and an idealist tail, which has a disconcerting tendency of disappearing when it thinks, as if the effect of synthesis was too much for it" (vii).

77. Reynolds argued that "both the assertion that history is a mode of experience and the assertion that a historical argument is a re-experiencing of the thought of the historical agent in terms of the historian's own experience result in incommunicable explanations" (ibid., 335).

78. Ibid., 340–341.

79. Ibid., 354.

80. Donelan, introduction to *Reason of States*, 11. For an astute reading of Donelan's commitments, see Gene M. Lyons, "The Study of International Relations in Great Britain: Further Connections," *World Politics* 38:4 (1986), 626–645.

81. R.L. Borthwick, "Peter Savigear," *The Independent*, 24 October 1992. Savigear spent his academic career, from 1966 to 1989, at the University of Leicester.

82. Suganami, "Structure of British Institutionalism," 2365.

83. Ibid., 2374–2375. See also Bull, *Anarchical Society*, xxx, 127–130.

84. Quoted in Hall, *International Thought of Martin Wight*, 51. Wight here followed Collingwood's distinction between historical and scientific facts.

85. Instead, Bull merely chastised social scientists for not realizing that historical study, "even one of a purely narrative kind, has its own intellectual structure of hypothesis and argument" ("International Relations as an Academic Pursuit," in Alderson and Hurrell [eds.], *Hedley Bull on International Society*, 254).

86. Keens-Soper to Wight, 9 August 1971[?], Wight MS 233 6/9.

87. Gilbert Murray, *Advance under Fire* (London: Victor Gollancz, 1951), 17.

88. Robert Latham, *The Liberal Moment: Modernity, Security and the Making of the Postwar International Order* (New York: Columbia University Press, 1997).

89. Murray, *Advance under Fire*, 8.

90. Ibid., 10.

91. Sir Alfred E. Zimmern, *The American Road to World Peace* (New York: E. P. Dutton & Co., 1953), 30–31. For a critical view of Zimmern's late work and its political impact, see Mark Mazower, *No Enchanted Palace: The End of Empire and the Ideological Origins of the United Nations* (Princeton, NJ, and Oxford: Princeton University Press, 2009), 66–103.

92. Zimmern, "The Legacy of Two Wars," first of three addresses delivered at the Connecticut Teachers College, New Britain, 13, 20, 27 January 1948, Zimmern MS 148/13–50, 20, Bodleian Library, Oxford.

93. See Toynbee's *The World and the West* (London: Oxford University Press, 1953), as well as the criticisms that book attracted in Douglas Jerrold's *The Lie about the West: A Response to Professor Toynbee's Challenge* (London: J. M. Dent & Co., 1953) and in the pages of the *Times Literary Supplement*, reprinted in *Counsels of Hope: The Toynbee-Jerrold Controversy* (London: Times Publishing Company, 1954). For a discussion of this controversy, see Ian Hall, "The 'Toynbee Convector': The Rise and Fall of Arnold J. Toynbee's Anti-Imperial Mission to the West," *The European Legacy* 17:4 (2012).

94. Wight, "Western Values in International Relations," in Butterfield and Wight (eds.), *Diplomatic Investigations*, 89.

95. Frederick Watkins, *The Political Tradition of the West: A Study in the Development of Modern Liberalism* (London: Oxford University Press, 1948) and Barbara Ward, *Policy for the West* (Harmondsworth: Penguin, 1951).

96. E. L. Woodward, "The Heritage of Western Civilization," *International Affairs* 25:2 (1949), 146.

CHAPTER 5

EPIGRAPHS: Friedrich Hayek, *The Road to Serfdom* (London: Routledge & Kegan Paul, 1979 [1944]), 163; Martin Wight, *Four Seminal Thinkers in International Theory: Machiavelli, Grotius, Kant and Mazzini*, ed. Gabrielle Wight and Brian Porter (Oxford: Oxford University Press, 2004), 44.

1. Fred Halliday famously argued for three slightly different categories: liberal, "hegemonic," and "revolutionary" internationalism, with the hegemonic category embracing overt and indirect imperialism. This seems to me to blur the complex relationship between liberalism and imperialism. See Halliday's "Three Concepts of Internationalism," *International Affairs* 64:2 (1988), 187–198; and, on conservative internationalism, see George Egerton, "Conservative Internationalism: British Approaches to International Organization and the Creation of the League of Nations," *Diplomacy and Statecraft* 5:1 (1994), 1–20.

2. Powell acknowledged that the cost was a slide into shabby and impov-

erished irrelevance, but he favored that over what he regarded as the even more humiliating alternatives. On Powell's shifting views on British foreign policy, see especially Simon Heffer, *Like the Roman: The Life of Enoch Powell* (London: Weidenfeld & Nicolson, 1998).

3. Halliday, "Three Concepts," 188.

4. Russell to Murray, 9 April 1943, Murray MS 166/61.

5. In Carr's account, supporters of the League were utopian because they sought to resurrect a past international order of Western European dominance, laissez-faire, and liberal international law, not because they sought to create a wholly new order. Here the flexibility of Mannheim's category of utopianism, on which Carr relied, is what has led some later readers astray. For Mannheim even a reactionary could be a "utopian"—what made one utopian was the desire for anything not found in the present rather than, in the more orthodox understanding of the term, something to be achieved in the future. See Carr's *Twenty Years' Crisis*, 1st ed., part 2, and Mannheim's *Ideology and Utopia*, especially part 4.

6. Lucian M. Ashworth, "Who Are the Idealists in Interwar IR?," *Review of International Studies* 32:2 (2006), 298–299. See, inter alia, Kenneth Waltz's *Man, the State, and War: A Theoretical Analysis* (New York: Columbia University Press, 1959), 16–41. Waltz's discussion is telling because he does not actually cite any authors who state in an explicit way that human nature is essentially good or that it can be modified. Rather, he cites a silly comment by the pacifist Beverly Nichols about the possibilities of education, the Quaker vision of a world without war, and Bertrand Russell's belief that, in Waltz's words, "a decline in the possessive instincts . . . [is] . . . a prerequisite to peace" (17).

7. Ashworth has catalogued a number of earlier uses of the realist-Idealist distinction in British writing on international politics, noting that their meanings are far from fixed in the interwar years. See his "Who Are the Idealists in Interwar IR?," 293–298.

8. Bull, "Theory of International Politics," 34. For Bull, the Idealists had said little that was "profound," were generally "superficial," and were "not remarkable for their intellectual depth or powers of explanation, only for their intense commitment to a particular vision of what should happen" (34–35).

9. It is notable, I think, that the only thinkers whom Wight thought had believed in the perfectibility of human nature were Rousseau and Marx. See his *International Theory*, 27–28.

10. The emphasis placed by interwar internationalists on education is well known and often discussed. See, for example, Eileen Power, "The Teaching of History and World Peace," in F. S. Marvin (ed.), *The Evolution of World-Peace* (London: Oxford University Press, 1921), 179–191; or, for a more extensive argument along the same lines, Angell's *The Unseen Assassins* (1932).

11. Murray to Russell, 14 May 1940, Murray MS 166/45.

12. Lionel Curtis, *Civitas Dei: The Commonwealth of God* (London: Mac-

millan, 1938), 891; Norman Angell, *The Steep Places: An Examination of Political Tendencies* (London: Hamish Hamilton, 1947), 31.

13. Zimmern, "The Legacy of Two Wars," [1st of] Three Addresses Delivered at the Connecticut Teachers College, New Britain, 13, 20, 27 Jan 1948, Zimmern MS 148/13–50, 21.

14. Herbert Butterfield, *Christianity and History* (London: Fontana, 1957 [1949]), 47.

15. For evidence of Carr's progressivism, see his *What Is History?* (London: Macmillan, 1961).

16. Murray, *Advance under Fire*, 11. Murray observed: "In itself, I suppose, this Wille zur Macht is an instinct necessary to life and growth, present in all normal men and nations, individuals and groups. That is why it is so strong, and why in excess it is so deadly . . ."

17. Ibid., 12. Here Murray had in mind the thought of E. H. Carr.

18. Ibid., 17. See also the observations of another veteran liberal, G. P. Gooch, to whom the "common man" was "selfish, short-sighted and quarrelsome" (*Under Six Reigns* [London: Longman, Green, 1958], 327).

19. Murray, *Advance under Fire*, 22.

20. For a wider discussion of these points, see Deborah Boucoyannis, "The International Wanderings of a Liberal Idea, Or Why Liberals Can Learn to Stop Worrying and Love the Balance of Power," *Perspectives on Politics* 5:4 (2007), 703–727.

21. Alfred Cobban, "The Nation-State," *History* 29:109 (1944), 55. Cobban (1901–1968) was educated at Latymer Upper School and Gonville and Caius College, Cambridge. Thereafter he taught at King's College, Newcastle, and then University College London, where he spent most of his career and where he wrote on France and on the history of ideas.

22. For a survey of British thinking on this topic, see Charles King, "Nations and Nationalism in British Political Studies," in Hayward, Barry, and Brown (eds.), *British Study of Politics*, 313–343.

23. This position is captured well in Wight's discussion of the reception of Guiseppe Mazzini, whom he thought of as quintessentially "Victorian . . . in every sense except that he was not a British subject" (*Four Seminal Thinkers*, 90).

24. Keith Hancock, *Argument of Empire* (Harmondsworth: Penguin Special, 1943), 12. On Mazzini, see Wight, *Four Seminal Thinkers*, 89–119.

25. Arnold J. Toynbee, *Nationality and the War* (London: J. M. Dent & Co., 1915), and "The Idolatry of Nationalism," *The Listener* (26 November 1930), 873–874.

26. Gilbert Murray, "Self-Determination of Nationalities," *Journal of the British Institute of International Affairs* 1:1 (January 1922), 6–13.

27. Lewis Namier, "Nationality and Liberty," in his *Avenues of History* (London: Hamish Hamilton, 1952), 20–44. See also Cobban's "Nation-State," which distinguishes between true "nations" and false cultural nationalisms.

28. Lewis Namier, *1848: The Revolution of the Intellectuals* (London: Geoffrey Cumberledge, 1944), 27.

29. Elie Kedourie, *Nationalism* (London: Hutchinson, 1960), 18.

30. Arnold J. Toynbee, *Survey of International Affairs, 1931* (London: Oxford University Press, 1932), 17.

31. Toynbee argued that fascism and communism were also species of idolatry. See his "Post-War Paganism versus Christianity," *The Listener* 17:419, 20 January 1937, 123–124. Zimmern's argument may be found in his *Spiritual Values and World Affairs*.

32. As Adrian Hastings has noted, "The central tide of English thought and culture in the 1930s was flowing quite perceptibly in one large direction: from irreligion to religion, from liberal or modernist religion to neo-orthodoxy, and from Protestantism to Catholicism" (*A History of English Christianity, 1920–1985* [London: Collins, 1986], 289.

33. See Toynbee, *A Study of History*, vol. 3 (London: Oxford University Press, 1934), 217–376; Angell, *Unseen Assassins*, 24–37.

34. Murray to Russell, 21 May 1955, Murray MS 166/133.

35. F. H. Hinsley, *Nationalism and the International System* (Dobbs Ferry, NY: Oceana Publications, 1973), 172. See also Hedley Bull's untitled review of this book in the *American Political Science Review* 69:1 (1975), 374.

36 Wight, *Power Politics*, 1st ed., 62.

37. Webster's part in the making of the UN is detailed in Charles Reynolds and E.J. Hughes, *The Historian as Diplomat: Charles Kingsley Webster and the United Nations* (London: Martin Robertson, 1976).

38. See Hall, "Art and Practice of a Diplomatic Historian."

39. Webster, diary, January 11, 1944, Webster MS 29/11, 275, British Library of Political and Economic Sciences, London.

40. Webster, quoted in Reynolds and Hughes, *The Historian as Diplomat*, 71. On the "education" Webster gave the government, see 36.

41. Webster, "British Foreign Policy since the Second World War," in Royal Institute of International Affairs, *United Kingdom Policy: Foreign, Strategic and Economic* (London: RIIA & Oxford University Press, 1950), 30–31.

42. Webster, quoted in Reynolds and Hughes, *The Historian as Diplomat*, 70.

43. J.L. Brierly, *The Covenant and the Charter* (Cambridge: Cambridge University Press, 1947), 17.

44. Webster, "Some Problems of International Institutions," unpublished lecture dated 1944, Webster MS 1/23/59–72, 1.

45. Webster to Bennett, June 29, 1950, Webster MS 1/30/42.

46. Murray to Russell, 16 September 1955, Murray MS 166/143.

47. Wight, lecture notes on the United Nations, probably post-1955, Wight MS 119, 84, 92.

48. Wight, lecture on United Nations, Wight MS 123, 29–30.

49. Wight, "The United Nations," talk at Royal Naval College, Greenwich, 15 July 1947, Wight MS 226, 2. Morgenthau, interestingly, held a similar view (see William E. Scheuerman, *Morgenthau* [Cambridge: Polity, 2009], 120).

50. Geoffrey Goodwin, "The Political Role of the United Nations: Some British Views," *International Organization* 15:4 (1961), 581–582. On British official attitudes, see also C. M. Woodhouse, *British Foreign Policy since the Second World War* (London: Hutchinson, 1961), 185–199.

51. See Schwarzenberger, *Power Politics*, 2nd ed., especially 695–724.

52. Courtney (1878–1974) was educated at Lady Margaret Hall, Oxford, and became a prominent suffragette. She was a member of the League of Nations Union executive committee from 1928 until its dissolution, then deputy chairman of the United Nations Association, under Murray, in 1945. She held the post until 1951.

53. See Alfred E. Zimmern, *The American Road to World Peace* (New York: E. P. Dutton & Co, 1953), 205–210.

54. Murray to Cecil, 15 May 1952, Murray MS 372/32.

55. Bertrand Russell, *Portraits from Memory* (London: George Allen & Unwin, 1956), 220.

56. See Toynbee's *Study of History*, especially vols. 7 to 9, and, for a more concise treatment, his Gifford Lectures, *A Historian's Approach to Religion* (London: Oxford University Press, 1956).

57. For a discussion of this movement and some of its effects, see John Nurser, "The 'Ecumenical Movement' Churches, 'Global Order,' and Human Rights, 1938–1948," *Human Rights Quarterly* 25:4 (2003), 841–881.

58. Murray to Russell, 23 April 1941, Murray MS 166/50.

59. See McNeill, *Toynbee*, 205–261.

60. For a comprehensive survey of federalist ideas and practices, see Andrea Bosco (ed.), *The Federal Idea*, 2 vols. (London & New York: Lothian Foundation, 1991/1992).

61. See, inter alia, Andrea Bosco, "Lothian, Curtis, Kimber and Federal Union Movement (1938–1940)," *Journal of Contemporary History* 23:3 (1988), 465–502.

62. On the origins of the latter, see Bell, *Idea of Greater Britain*.

63. Bosco, "Lothian."

64. On Lothian, see John Turner (ed.), *The Larger Idea: Lord Lothian and the Problem of National Sovereignty* (London: The Historians' Press, 1988); and on the 1940 proposal, see John Pinder's chapter in that volume, "Prophet Not without Honour: Lothian and the Federal Idea," 137–152.

65. An Atlantic Union had been proposed by the American writer Clarence Streit in his *Union Now* (New York: Harper's, 1939).

66. See Schwarzenberger, *Power Politics*, 2nd ed. (1951), 804–816.

67. Ward, *Policy for the West*.

68. For overviews, see Michael Burgess, *Federalism and the European Union: Political Ideas, Influences and Strategies in the European Community, 1972–1987* (London: Routledge, 1989); Hugo Young, *This Blessed Plot: Britain and Europe from Churchill to Blair* (London & Basingstoke: Macmillan, 1998); and Oliver Daddow, *Britain and Europe since 1945: Historiographical Perspectives on Integration* (Manchester: Manchester University Press, 2004), 84–85.

69. Karl Mannheim, *Man and Society in an Age of Reconstruction: Studies in Modern Social Structure*, trans. Edward Shils (London: Routledge & Kegan Paul, 1940), 2.

70. Ibid., 7.

71. Ibid., 17.

72. Ibid., 63.

73. Ibid., 156.

74. See the discussion in ibid., chapter 9, 199–236.

75. For a brief account of the origins of functionalism and its uses in political science, see Roy E. Jones, *The Functional Analysis of Politics: An Introductory Discussion* (London: Routledge & Kegan Paul, 1967).

76. David Mitrany, *A Working Peace System* (London: RIIA, 1943), 21. See also Mitrany's "The Functional Approach to World Organization," *International Affairs* 24:3 (1948), 350–363.

77. Mitrany, *Working Peace System*, 27. On Mitrany's conservatism, see Mark F. Imber, "Re-Reading Mitrany: A Pragmatic Assessment of Sovereignty," *Review of International Studies* 10:2 (1984), 103–123.

78. That formal institutions were too often unequal to the tasks required of them was a "lesson" the functionalists drew from the interwar period, when, as Jones put it, "Time and again it was demonstrated that the problems of politics could not be solved by formal institutions, however well-intentioned, fair, and honourable they might be" (*Functional Analysis of Politics*, 10).

79. Mitrany called this the "virtue of technical self-determination" (*Working Peace System*, 35).

80. Mitrany, *Working Peace System*, 40.

81. See especially Ernst Haas, *Beyond the Nation-State: Functionalism and International Organization* (Stanford: Stanford University Press, 1964); and Jones, *Functional Analysis of Politics*.

82. Wight, "Western Values," 130.

83. See especially Berlin's *Four Essays on Liberty* (Oxford: Oxford University Press, 1969); and Popper's *The Open Society and its Enemies*, 2 vols. (London: Routledge, 1974).

84. Hayek, *Road to Serfdom*, 163.

85. Ibid.

86. Ibid., 164.

87. Ibid.

88. Ibid., 165–166.

89. Ibid., 169.

90. Ibid., 170.

91. Ibid., 171.

92. Ibid., 173.

93. Ibid.

94. Ibid., 174.

CHAPTER 6

EPIGRAPH: Herbert Butterfield, *The Englishman and His History* (Cambridge: Cambridge University Press, 1944), 138.

1. Hermann Kantorowicz, *The Spirit of British Policy and the Myth of the Encirclement of Germany* (London: George Allen & Unwin, 1931), 35.
2. Ibid., 362.
3. See especially David Reynolds, *In Command of History: Churchill Fighting and Writing the Second World War* (Harmondsworth: Penguin, 2005).
4. David Cannadine, *In Churchill's Shadow: Confronting the Past in Modern Britain* (Oxford: Oxford University Press, 2003), 197.
5. Dorothy Ross, "Anglo-American Political Science, 1880–1920," in Adcock, Bevir, and Stimson (eds.) *Modern Political Science*, 22.
6. For one representative version of this view of whig foreign policy, see A. L. Rowse, "The Tradition of British Policy," *Political Quarterly* 10:4 (1939), 489–501. For a later view, see Jeremy Black, "Britain's Foreign Alliances in the Eighteenth Century," *Albion: A Quarterly Journal Concerned with British Studies* 20:4 (1988), 573–602.
7. For a reinterpretation of British foreign policy in the eighteenth century, see Brendan Simms, *Three Victories and a Defeat: The Rise and Fall of the First British Empire, 1714–1783* (Harmondsworth: Penguin, 2008). This view of Britain's "traditional" foreign policy was shared by American political realists. See, for example, Morgenthau, *Politics among Nations*, 6th ed. (New York: Knopf, 1985), 211–212.
8. Churchill, *The Second World War*, vol 1: *The Gathering Storm*, 178.
9. Ibid., 180.
10. It took until the 1970s before this argument could be made in full. See Paul Kennedy, "The Tradition of Appeasement in British Foreign Policy, 1865–1939," *British Journal of International Studies* 2:3 (1976), 195–215.
11. British scholars are unusual in the interest they have shown for the practice of diplomacy. It features prominently in the earliest efforts of British scholars to analyze international politics—see, for example, the Edinburgh historian D. P. Heatley's *Diplomacy and the Study of International Relations* (Oxford: Clarendon, 1919); or R. B. Mowat's *Diplomacy and Peace* (London: Williams and Norgate, 1935). The classic manual of diplomacy remains Sir Ernest Satow's *A Guide to Diplomatic Practice*, 4th ed. (New York: Longmans, Green, 1957), first published in 1916.
12. For a new take on this old argument, see Paul Sharp, *Diplomatic Theory of International Relations* (Cambridge: Cambridge University Press, 2009); and for a wider discussion of diplomacy, see Ian Hall, "Diplomacy, Anti-Diplomacy and International Society," in Richard Little and John Williams (eds.) *The Anarchical Society in a Globalized World* (Basingstoke: Palgrave, 2006), 141–161.
13. For a brief account of the whig tradition, see Mark Bevir and R. A. W.

Rhodes, "Decentering Tradition: Interpreting British Governance," *Administration and Society* 33:2 (2001), 120–121.

14. A certain philosophical idealism is inherent in this kind of thinking. On this point, see Andrew Gamble, "Theories of British Politics," *Political Studies* 38 (1990), 408–9.

15. Butterfield and Wight, preface to their edited *Diplomatic Investigations*, 12–13.

16. Herbert Butterfield, "Harold Temperley and George Canning," in Harold Temperley, *The Foreign Policy of Canning, 1822–27: England, the Neo-Holy Alliance, and the New World*, 2nd ed. (London: Cass, 1966), xvi.

17. Temperley, *The Foreign Policy of Canning;* and Charles Webster, *The Foreign Policy of Castlereagh*, 2 vols (London: Bell, 1931–35).

18. On the decline of diplomatic history, see Butterfield, "Harold Temperley and George Canning," vii–xxvi. For international and contemporary histories, see Gordon Connell-Smith, *Pattern of the Post-War World* (Harmondsworth: Penguin, 1957); Hugh Seton-Watson, *Neither War nor Peace: The Struggle for Power in the Post-War World* (London: Methuen, 1960); G. F. Hudson, *The Hard and Bitter Peace: World Politics since 1945* (London: Pall Mall, 1966); or Peter Calvocoressi, *International Politics since 1945* (New York: Frederick A. Praeger, 1968). The rise of "contemporary history" was controversial in Britain, especially after 1945, when the debate over Munich and the origins of the war was at its height. See R. W. Seton-Watson, "A Plea for the Study of Contemporary History," *History* 14 (1929), 1–18, and for a more skeptical view, Max Beloff, "The Study of Contemporary History: Some Further Reflections," *History* 30 (1945), 75–84.

19. Kathleen Burk details Taylor's successes in *Troublemaker: The Life and History of A. J. P. Taylor* (New Haven & London: Yale University Press, 2000).

20. Wight's view that contemporary history was "one of the two poles of our subject" was widely shared—the other he called the "Sociology of the International Community." See his "What Is International Relations?" (1950), Wight MS 112, 15.

21. For a full account of "modernist empiricism" in British political studies, see Bevir, "Prisoners of Professionalism," 469–509; and for a wider discussion of "modernism" in British historiography, see Michael Bentley, *Modernizing England's Past: English Historiography in the Age of Modernism, 1870–1970* (Cambridge: Cambridge University Press, 2005).

22. See Lewis Namier, *The Structure of Politics at the Accession of George III* (London: Macmillan, 1929); S. E. Finer, *Comparative Government* (London: Allen Lane, 1970).

23. Geoffrey Goodwin, *Britain and the United Nations* (London: Oxford University Press, 1957); F. H. Hinsley, *Nationalism and the International System* (Dobbs Ferry, NY: Oceana Publications, 1973).

24. Mark Bevir, "Meta-Methodology: Clearing the Underbrush," in J. Box-Steffensmeier, H. Brady, and D. Collier (eds.), *The Oxford Handbook of Political Methodology* (Oxford: Oxford University Press, 2008), 51.

25. Bevir, "Prisoners of Professionalism," 476.
26. Bentley, *Modernizing England's Past*, 11.
27. See Geoffrey Barraclough, *An Introduction to Contemporary History* (Harmondsworth: Penguin, 1988 [1964]); Herbert Butterfield, *Christianity and History* (London: G. Bell & Sons, 1949); Lewis Namier, *Avenues of History* (London: Hamish Hamilton, 1952), 1–10; and Paul W. Schroeder, "A. J. P. Taylor's International System," *International History Review* 23:1 (2001), 3–27.
28. On Butterfield's historical thought, see especially Michael Bentley, "Butterfield at the Millennium: The Sir Herbert Butterfield Lecture, 1999," *Storia della Storiografia* 38 (2000), 17–32; and on his international thought, see Ian Hall, "History, Christianity and Diplomacy: Sir Herbert Butterfield and International Relations," *Review of International Studies* 28:4 (2002), 719–736.
29. Herbert Butterfield, *Man on His Past: The Study of the History of Historical Scholarship* (Cambridge: Cambridge University Press, 1955); Butterfield, *History and Human Relations* (London: Collins, 1951).
30. Herbert Butterfield, *The Whig Interpretation of History* (New York: W. W. Norton, 1965 [1931]), 103.
31. Butterfield, *History and Human Relations*, 165.
32. Butterfield, *The Study of Modern History* (London: G. Bell & Sons, 1944), 17.
33. The British historical profession was in this respect no different from its American counterpart, best described in Peter Novick, *That Noble Dream: The "Objectivity" Question and the American Historical Profession* (Cambridge: Cambridge University Press, 1988), 361–414.
34. Bull, "International Theory."
35. Bull's attack elicited a withering reply—Morton Kaplan's "The New Great Debate: Traditionalism vs. Science in International Relations," *World Politics* 19:1 (1966), 1–20.
36. Bull, "International Theory," 361.
37. Ibid., 361.
38. Ibid., 375.
39. Ibid.
40. Bevir, "Prisoners of Professionalism," 483.
41. Jones, "The English School," 7.
42. Bevir has argued that "the contrast between modernist empiricism and positivism obscures as much as it reveals. It obscures the way in which both arose as part of the modernist break with Enlightenment and romantic theories; it obscured their shared origins in the dilemmas posed by things such as World War One for nineteenth-century notions of character, reason and progress. In addition, it obscures the way in which modernist empiricism has absorbed aspects of the positivist agenda" ("Prisoners of Professionalism," 477).
43. Lord Vansittart, "The Decline of Diplomacy," *Foreign Affairs* 28:2 (1950), 177.
44. Butterfield to Beloff, 15 June 1950, Butterfield MS 531:B55.

45. Charles Webster, *The Study of International Politics* (London: Humphrey Milford, 1923), 19.

46. Butterfield observed of Webster's histories that "the real hero was British foreign policy, defended authoritatively and almost officially—always too unquestionably right, and with Continental diplomacy somewhat as a foil" ("Harold Temperley and George Canning," xxv).

47. Harold Nicolson, *Curzon: The Last Phase, 1919–1925: A Study in Post-War Diplomacy* (London: Constable, 1934), 40.

48. See especially Bull's *Anarchical Society* (1977), which discusses diplomacy in exactly these terms.

49. Nicolson (1886–1968), whose father Arthur Nicolson, 1st Baron Carnock, had himself been a distinguished diplomat, was educated at Wellington and Balliol College, Oxford, and joined the diplomatic service in 1909. He attended Versailles, served for a brief period at the League and for a longer one at the Foreign Office, and then (in 1925) was posted to Tehran, only to be recalled two years later. He resigned in 1930 and committed himself to a career as a writer. On Nicolson's thought, see Derek Drinkwater, *Sir Harold Nicolson and International Relations: The Practitioner as Theorist* (Oxford: Oxford University Press, 2005).

50. See the following by Nicolson: *Sir Arthur Nicolson, Bart, First Lord Carnock: A Study in the Old Diplomacy* (London: Constable, 1930); *Peacemaking 1919* (London: Constable, 1945 [1933]); *Diplomacy*, 2nd ed. (London: Oxford University Press, 1950 [1st ed. 1939]); and *The Congress of Vienna: A Study in Allied Unity, 1812–1822* (London: Constable, 1946).

51. Nicolson, *Diplomacy*, 2nd ed., 7.
52. Ibid., 58.
53. Ibid., 70.
54. Ibid., 82.
55. Ibid., 90.
56. Nicolson railed that "[t]he ordinary elector is not merely ignorant, lazy and forgetful . . . but he does not apply to the general theory of foreign affairs that thought and intelligence which he devotes to domestic matters." (Ibid., 92–93).
57. Ibid., 91.
58. Ibid., 100.
59. Ibid., 131.
60. Ibid., 132.
61. Ibid., 135.
62. Ibid., 139.
63. Ibid., 143–144.
64. Ibid., 144–145.
65. Ibid., 150.
66. Butterfield, "The Balance of Power and the Development of the Theory of International Relations" (April 1959), Papers of the British Committee on the Theory of International Politics, box 2, 36, Chatham House.

67. Butterfield was educated at Keighley Grammar School and Peterhouse, Cambridge. He was elected a Fellow of Peterhouse in 1923 and remained there for the rest of his career, rising to become first professor of modern history (1944–63), then master of Peterhouse (1955–68) and Regius Professor of History (1963–68). His thought is explored in Bentley, *Modernizing England's Past*; C. T. McIntire, *Herbert Butterfield: The Historian as Dissenter* (New Haven & London: Yale University Press, 2004); and Keith Sewell, *Herbert Butterfield and the Interpretation of History* (New York: Palgrave, 2005). In 1959 he also became the first chairman of the British Committee on the Theory of International Politics—see Dunne, *Inventing International Society*; as well as Vigezzi, *The British Committee on the Theory of International Politics*; and Adam Watson, *Hegemony and History* (London & New York: Routledge, 2007), 10–13. Butterfield's major writings on international relations are collected in Karl W. Schweizer and Paul Sharp (eds.), *The International Thought of Herbert Butterfield* (New York: Palgrave, 2007).

68. This is the central theme of Butterfield's *The Englishman and His History* (1944).

69. Butterfield, *The Whig Interpretation of History* (New York: Norton, 1965 [1931]), 1.

70. Butterfield, *The Englishman and His History*, vii.

71. Ibid., 9.

72. Ibid., 16.

73. Butterfield, *Christianity and History*, 41.

74. Ibid., 44.

75. Ibid.

76. Ibid., 45–46.

77. Ibid., 47.

78. Ibid.

79. Butterfield, "The Tragic Element in Modern International Conflict," *The Review of Politics* 12:2 (1950), 147–164 (reprinted in *History and Human Relations* [London: Collins, 1951], 9–36); and his "The Scientific versus the Moralistic Approach in International Affairs," *International Affairs* 27 (1951), 411–422.

80. Butterfield, "Tragic Element," in *History and Human Relations*, 10.

81. Ibid., 19.

82. Ibid.

83. Butterfield, "Tragic Element," in *History and Human Relations*, 22.

84. Wight noted that while some teased Butterfield by calling him a "neo-Machiavellian" he was in fact hampered by a "certain sentimentality of outlook." Rather than a realist, Wight thought him an "Inverted Revolutionist" or even a pacifist at heart ("Christianity and Power Politics," Wight MS 39, 23–24).

85. Butterfield, "Tragic Element," in *History and Human Relations*, 31.

86. Butterfield, *Christianity, Diplomacy and War* (London: Wyvern Books 1962 [1953]), 76.

87. Ibid., 78.
88. Ibid., 99.
89. Ibid.
90. Butterfield, "The New Diplomacy and the Historical Diplomacy," in Butterfield and Wight (eds.), *Diplomatic Investigations*, 183.
91. Ibid.
92. See Butterfield, *The Statecraft of Machiavelli* (London: G. Bell & Sons, 1960 [1940]); and his introduction to Machiavelli's *The Prince*, trans W. R. Marriott (London: J. M. Dent & Sons, 1958), v–xi.
93. For Butterfield's views on the "rise of the inductive method," see his *Statecraft of Machiavelli*, 59–86, and for Machiavelli's weakness for deductive thinking, 115.
94. Butterfield, *Statecraft of Machiavelli*, 129.
95. Butterfield, "The Tragic Element," in *History and Human Relations*, 30.
96. Ibid.
97. Ibid., 28.
98. Ibid., 28–29.
99. Butterfield, *International Conflict in the Twentieth Century* (London: Routledge & Kegan Paul, 1960), 119.
100. Martin Wight, handwritten note from British Committee meeting, 15 April 1961, Papers of the British Committee on the Theory of International Politics, box 5.
101. Butterfield, undated notes, probably from 1965, Butterfield MS 109/3.
102. Butterfield, untitled paper given at Villa Serbelloni, Bellagio, 1–7 April 1968, Butterfield MS 109/2, n.p.
103. Wight, *Power Politics*, 1st ed., 63–64.
104. Martin Wight, "The Whig Tradition in International Theory and Western Values," British Committee paper delivered on 7 October 1961, Butterfield MS 337.
105. Only a few scholars have noted the "whig" connection to Wight's international theory. A rare exception is Daniel Edward Young, whose "Martin Wight: Politics in the Era of Leviathan," in Eric Petterson (ed.), *The Christian Realists: Reassessing the Contribution of Niebuhr and His Contemporaries* (Lanham, MD: University Press of America), treats Wight as a "whig realist."
106. Wight, *Power Politics*, 1st ed., 65.
107. Ibid.. The implication is evident in Wight's naming of William Gladstone and Franklin D. Roosevelt as exemplars of this tradition.
108. Wight, "The Balance of Power," in Arnold Toynbee and F. T. Ashton-Gwatkin (eds.), *Survey of International Affairs: The World in March 1939* (London: Oxford University Press, 1952), 508–531. This essay casts Britain and France as the "two senior nation-states of Western Christendom" and Russia and Germany as having "lacked or rejected the traditions of Western Civilization" (510).
109. Wight, "Western Values," 89.
110. Ibid., 90.

111. Wight, "The Balance of Power," 516.

112. Dan Young has rightly questioned whether Wight ever used the term "Grotian" or whether it was a later interpolation by his followers: Young, "Escape from Machiavellianism? Thomist Themes in Twentieth Century Political Realism," *Politics and Religion* 4 (2011), 526–549. Wight did use the term in the lectures recently published as *Four Seminal Thinkers*.

113. Wight, *International Theory*.

114. See Hall, *International Thought of Martin Wight*, 133–156.

115. This is not to say that it has not led to some significant studies. See especially Hedley Bull, Benedict Kingsbury, and Adam Roberts (eds.), *Hugo Grotius and International Relations*, new edition (Oxford: Clarendon, 1992); Edward Keene, *Beyond the Anarchical Society: Grotius, Colonialism and Order in World Politics* (Cambridge: Cambridge University Press, 2002); and Renée Jeffery, *Hugo Grotius in International Thought* (New York: Palgrave, 2006).

116. Not everyone has missed this connection. See especially Callahan, "Nationalising International Society."

117. Wight, "Western Values," 90.

118. Ibid.

119. Ibid., 90–91.

120. Ibid., 91.

121. Wight, *Power Politics*, 1st ed., 65; *International Theory*, 123–124, 243; "Western Values," 91, 111.

122. Barry Buzan, *From International to World Society? English School Theory and the Social Structure of Globalization* (Cambridge: Cambridge University Press, 2004), 167–176.

123. Wight, "The Power Struggle within the United Nations," *Proceedings of the Institute of World Affairs*, 33rd session (Los Angeles: University of Southern California, 1956), 258–259. See also Wight's less forthright comments on the UN in *International Theory*, 144.

124. Wight, "An Anatomy of International Thought," *Review of International Studies* 13 (1987), 223; Hall, *International Thought of Martin Wight*, 123–126.

125. Wight, "Western Values," 96–97.

126. See Hall, *International Thought of Martin Wight*, 147–151.

127. See, for instance, the approach taken by Tim Dunne, Milja Kurki, and Steve Smith in their edited *International Relations Theories: Discipline and Diversity* (Oxford: Oxford University Press, 2007), which treats each theory—from "classical realism" to "green theory"—discretely and in turn.

128. See Wight, *International Theory*, especially chapters 7–9 (on diplomacy), 10 (on war) and 11 (on international law, obligation, and ethics).

129. Wight, "Western Values," 98, 93.

130. Ibid., 103–104.

131. Ibid., 107.

132. Wight, *International Theory*, 180–188.

133. Ibid., 206–207.

134. Ibid., 233–244.
135. Adam Watson, *Diplomacy: The Dialogue between States* (London: Eyre Methuen, 1982), 20.
136. Report for Cambridge University Press contained in David to Butterfield, 11 August 1965, Wight MS 248.
137. *International Affairs* 43:1 (1967), 125–127; Hans J. Morgenthau, review of *Diplomatic Investigations*, *Political Science Quarterly* 82:3 (1967), 461–463. Morgenthau called it a "healthy corrective to present academic priorities" (463). The book went unreviewed in *International Relations, Political Quarterly, Political Studies*, and *Government and Opposition*.
138. Frank Spencer, untitled review of *Diplomatic Investigations*, *History* 54:180 (1969), 156–157.
139. See Bull, *Anarchical Society*, especially 3–50.
140. See Watson, *Diplomacy*, as well as Hedley Bull and Adam Watson (eds.), *The Expansion of International Society* (Oxford: Clarendon, 1984); and Adam Watson, *The Evolution of International Society: A Comparative Historical Analysis* (London & New York: Routledge, 1992).
141. See especially Adam Watson, *The Limits of Independence: Relations between States in the Modern World* (London & New York: Routledge, 1997).

CHAPTER 7

EPIGRAPH: John Le Carré, *Tinker Tailor Soldier Spy* (London: Sceptre, 1999 [1974]), 370.

1. A. J. P. Taylor, *The Troublemakers: Dissent over Foreign Policy, 1792–1939* (Harmondsworth: Pelican, 1985 [1957]), 9.
2. Whether Taylor was as radical as he claimed is the subject of much dispute. Chris Wrigley has put the case for the defense in his *A. J. P. Taylor: Radical Historian of Europe* (London & New York: I. B. Tauris, 2006), while the prosecution's case is presented in Stefan Collini, *Absent Minds: Intellectuals in Britain* (Oxford: Oxford University Press, 2006), 375–392.
3. Taylor, *Troublemakers*, 13.
4. On Liberal Radicalism in the late nineteenth century, see especially Peter Cain, "Radicalism, Gladstone and the Liberal Critique of Disraelian 'Imperialism'," in Duncan Bell (ed.), *Victorian Visions of Global Order: Empire and International Relations in Nineteenth-Century Political Thought* (Cambridge: Cambridge University Press, 2007), 215–238.
5. Alan Bullock and F. W. Deakin, general preface to S. Macoby (ed.), *The English Radical Tradition, 1763–1914* (London: Adam & Charles Black, 1966 [1952]), vii.
6. See Wight, *International Theory*, especially 8–12.
7. Stephen Walt, "International Relations: One World, Many Theories," *Foreign Policy* 110 (1998), 29–46; Ole Wæver, "The Rise and Fall of the Inter-Paradigm Debate," in Ken Booth, Steve Smith, and Marysia Zalewski (eds.),

International Theory: Positivism and Beyond (Cambridge: Cambridge University Press, 1996), 149–185.

8. See John G. Gunnell, "The Myth of the Tradition," *American Political Science Review* 72:1 (1978), 122–134.

9. See Philip Bounds, "Orwell and Englishness: The Dialogue with British Marxism," *Cultural Logic: Marxist Theory and Practice* (2007), 6, online at http://clogic.eserver.org/2007/Bounds.pdf (accessed 6 April 2009). For a flavor of communist writing on English radicalism, see Christopher Hill, *The English Revolution, 1640* (London: Lawrence & Wishart, 1940); and Harvey J. Kaye, *The British Marxist Historians: An Introductory Analysis*, new edition (Houndmills: Palgrave Macmillan, 1995 [1984]).

10. Burk, *Troublemaker*, 298. See also Wrigley, *A.J.P. Taylor*, 253–257.

11. Taylor, *Troublemakers*, 12.

12. Ibid., 13.

13. Ibid.

14. Thomas Paine, "Common Sense," in his *Rights of Man, Common Sense and Other Political Writings*, ed. Mark Philip (Oxford: Oxford University Press, 2008), 14.

15. See Mark Bevir, "Republicanism, Socialism, and Democracy in Britain: The Origins of the Radical Left," *Journal of Social History* 34:2 (2000), 351–368.

16. For an authoritative account of Bentham's notion of "sinister interests," see Philip Schofield, *Utility and Democracy: The Political Thought of Jeremy Bentham* (Oxford: Oxford University Press, 2006). On radical hostility to "special interests" more generally, see Samuel H. Beer, *Modern British Politics: A Study of Parties and Pressure Groups*, 2nd ed. (London: Faber & Faber, 1969), 40.

17. Paine, "Common Sense," 5.

18. Paine held this view, but it is not shared by all radicals. See T. C. Walker, "The Forgotten Prophet: Tom Paine's Cosmopolitanism and International Relations," *International Studies Quarterly* 44 (2000), 51–72.

19. Beer, *Modern British Politics*, 41.

20. Leon Trotsky, *My Life: An Attempt at an Autobiography* (New York: C. Scribner's Sons, 1930), 341.

21. Gordon K. Lewis, "America and the New British Radicalism," *Western Political Quarterly* 6:1 (1953), 11.

22. Ibid., 11.

23. Ibid., 1.

24. Ibid., 9.

25. Taylor, *Troublemakers*, 189.

26. Ibid., 197.

27. Ibid., 178.

28. J.M. Keynes, *The Economic Consequences of the Peace* (London: Macmillan, 1919).

29. Taylor, *Troublemakers*, 197.

30. Ibid., 197–198.

31. On Laski's changing views of Marx, see Peter Lamb, *Harold Laski: Problems of Democracy, the Sovereign State, and International Society* (New York: Palgrave, 2004), especially 27–38; and on Carr and Marx, see Jones, *E.H. Carr and International Relations*, 58–59, as well as Haslam, *Vices of Integrity*, 52–54.

32. Ernest Barker provided the most succinct expression of this position in "The Discredited State," *Political Quarterly* 5 (1915), 101–121, written prior to the outbreak of war, in May 1914. See also David Runciman, *Pluralism and the Personality of the State* (Cambridge: Cambridge University Press, 1997).

33. Runciman, *Pluralism and the Personality of the State*, 158.

34. Laski, *Studies in the Problem of Sovereignty* (New Haven: Yale University Press, 1917). See also Jeanne Morefield, "States Are Not People: Harold Laski on Unsettling Sovereignty, Rediscovering Democracy," *Political Research Quarterly* 58:4 (2005), 659–669.

35. It also satisfied his belief that "[a] new political philosophy is necessary to a new world" (*A Grammar of Politics*, 3rd ed. [London: George Allen & Unwin, 1934], 15).

36. Laski, "Nationalism and the Future of Civilization" (1932), in his *The Danger of Being a Gentleman and Other Essays* (London: George Allen & Unwin, 1939), 190.

37. Ibid., 191.

38. Ibid. See also Laski's account of the "The State and the International Community" in his *An Introduction to Politics* (London: George Allen & Unwin, 1931), 92–107.

39. Laski, "Nationalism and the Future of Civilization," 218.

40. Ibid., 225.

41. Russell, *Power*, 184.

42. Ibid., 186.

43. Ibid., 196.

44. Ibid., 201.

45. Ibid., 202–204.

46. Ibid., 202.

47. Ibid., 206.

48. The distinctly unradical Hugh Seton-Watson, for example, was also an admirer of Carr's *Twenty Years' Crisis* (see Seton-Watson, *Neither War nor Peace*, 11). On the breadth of Carr's appeal, see Peter Wilson, "Radicalism for a Conservative Purpose: The Peculiar Realism of E.H. Carr," *Millennium: Journal of International Studies* 20:1 (2001), 123–136.

49. See Hans J. Morgenthau, "The Political Science of E.H. Carr," *World Politics* 1:1 (1948), 127–134; and W.T.R. Fox, "E.H. Carr and Political Realism: Vision and Revision," *Review of International Studies* 11:1 (1985), 1–16.

50. See also Carr's comment in *The Soviet Impact on the Western World*: "The view that 'ideals' are a cloak for 'interests' is Marxist, though by no means exclusively Marxist. In some measure it is obviously well founded,

and nowhere has it probably been truer than in the conduct of international relations" (Carr, *The Soviet Impact on the Western World* [London: Macmillan & Col, 1946], 80).

51. Carr, *Twenty Years' Crisis*, 1st ed., 187. See also Carr's remarks about how the "post-War Utopia became the tool of vested interests" (289).

52. Ibid., 215.

53. Morgenthau, "Political Science of E. H. Carr," 130.

54. "Few people are yet willing," Carr observed, "to recognise that the conflict between nations like the conflict between classes cannot be resolved without real sacrifices, involving in all probability a substantial reduction in consumption by privileged groups and in privileged countries. . . . Ultimately the best hope of progress towards international reconciliation seems to lie along the path of economic reconstruction" (*Twenty Years' Crisis*, 1st ed., 304).

55. Ibid., 306.

56. This is a vexed issue. For one sympathetic appraisal of Carr's position on this topic, see R. W. Davies, "Carr's Changing Views of the Soviet Union," in Cox (ed.), *E. H. Carr*, 91–108.

57. Carr, *Soviet Impact*, 3–4. Carr's rose-tinted view of the popularity of communist governments in Eastern Europe was matched by his sympathetic appraisal of Soviet government: "The broad lines of Soviet policy may be dictated from the centre. But the Soviet Union has never ignored the human element, or underestimated the extent to which the execution of any given policy depends on the enthusiasm and initiative of the individual citizen" (19).

58. Ibid., 7–9.

59. Ibid., 17–18.

60. Carr's *Twenty Years' Crisis* ends with an appeal for a "new international order" based on what he calls "economic reconstruction"—planning intended to subordinate "economic advantage to social ends" (302–307).

61. Carr, *Soviet Impact*, 20.

62. Ibid., 43.

63. On the strengths of Marxist thought, see Carr, *Soviet Impact*, 88.

64. Ibid., 114.

65. Anthony Hartley, *A State of England* (London: Hutchinson, 1963), 47–48.

66. See, for example, George Orwell's notorious argument that pacifism was "objectively pro-Fascist" ("London Letter," March–April 1942, in Sonia Orwell and Ian Angus [eds.], *The Collected Essays, Journalism and Letters of George Orwell, II: My Country Right or Left, 1940–43* [London: Secker & Warburg, 1968], 182). The number of conscientious objectors (COs) during the Second World War reached 62,301—a high figure in comparison to the American total of around 37,000. Between 1948 and 1957, between 600 and 700 registered as COs in accordance with the National Service Act. See Edward R. Cain, "Conscientious Objection in France, Britain, and the United States," *Comparative Politics* 2:2 (1970), 289.

67. Edward Shils, "British Intellectuals in the Mid-Twentieth Century," in

his *The Intellectuals and the Powers and Other Essays* (Chicago: University of Chicago Press, 1972), 137. The article was first published in *Encounter* in April 1955.

68. Ibid., 137.
69. Ibid., 138.
70. Hartley, *State of England*, 47–48.
71. For a broad survey of radical anti-imperialism, see Bernard Porter, *Critics of Empire: British Radicals and the Imperial Challenge* (London & New York: I. B. Tauris, 2008 [1968]).
72. For a survey of Labour's postwar foreign policy, see Vickers, *The Labour Party and the World*, vol. 1, 159–191.
73. Lamb, *Harold Laski*, 12.
74. For an account that emphasized both of these points, see John Saville, *The Politics of Continuity: British Foreign Policy and the Labour Government, 1945–51* (London: Verso, 1993).
75. Denis Healey, "Power Politics and the Labour Party," 179.
76. E. J. Hobsbawm, "The British Communist Party," *Political Quarterly* 25:1 (1954), 39.
77. Ibid.
78. The overall weakness of communism in postwar Britain is made clear in Neal Wood, "The Empirical Proletarians: A Note on British Communism," *Political Science Quarterly* 74:2 (1959), 259–260.
79. Unusually for European communist parties, the CPGB was dominated by working-class leaders rather than intellectuals. See Wood, "Empirical Proletarians," 268.
80. Bernal was Irish by birth but was educated at Stonyhurst, Bedford College, and then Emmanuel College, Cambridge. He was professor of physics at Birkbeck College, University of London, from 1937. He left the CPGB sometime in the 1930s but remained consistently pro-Soviet and was awarded the Lenin Peace Prize in 1953. He was the author of a number of works on international relations, including *World without War* (London: Routledge and Kegan Paul, 1958).
81. Haldane was educated at Eton and New College, Oxford. After four years as a fellow of New College, he moved to Trinity College, Cambridge, and then to University College London. He joined the CPGB in 1942 and left in 1950. He remained, however, a communist and critic of British foreign policy and the West.
82. Dobb was an historian and economist. He was educated at Pembroke College, Cambridge, and taught briefly at the LSE before returning to his old college and then Trinity College, where he remained for the rest of his career.
83. Hill was educated at Balliol College, Oxford, and was later master of Balliol. His books include *The Intellectual Origins of the English Revolution* (Oxford: Clarenden, 1965).
84. Hobsbawm was educated in Berlin and London, and at King's College, Cambridge. He wrote his Ph.D. thesis on the Fabians, was a member

of the rarefied Cambridge intellectual club, the Apostles, and after war service taught at Birkbeck College London for most of his academic life. His works include a four-part history of Europe, comprising *The Age of Revolution* (1962), *The Age of Capital* (1975), *The Age of Empire* (1987), and *The Age of Extremes* (1994). On his life, see Eric Hobsbawm, *Interesting Times: A Twentieth-Century Life* (London: Pantheon Books, 2003).

85. Kiernan was educated at Manchester Grammar School and Trinity College, Cambridge. He taught at Edinburgh until his retirement in 1977. His best-known work is *The Lords of Human Kind: European Attitudes towards the Outside World in the Imperial Age* (London: Weidenfeld and Nicolson, 1969).

86. Thompson was educated in Oxford and at Corpus Christi College, Cambridge. He was the author of *The Making of the English Working Class* (London: Victor Gollancz, 1963).

87. For a contemporary assessment from a sympathetic critic, see Herbert Butterfield, "Marxist History," in *History and Human Relations*, 66–100. The essay was first published in *Scrutiny* in 1933 under the title "History and the Marxian Method."

88. On this group, see Kaye, *British Marxist Historians*, as well as Christopher Parker, *The English Historical Tradition since 1850* (Edinburgh: John Donald, 1990), 177–201.

89. The impact on history was more dramatic and broad. British historiography was revolutionized under Marxist influence in the 1950s and especially the 1960s, leading to the near-complete displacement of political and diplomatic history and their replacement by social and economic history through vehicles such as the journal *Past and Present* (1952–).

90. See especially Cole's *What Marx Really Meant* (Westport, CT: Greenwood, 1970 [1934]). Cole was educated at St Paul's School, Oxford, and Balliol College, Oxford. He became a fellow of University College, Oxford, in 1925 and the first Chichele Professor of Social and Political Theory in 1944.

91. See Vickers, *Labour Party and the World*, vol. I, 169–173.

92. Crossman, Foot, and Mikardo, *Keep Left*.

93. Kenneth O. Morgan, *Michael Foot: A Life* (London: HarperCollins, 2007), 122–123. Morgan notes that "Foot's viewpoint" on international affairs was "an amalgam of socialism, patriotism and anti-militarism."

94. The arguments of Keep Left were also the subject of rebuttals from Denis Healey, acting at Bevin's behest, not least in the Labour pamphlet *Cards on the Table* (London: Labour Party, 1947). For context, see Vickers, *Labour Party and the World*, vol. I, 180–181.

95. Morgan has described this book as "really a series of personal statements on behalf of a libertarian form of democratic socialism and tackling global poverty. Full of beguiling phrases, they hardly offered any ideological structure firm enough for his principles to embrace" (*Michael Foot*, 162).

96. Aneurin Bevan, *In Place of Fear* (London: Hutchinson, 1952), 122. Bevan came from a nonconformist mining background in South Wales. He

came to prominence as a trade union leader during the 1926 general strike and became MP for Ebbw Vale in 1931.

97. Ibid., 124–125.

98. Ibid., 126 (on "American Big Business") and 128 (on "The right of military chiefs to conduct political propaganda . . . ").

99. Ibid., 142, 144.

100. Brian Magee, *The New Radicalism* (New York: St Martin's Press, 1963 [1962]), 108.

101. See, for example, Hartley's *State of England*.

102. For a contemporary discussion, see F. S. Northedge, *British Foreign Policy: The Process of Readjustment, 1945–1961* (London: George Allen & Unwin, 1962), 239–240.

103. See, for example, Richard Cobden's objections, expressed in 1836, to "standing armaments by land and sea" in his *Political Writings*, quoted in Chris Brown, Terry Nardin, and Nicholas Rengger (eds.), *International Relations in Political Thought: Texts from the Ancient Greeks to the First World War* (Cambridge: Cambridge University Press, 2002), 539.

104. See Philip Noel-Baker, *Disarmament* (London: The Hogarth Press, 1926); as well as his *The Arms Race* (London: John Calder, 1958), which won its author the 1959 Nobel Peace Prize.

105. Raymond Williams, "The British Left," *New Left Review* I/30 (1965), 25.

106. See David Cortright, *Peace: A History of Movements and Ideas* (Cambridge: Cambridge University Press, 2008), especially 126–154.

107. See McIntire, *Herbert Butterfield*, 346.

108. See Russell, *The Basic Writings of Bertrand Russell* (London & New York: Routledge, 2006 [1961]), 726–728; and Butterfield, *International Conflict in the Twentieth Century*, especially 88–98.

109. Butterfield was invited in 1961 to be president of the Cambridge University branch of CND. He refused on the grounds that "though all movements in favour of nuclear disarmament have my sympathy, I don't personally feel that the thing ought to be the subject of campaigns and pressure groups" (Butterfield to Southall, 30 November 1960, Butterfield MS, 425).

110. On the founding of CND, see Cortright, *Peace*, 134–135.

111. A. J. P. Taylor, *A Personal History* (London: Hamish Hamilton, 1984), 290.

112. Ibid., 291–292.

113. For a detailed analysis of the rise of CND, see Henry J. Steck, "The Re-Emergence of Ideological Politics in Great Britain: The Campaign for Nuclear Disarmament," *Western Political Quarterly* 18:1 (1965), 87–103.

114. John Rex and Peter Worsley, "Campaign for a Foreign Policy," *New Left Review* 4 (1960), 49–53, emphasis in original.

115. Anderson was educated at Eton and Worcester College, Oxford. He twice served as editor of the *New Left Review*, between 1962 and 1982, and again from 2000 to 2003.

116. Nairn was educated at Dunfermline High School, Edinburgh College

of Art, and Edinburgh University. He taught at various colleges and universities, and joined the *New Left Review* in 1962.

117. Thompson was educated at Kingswood School, Bath, and Corpus Christi, Cambridge, and subsequently taught at Warwick University, from which he resigned in 1971.

118. Williams was educated at Grammar School in Abergavenny and Trinity College, Cambridge. He served in the Army in the Second World War but registered as a Conscientious Objector when called up for the Korean War. He taught in adult education in Oxford and returned to Cambridge in 1961 to take a chair in modern drama. He retired in 1983.

119. Worsley was educated at Wallasey Grammar School and Emmanuel College, Cambridge, where he read first literature, and then, after a period of war service, social anthropology. He was the first professor of sociology at Manchester. See his *An Academic Skating on Thin Ice* (Oxford & New York: Berghahn, 2008).

120. Williams, "The British Left," 26.

121. For a survey of the origins of the New Left, see Michael Kenny, *The First New Left: British Intellectuals after Stalin* (London: Lawrence & Wishart, 1995).

122. Prior to 1956, it was possible to argue in favor of an ordinary diplomatic relationship with Russia; after, it was far more difficult. See, for example, Kingsley Martin, "Britain and Russia," *Political Quarterly* 17:1 (1946), 38–48.

123. Kenny, *The First New Left*, 19.

124. Perry Anderson, "The Left in the Fifties," *New Left Review* I/29 (1965), 3–18.

125. Perry Anderson, "Origins of the Present Crisis," *New Left Review* I/23 (1964), 47. For Anderson's debt to Gramsci, see the discussion on page 39.

126. For a contemporary survey, see A. P. Thornton, *The Imperial Idea and Its Enemies: A Study in British Power* (London: Macmillan, 1966); as well as Porter, *Critics of Empire*.

127. Lenin, *Imperialism: The Highest Stage of Capitalism*, online at http://www.marxists.org/archive/lenin/works/1916/imp-hsc/ (accessed 16 October 2009).

128. Michael Barrett Brown, "Imperialism Yesterday and Tomorrow," *New Left Review* I/5 (1960), 45.

129. Ibid., 48.

130. Tom Nairn, "Labour Imperialism," *New Left Review* I/32 (1965), 3–15.

131. See Peter Worsley, *The Third World* (London: Weidenfeld & Nicolson, 1964), 14.

132. Ibid., 14–15.

133. See Colin Crouch, *The Student Revolt* (London: Bodley Head, 1970).

134. Gareth Stedman Jones, "The Meaning of the Student Revolt," in Alexander Cockburn and Robin Blackburn (eds.), *Student Power: Problems, Diagnosis, Action* (Harmondsworth: Penguin, 1969), 37. Stedman Jones (1942–)

was educated at St Paul's School, Oxford, and St John's and Nuffield Colleges, Oxford. He has taught at Cambridge since 1974 and is presently professor of political science.

135. Shils, "British Intellectuals," 142.

136. Bob Rowthorn, "Imperialism in the Seventies—Unity or Rivalry?," *New Left Review* I/69 (1971), 31. See also Gareth Stedman Jones, "The Specificity of US Imperialism," *New Left Review* I/60 (1970), 59–86.

137. Stedman Jones, "The Meaning of the Student Revolt," 38.

138. Ibid., 38. See also the manifesto of the Trotskyite "Revolutionary Socialist Students' Federation" (RSSF), which committed the group "on principle" to "all anti-imperialist, anti-capitalist and anti-fascist struggles."

139. Roy E. Jones, *The Functional Analysis of Politics: An Introductory Discussion* (London & New York: Routledge & Kegan Paul, 1967), 10.

140. There were, of course, academics and intellectuals who were part of such a complex, but they tended to be economists, operational researchers, engineers, and scientists, not specialists in international relations. See David Edgerton, *Warfare State: Britain, 1920–1970* (Cambridge: Cambridge University Press, 2006).

141. Michael Nicholson, "The Continued Significance of Positivism," in Booth et al., *International Theory*, 130.

142. Michael Banks, "Two Meanings of Theory in Study of International Relations," *Year Book of World Affairs* 20 (1966), 220.

143. Ibid., 223.

144. Ibid., 235.

145. Banks cited Nicholson's article on Richardson, "A Meteorology of War and Peace," *The Listener*, 18 November 1965. Nicholson's "Tariff Wars and a Model of Conflict" appeared after Banks' piece (*Journal of Peace Research* 4:1 [1967], 26–38), as did his "Mathematical Models in the Study of International Relations," *Year Book of World Affairs* 22 (1968), 47–63.

146. John W. Burton, *International Relations: A General Theory* (Cambridge: Cambridge University Press, 1965).

147. See Jones's *Functional Analysis of Politics* and his *Principles of Foreign Policy: The Civil State in Its World Setting* (New York: St Martin's Press, 1979).

148. Michael Nicholson, "The Enigma of Martin Wight," *Review of International Studies* 7 (1981), 20.

149. Taylor, *Troublemakers*, 17.

150. Michael Banks, "The Evolution of International Relations Theory," in his edited *Conflict in World Society: A New Perspective on International Relations* (New York: St Martin's Press, 1984), 17.

CHAPTER 8

EPIGRAPH: Anthony Sampson, *Anatomy of Britain* (London: Hodder & Stoughton, 1962), 620.

1. See Hall, "The 'Toynbee Convector.'"

2. Margery Perham, *The Colonial Reckoning: The End of Imperial Rule in Africa in the Light of British Experience* (New York: Alfred P. Knopf, 1962), 15.

3. For a discussion of this point, see Ian Hall, "The Imperial Paradox in Liberal International Theory," *Journal of International Political Theory* 4:1 (2008), 146–156.

4. For Mill's views on empire, see Jennifer Pitts, *A Turn to Empire: The Rise of Imperial Liberalism in Britain and France* (Princeton, NJ, & Oxford: Princeton University Press, 2005), 133–162; and for Murray's, see Morefield, *Covenants without Swords*.

5. On this point, see especially Bell, *Idea of Greater Britain*.

6. Geoffrey Barraclough, *An Introduction to Contemporary History* (Harmondsworth: Penguin, 1988 [1964]), 154.

7. Gilbert Murray, untitled address to the annual general meeting of the United Nations Association, 16 September 1952, Murray MS 372/45–46.

8. Murray to Russell, 16 September 1955, Murray MS 166/143.

9. Murray to Russell, 1 January 1957, Murray MS 166/157.

10. Perham (1895–1982) was educated at St Hugh's College, Oxford, where she took a First in Modern History. She taught briefly at Sheffield, then traveled to Africa in 1920, where her sister lived, returning four years later to teach history and philosophy, politics, and economics (PPE) at St Hugh's. In 1928 she set out again for Africa, resigning her teaching post at St Hugh's in 1930, but remaining a non-stipendiary fellow. In 1935 she became a research lecturer (later reader) in colonial administration at Oxford, and was appointed to the first official fellowship of the new Nuffield College in 1939. She left Oxford in 1948, but continued to advise Arthur Creech-Jones, the Labour colonial secretary in the Attlee governments. For a full account, see Patricia M. Pugh, "Perham, Dame Margery Freda (1895–1982)," *Oxford Dictionary of National Biography*, online.

11. Perham, *Colonial Reckoning*, 43.

12. Ibid., 21 (on critics of colonialism) and 200–201 (on hopes for the future).

13. Ibid., 43, 203.

14. C.E. Carrington, *The British Overseas: Exploits of a Nation of Shopkeepers*, vol. 1: *Making of the Empire*, 2nd ed. (Cambridge: Cambridge University Press, 1968 [1950]). The second volume, which would have addressed decolonization, was never published.

15. C.E. Carrington, "A New Theory of the Commonwealth," *International Affairs* 31:2 (1955), 138.

16. C.E. Carrington, "Between the Commonwealth and Europe," *International Affairs* 38:4 (1962), 449–459.

17. C.E. Carrington, *The Liquidation of the British Empire* (Toronto & Vancouver: Clarke, Unwin & Company, 1962), 11. Churchill had declared: "I have not become the King's First Minister in order to preside over the liquidation of the British Empire." On the "vogue-word" *liquidation* and its relation to totalitarian practices of government, see 13.

18. Ibid., 13.
19. Ibid., 21–22.
20. For Murray's refutation, see "Self-Determination of Nationalities," *Journal of the British Institute of International Affairs* 1:1 (1922), 6–13.
21. Carrington, *The Liquidation of the British Empire*, 23.
22. Ibid., 23.
23. Ibid., 26.
24. Ibid., 39.
25. Ibid., 21, 87.
26. Seton-Watson was the son of the historian R. W. Seton-Watson and was educated at Winchester and New College, Oxford, where he read classics and PPE. He served in the Special Operations Executive (SOE) during the Second World War, became a fellow of University College, Oxford, afterward, and then became professor of Russian history at the School of Slavonic and East European Studies, University of London, in 1951. See also D. Obolensky, "George Hugh Nicholas Seton-Watson," *Proceedings of the British Academy* 73 (1987), 631–642.
27. Hugh Seton-Watson, *Neither War nor Peace: The Struggle for Power in the Postwar World* (London: Methuen, 1960), 269.
28. Ibid., 269.
29. Martin Wight praised the book's "level gaze at the struggle for power" and Seton-Watson's "knowledge that a victory for justice and freedom is not guaranteed by history." Review of *Neither War nor Peace*, *International Affairs* 36:4 (1960), 495–496.
30. Seton-Watson, *Neither War nor Peace*, 269.
31. Ibid., 270.
32. Ibid., 461–462.
33. Ibid., 459.
34. Richard Crossman, *Government and the Governed: A History of Political Ideas and Political Practice* (London: Chatto & Windus, 1969), 338.
35. The phrase "revolt against the West" is often associated with Hedley Bull, who used it in a late essay ("The Revolt against the West," in Bull and Watson [eds.], *Expansion of International Society*), but it was common in the 1960s. See, for example, Barraclough's *Introduction to Contemporary History* (1964), chapter 6.
36. Butterfield, *International Conflict in the Twentieth Century*, 28.
37. Ibid., 29.
38. Ibid., 31.
39. Ibid., 104.
40. For a lengthier discussion of Wight's views on the "crisis of modern politics," see Hall, *International Thought of Martin Wight*, 65–86.
41. W. Arthur Lewis, Michael Scott, Martin Wight, and Colin Legum, *Attitude to Africa* (Harmondsworth: Penguin, 1951), 36, 39.
42. Wight, "The United Nations," undated lecture notes, probably 1956, Wight MS 119, 96–97.

43. Wight, "Power Struggle," 248.
44. Ibid., 249–250.
45. Ibid., 250.
46. Wight, "Is the Commonwealth a Non-Hobbesian Institution?," *Journal of Commonwealth and Comparative Politics* 16:2 (1978), 123.
47. Ibid., 133.
48. Ibid.
49. Wight, "Brutus in Foreign Policy: The Memoirs of Sir Anthony Eden," *International Affairs* 36:3 (1960), 308.
50. Ibid., 307–308.
51. Ibid., 308.
52. Ibid., 309.
53. Ibid., 308–309.
54. Wight, "International Legitimacy," in his *Systems of States*, 163.
55. Ibid., 165–168. On Wight's religious views, see Hall, *International Thought of Martin Wight*, 21–42.
56. Wight, "International Legitimacy," 172.
57. Bull, "What is the Commonwealth?," *World Politics* 11:4 (1959), 579.
58. Ibid., 582.
59. Ibid., 585–586.
60. Bull, "Society and Anarchy in International Relations," in Butterfield and Wight (eds.), *Diplomatic Investigations*, 50. On this point, see also Tim Dunne and Nicholas Wheeler, "Hedley Bull's Pluralism of the Intellect and Solidarism of the Will," *International Affairs* 72:1 (1996), 91–107.
61. Hedley Bull, "The State's Positive Role in World Affairs," *Daedalus* 108:4 (1977), 111–123; reprinted in Alderson and Hurrell (eds.), *Hedley Bull on International Society*, 139–157.
62. Adam Watson, *Hegemony and History* (London & New York: Routledge, 2007), 37.
63. Bull, *Anarchical Society*, 90–94.
64. Ibid., 149.
65. Ibid., 290–305.
66. Ibid., 303, 308. See also the discussion about "haves" and "have-nots" in the contemporary world in Bull, "*The Twenty Years' Crisis* Thirty Years On," in Alderson and Hurrell (eds.), *Hedley Bull on International Society*, especially 134–137.
67. Bull, "State's Positive Role," in Alderson and Hurrell (eds.), *Hedley Bull on International Society*, 154.
68. Ibid.
69. Ibid., 156.
70. Watson was educated at Rugby and King's College, Cambridge, and joined the Diplomatic Service in 1937, serving in the Balkans, Egypt, and the USSR. He was head of the African department at the Foreign Office in 1956–59, and subsequently held a number of ambassadorships, including that to Cuba in 1963–66, whereupon he returned to London to become under-

secretary at the Foreign Office. He resigned in 1968 and subsequently was involved in business and academia.

71. Watson, *Hegemony and History*, 12.

72. Adam Watson, "Problems of Adjustment in the Middle East," *Annals of the American Academy of Political and Social Science* 282 (1952), 62–63.

73. Adam Watson, "The Aftermath of Suez: Consequences for French Decolonization," in Wm. Roger Louis and Roger Owen (eds.), *Suez 1956: The Crisis and Its Consequences* (Oxford: Clarendon, 1989), 344–345.

74. Adam Watson (as "Scipio"), *Emergent Africa* (London: Chatto & Windus, 1965), 61.

75. Ibid., 65.

76. Ibid., 61.

77. Ibid., 62.

78. Ibid., 66.

79. Ibid., 128–129.

80. Ibid., 143.

81. Ibid.

82. Ibid., 145.

83. Ibid., 143.

84. Ibid., 166.

85. Ibid., 175.

86. Watson, *The Nature and Problems of the Third World* (Claremont, CA: Claremont Colleges, 1968), 4, 7.

87. Ibid., 15–16, my emphasis.

88. Ibid., 35.

89. Ibid., 39.

90. Watson, *Hegemony and History*, 5.

91. Watson, *The Limits of Independence: Relations between States in the Modern World* (London & New York: Routledge, 1997), 126.

92. Ibid., 127, 139.

93. Watson, *Hegemony and History*, 19.

94. Worsley, *Third World*, 45.

95. See Carrington's *The British Overseas*, Curtis's *Civitas Dei*, Hancock's *Argument of Empire*, and Mansergh's *The Commonwealth Experience* (London: Weidenfeld & Nicolson, 1969). Mansergh (1910–1991) was born in Ireland, educated at St Columba's College in Dublin, and Pembroke College, Oxford, where he was taught by R. B. McCallum, the author of *Public Opinion and the Last Peace* (London: Oxford University Press, 1944) and other works. Mansergh served as professor of Commonwealth Relations at Chatham House until being elected as the first holder of the Smuts Chair of the History of the British Commonwealth in 1953, a post he held until 1970. He was master of St John's College, Cambridge, from 1969 to 1979.

96. John Gallagher and Ronald Robinson, "The Imperialism of Free Trade," *Economic History Review*, 2nd series, 6:1 (1953), 1–15. For Hobson's view, see his *Imperialism: A Study*, 3rd ed. (London: Allen & Unwin, 1938). For com-

mentaries on Gallagher and Robinson's thesis, see Wm. Roger Louis (ed.), *Imperialism: The Robinson and Gallagher Controversy* (New York: New Viewpoints, 1976); and Wm. Roger Louis, "Robinson and Gallagher and Their Critics," in his *Ends of British Imperialism: The Scramble for Empire, Suez and Decolonization* (London & New York: I. B. Tauris, 2006), 907–954.

97. Gallagher and Robinson, "Imperialism of Free Trade," 1.
98. Ibid., 4–5.
99. Ibid., 5.
100. Ibid., 6.
101. Ibid., 7.
102. Ronald Robinson and John Gallagher, with Alice Denny, *Africa and the Victorians: The Official Mind of Imperialism* (London: Macmillan, 1961)
103. These various criticisms are discussed in Louis, "Robinson and Gallagher and Their Critics," especially 916–921.
104. Strachey was educated at Eton and Magdalen College, Oxford. He worked briefly as a journalist before going into politics, flirted for a while with Oswald Mosley's New Party, but returned to the Labour Party, serving under Attlee. He opposed the CND movement and argued against unilateralism.
105. John Strachey, "Tasks and Achievements of British Labour," in Crossman (ed.), *New Fabian Essays*, 184–185. See also his *The End of Empire* (London: Gollancz, 1959).
106. Strachey, "Tasks and Achievements of British Labour," 210.
107. Michael Barratt Brown, "Imperialism Yesterday and Today," *New Left Review* I/5 (1960), 48.
108. Ibid., 48.
109. For a survey of this movement and its precursors, see Lyon, *Neutralism*, and for a New Left response, see Ian Campbell's review of the book in *New Left Review* I/25 (1964), 94–95.
110. Worsley, *Third World*, 242.
111. Worsley, "Revolution of the Third World," *New Left Review* I/12 (1961), 22.
112. Ibid., 25. See also Worsley, *Third World*, 232–275.
113. Burton, *International Relations*, especially 163–242. For an indication of Burton's change of views on nonalignment, see his suggestion in *World Society* (Cambridge: Cambridge University Press, 1972) that it was more a "useful model and theory" than a practical course of action (96).
114. See Fanon's *The Wretched of the Earth*, trans. Catherine Farringdon (Harmondsworth: Penguin, 1967); and, for a wider discussion, Sebastian Kaempf, "Violence and Victory: Guerrilla Warfare, 'Authentic Self-Affirmation' and the Overthrow of the Colonial State," *Third World Quarterly* 30:1 (2009), 129–146.
115. Stedman Jones, "Meaning of the Student Revolt," 44.
116. Ibid., 44.
117. J.G. Darwin, "The Fear of Falling: British Politics and Imperial De-

cline since 1900," *Transactions of the Royal Historical Society*, fifth series, 36 (1986), 39.

118. Ibid., 42.

CHAPTER 9

EPIGRAPH: E. F. Penrose, "Britain's Place in the Changing Structure of International Relations," in E. F. Penrose, Peter Lyon, and Edith Penrose (eds.), *New Orientations: Essays in International Relations* (London: Frank Cass, 1970), 29.

1. It should be noted that Bull became a British subject in 1965, and although he returned to Canberra to teach at the Australian National University from 1967 to 1977, he remained so until his death in 1985.

2. Burton, *International Relations*, 25.

3. Ibid., 7.

4. Ibid., 12. On the "frontiersmen," see 29.

5. See especially Bernard Brodie, "Strategy as a Science," *World Politics* 1:4 (1949), 467–488.

6. Ibid., 484.

7. See, for example, R. G. Collingwood's contemporary judgment that "[t]he pacifist does nothing to decrease war. On the contrary, he promotes it to the utmost of his power by ensuring . . . that the war-makers will have their reward" (*The New Leviathan, Or Man, Society, Civilization and Barbarism* [Oxford: Clarendon, 1942], 232).

8. Michael Howard, "Military Power and International Order," *International Affairs* 40:3 (1964), 400–401.

9. Fuller was educated at Sandhurst and commissioned into the Oxfordshire Light Infantry. He fought in the Boer War and served in India and then in the First World War. Finishing the war as a colonel, he worked in the War Office promoting his ideas about tank warfare, published *The Reformation of War* (1923), and building his reputation as a strategist. He retired from the Army in 1933 and joined Mosley's British Union of Fascists (BUF), attending Hitler's fiftieth birthday party in 1939. For a full biography, see Brian Holden Reid, "Fuller, John Frederick Charles (1878–1966)," *Oxford Dictionary of National Biography*, online.

10. Liddell Hart was educated at St Paul's and Corpus Christi, Cambridge. He fought in the First World War, but having been concussed and gassed he was judged unfit for further service in 1916. In the early 1920s he was influenced by Fuller's ideas on mechanized mobile warfare, especially by *The Reformation of War*. He was officially retired from the Army in 1927. He became a journalist and writer, famously becoming a noted critic of fashion as well as strategy, and became defense correspondent of *The Times* in 1935, but left in 1939. See Brian Holden Reid, "Hart, Sir Basil Henry Liddell," *Oxford Dictionary of National Biography*, online.

A few others do deserve note, especially C. R. M. F. Cruttwell, author of *The Role of British Strategy in the Great War* (Cambridge: Cambridge University

Press, 1936); as well as his better-known *A History of Peaceful Change in the Modern World* (London: Oxford University Press & RIIA, 1937).

11. See also Azar Gat, *A History of Military Thought: From the Enlightenment to the Cold War* (Oxford: Oxford University Press, 2001), 531–561 (on Fuller) and 643–784 (on Liddell Hart). Liddell Hart continues to be the subject of much criticism. See, for example, John Mearsheimer, *Liddell Hart and the Weight of History* (Ithaca: Cornell University Press, 1988). For a more friendly assessment, see Alex Danchev, *Alchemist of War: The Life of Basil Liddell Hart* (London: Phoenix, 1989).

12. See especially Fuller's *The Reformation of War* (London: Hutchinson, 1923).

13. Gat, *History of Military Thought*, 680. On Liddell Hart's preference for a small "New Model Army" rather than a mass force, see his letter to Kingsley Martin, 9 August 1942, Liddell Hart MS 1/494/64–65.

14. Wilkinson was educated at Owens College, Manchester, and Merton College, Oxford, became a lawyer and then a journalist, and wrote a treatise on *Imperial Defence* (1884) with Sir Charles Dilke. He retired from the Chichele Chair in 1923.

15. Wilkinson was succeeded by Sir Ernest Swinton (1868–1951, holder of the Chichele Chair 1925–1939), educated at various schools, and then commissioned into the royal Engineers.

16. Gibbs was educated at Magdalen College, Oxford, and taught at Merton College until the outbreak of the Second World War. He served in the Guards, but was seconded to the Cabinet Office to write part of the official history of the war, returning to Merton after the war. He was the author of a number of books, including the first volume of the histories of Allied Grand Strategy in the Second World War, *History of the Second World War: Grand Strategy*, vol 1: *Rearmament Policy* (London: HMSO, 1976).

17. Howard, *Captain Professor: A Life in War and Peace* (London: Continuum, 2006), 140.

18. Maurice was educated at St Paul's and Sandhurst, and served in the Boer War and subsequently at the Staff College. He was involved in a significant controversy toward the end of the First World War and left the Army in 1918 to become a journalist and educational administrator. He applied for, but was not given, the Chichele Chair in 1925.

19. Howard, *Captain Professor*, 140–144.

20. Oddly, Howard's substantial contributions to both the study of international relations and strategic studies have latterly been overlooked. He appears only briefly, for instance, in Dunne's *Inventing International Society* and not at all in Barry Buzan and Lene Hansen's *The Evolution of International Security Studies* (Cambridge: Cambridge University Press, 2009).

21. Howard, *Captain Professor*, 148. Wight's contribution was "War and International Politics," *The Listener* 54:1389, 13 October 1955, 584–585.

22. Charles K. Webster and Noble Frankland, *The Strategic Air Offensive against Germany, 1939–1945* (London: HMSO, 1961). Webster was instrumen-

tal in persuading Howard to write his study of the Franco-Prussian war. Howard has described Webster as the "true godfather of War Studies in London" (*Captain Professor*, 145). Frankland (1922–) was the official military historian to the Cabinet Office from 1951 until 1958 and director of the Imperial War Museum from 1960 to 1982.

23. See, for example, Sir Charles Webster, Major General Sir Ian Jacob, and E. A. G. Robinson, *United Kingdom Policy: Foreign, Strategic, Economic* (London: Royal Institute of International Affairs, 1950).

24. Howard, *Captain Professor*, 157–158. The ISS became the "International Institute for Strategic Studies" (IISS) in 1964.

25. Liddell Hart to Buchan, 11 December 1958, Liddell Hart MS 1/123/56. It should be noted that there was significant support, too, within the civil service. Howard recalls that Michael Palliser, then head of the Foreign Office Policy Planning Staff, was instrumental in ensuring good relations between the ISS and Whitehall. It helped, no doubt, that Palliser had been at Wellington with Howard, then Oxford, and that they served together in the Guards.

26. See http://www.rusi.org/history. Accessed 4 November 2009.

27. Butterfield's British Committee was funded in the initial stages by the Rockefeller Foundation, which had previously supported an equivalent American Committee. See Dunne, *Inventing International Society*, 90. For a discussion of the wider context of these funding initiatives, see Emily Hauptmann, "From Opposition to Accommodation: How Rockefeller Foundation Grants Redefined Relations between Political Theory and Social Science in the 1950s," *American Political Science Review* 100:4 (2006), 643–649.

28. Howard, *Captain Professor*, 160.

29. For the story of one such trip, see ibid., 169–175.

30. Butterfield traveled to Columbia University in 1956 at the invitation of Kenneth Thompson, who worked for Dean Rusk, the president of the Rockefeller Foundation (Dunne, *Inventing International Society*, 90–91). Wight visited the US in 1956–57 to lecture at the University of Chicago and attended a meeting of the equivalent American Committee (Hall, *International Thought of Martin Wight*, 9).

31. Alastair Buchan and Philip Windsor, *Arms and Stability in Europe* (New York: Praeger, 1963), ix.

32. On British official views, see Nicholas J. Wheeler, "British Nuclear Weapons and Anglo-American Relations, 1945–56," *International Affairs* 62:1 (1986), 71–86.

33. Esmond Wright, review of John Robinson Beal, *John Foster Dulles: A Biography*, *International Affairs* 33:4 (1957), 526.

34. Rear Admiral Sir Anthony Buzzard, Marshal of the RAF Sir John Slessor, and Richard Lowenthal, "The H-Bomb: Massive Retaliation or Graduated Deterrence," *International Affairs* 32:3 (1956), 148–165. Buzzard"s preference was for "graduated deterrence"—indeed, Howard notes that he was "obsessed" with the idea (*Captain Professor*, 157).

35. Reflective works about the atomic bomb are surprisingly uncommon

in Britain in the second half of the 1940s. Liddell Hart's epilogue to his *The Revolution in Warfare* (London: Faber, 1946), which was finished prior to the dropping of the bombs on Japan, is one exception; E. L. Woodward's pamphlet, *Some Political Consequences of the Atomic Bomb* (London: Geoffrey Cumberledge and Oxford University Press, 1946) is another. P. M. S. Blackett contributed a number of works, including *The Atom and the Charter* (London: Fabian Society, 1946).

36. From 1950 until 1959, to take one prominent outlet for strategic studies as an example, *Foreign Affairs* published half a dozen articles by British contributors on strategic issues, all by practitioners, including politicians (Anthony Eden), former or serving soldiers (Sir John Glubb, Fitzroy Maclean, John Slessor), journalists (Donald MacLachlan), or former civil servants (Sir Ian Jacob). From 1960 until 1975, the balance shifted toward scholars and academics, with Alastair Buchan, Hedley Bull, and Michael Howard all publishing pieces, along with Eden, Jacob, Slessor, Anthon Verrier, and Patrick Gordon Walker.

37. Sir John Slessor, *The Great Deterrent* (London: Cassells, 1957).

38. Philip Noel-Baker, *The Arms Race: A Programme for World Disarmament* (London: Atlantic, 1958), 561.

39. Stephen King-Hall, *Power Politics in a Nuclear Age: A Policy for Britain* (London: Victor Gollancz, 1962).

40. For a representative argument from one of the early architects of the British nuclear disarmament movement, see Wayland Young, *Strategy for Survival: First Steps in Nuclear Disarmament* (Harmondsworth: Penguin, 1959).

41. Bull made appeals to the authority of three realists: Machiavelli, on dirty hands; Hobbes, on international anarchy; and Kissinger, on the problems of verifying a nuclear test ban (see "Disarmament in the International System," *Australian Journal of Politics and History* 5:1 [1959], 50, 49, 44.

42. Bull, "Disarmament in the International System," 42–43. See John Herz, "Idealist Internationalism and the Security Dilemma," *World Politics* 2 (1950), 157–180; and Morgenthau, *Scientific Man versus Power Politics*. Bull's essay was also strongly influenced by the work of his fellow Australian Arthur Lee Burns.

43. Bull, "Disarmament in the International System," 41.

44. Ibid., 47.

45. Robert O'Neill, "Hedley Bull and Arms Control," in Coral Bell and Meredith Thatcher (eds.), *Remembering Hedley* (Canberra: Canberra Papers on Strategy and Defence 170, 2008), 33. O'Neill notes that the Rockefeller fellowship was arranged by Manning, who was "horrified at the prospect of losing Bull for two years" of military service.

46. Robert Ayson, "'A Common Interest in Common Interest': Hedley Bull, Thomas Schelling and Collaboration in International Politics," in Bell and Thatcher (eds.), *Remembering Hedley*, 62.

47. Thomas C. Schelling, review of Hedley Bull, *Control of the Arms Race, Survival* 3:4 (1961), 195–196.

48. Bull, "International Theory: The Case for a Classical Approach," 368. On this point, see also Bull's claim that Schelling's "exercises in game theory serve only to illustrate points that are independently arrived at . . . [not] to determine solutions to strategic problems" ("Strategic Studies and Its Critics," *World Politics* 20:4 [1968], 601–602).

49. Bull, "International Theory: The Case for a Classical Approach," 368.

50. Herman Kahn, *Thinking about the Unthinkable* (New York: Horizon, 1971 [1962]).

51. Bull, "Strategic Studies and Its Critics," 596–567. Howard entertained similar thoughts—see his *Captain Professor*, 173–174.

52. Hedley Bull, *The Control of the Arms Race: Disarmament and Arms Control in the Missile Age*, 2nd ed. (New York: Frederick A. Praeger, 1965), 20–21.

53. On Bull and Anderson, see Renée Jeffery, "Australian Realism and International Relations: John Anderson and Hedley Bull on Ethics, Religion and Society," *International Politics* 45:1 (2008), 52–71.

54. Bull, "Strategic Studies and Its Critics," 597.

55. Wight opens with a discussion of Herz's *International Politics in the Atomic Age* (New York: Columbia University Press, 1962).

56. Wight had sympathy with the case put by the CND, but thought its assumptions about what might happen after unilateral disarmament, in the event, for instance, of a Soviet invasion of Britain, were naïve. "It is easy to say 'Rather Red than dead'," he noted, "but not easy to apprehend its full meaning." ("War and Peace" [1963], Wight MS 204, A/29).

57. Bull, "Strategic Studies and Its Critics," 599.

58. Alastair Buchan, *War in Modern Society: An Introduction* (London: Fontana, 1968 [1966]), vii.

59. Buchan argued: "'Either war is a crusade or it is a crime' wrote R. H. Tawney. This is an exceedingly dangerous view for it leads directly away from all considerations of moderation in the use of force to protect the interests of the state, and toward those ideas of a moral or holy war, of one or a group of states arrogating to themselves the right to judge the rectitude of their own cause and to use unlimited force to prosecute it, the moralistic conceptions of the international order which the Europeans found so distasteful and alarming in the foreign policy of Mr. John Foster Dulles" (*War in Modern Society*, 22).

60. Alastair Buchan, *The End of the Postwar Era: A New Balance of World Power* (London: Weidenfeld & Nicolson, 1974), 14.

61. See the following by Buchan: "The Reform of NATO," *Foreign Affairs* 40:2 (1962), 165–182; "Partners and Allies," *Foreign Affairs* 41:4 (1963), 621–637; and "The Changed Setting of the Atlantic Debate," *Foreign Affairs* 43:4 (1965), 574–586.

62. See Bull, "What Is the Commonwealth?," *World Politics* 11:4 (1959), 577–587: as well as "International Theory: The Case for a Classical Approach"; "Strategic Studies and Its Critics"; and "Arms Control and World Order," *International Security* 1:1 (1976), 3–16. See also Bull, "The New Balance of Power in Asia and the Pacific," *Foreign Affairs* 49:4 (1971), 669–681.

63. See the following by Laurence W. Martin: "The Bournemouth Affair: Britain's First Primary Election," *Journal of Politics* 22:4 (1960), 654–681; "Woodrow Wilson's Appeals to the People of Europe: British Radical Influence on the President's Strategy," *Political Science Quarterly* 74:4 (1959), 498–516; and "The Market for Strategic Ideas in Britain: 'The Sandys Era,'" *American Political Science Review* 56:1 (1962), 23-41.

64. See especially Bull's "International Relations as an Academic Pursuit."

65. Bull, "Strategic Studies and Its Critics," 603.

66. Robert O'Neill, "Hedley Bull and Arms Control," in Coral Bell and Meredith Thatcher (eds.), *Remembering Hedley* (Canberra: ANU E-Press, 2008), 38.

67. Bull, "Strategic Studies and Its Critics," 605.

68. Michael Howard, "The Relevance of Traditional Strategy," *Foreign Affairs* 51:2 (1973), 253–266.

69. Michael Howard, "The Strategic Approach to International Relations," *British Journal of International Studies* 2:1 (1976), 73–75.

70. See Alastair Buchan, "A World Restored?," *Foreign Affairs* 50:4 (1972), 644–659; and "The Indochina War and World Politics," *Foreign Affairs* 53:4 (1975), 638–650.

71. For Bull's account of the "new medievalism," see *Anarchical Society*, 245–246 and 254–266. Similar anxieties were expressed by Alastair Buchan's Reith Lectures for 1973, published as *Change without War: The Shifting Structure of World Power* (London: Chatto & Windus, 1974), especially 99–112.

72. C. E. Callwell, *Small Wars: Their Principles and Practice*, 3rd ed. (Lincoln & London: University of Nebraska Press, 1996 [1st ed. 1896]); and T. E. Lawrence, *Seven Pillars of Wisdom* (London: Jonathan Cape, 1935 [1922]).

73. See, for example, Fitzroy Maclean, *Escape to Adventure* (Boston: Little, Brown, 1950).

74. See Sir Robert Thompson, *Defeating Communist Insurgency: Experiences from Malaya and Vietnam* (London: Chatto & Windus, 1964); and Richard Clutterbuck, *The Long Long War: The Emergency in Malaya, 1948-1960* (London: Cassell, 1967).

75. Crozier, *The Rebels: A Study of Post-War Insurrections* (London: Chatto & Windus, 1960); *The Struggle for the Third World* (London: Bodley Head, 1966); and *A Theory of Conflict* (London: Hamilton, 1974).

76. On the influence of these bodies on postwar British thinking, see Hugh Wilford, "The Information Research Department: Britain's Secret Cold War Weapon Revealed," *Review of International Studies* 24 (1998), 353–369. See also Crozier's autobiography, *Free Agent: The Unseen War, 1941-91* (New York: HarperCollins, 1993).

77. Paul Wilkinson, *Terrorism vs. Liberal Democracy: The Problems of Response* (London: Institute for the Study of Conflict, 1976). Much expanded and revised, this work later became *Terrorism versus Democracy: The Liberal State Response* (London & Portland, OR: Frank Cass, 2001). See also Wilkinson's *Political Terrorism* (London: Macmillan, 1974).

78. See, for instance, Philip Schlesinger, "On the Shape and Scope of Counter-Insurgency Thought," in Gary Littlejohn, Barry Smart, John Wakeford, and Nira Yuval-Davis (eds.), *Power and the State* (London: Croom Helm, 1978), 98–127.

79. Roger Morgan, "The Study of International Politics," in his edited *The Study of International Affairs: Essays in Honour of Kenneth Younger* (London: Oxford University Press for RIIA, 1972), 286.

80. Ibid., 283.

81. John Burton, *Systems, States, Diplomacy and Rules* (Cambridge: Cambridge University Press, 1968), xi.

82. It is significant, as he himself explained thirty years later, that the pioneering peace researcher Johan Galtung's first book was a study of Gandhi's political ethics: Johan Galtung and Arne Naess, *Gandhis politiske etikk* (Oslo: Tanum, 1955); cited in Galtung's "Twenty Five Years of Peace Research: Ten Challenges and Some Responses," *Journal of Peace Research* 22 (1985), 141–159.

83. Of crucial importance was Galtung's International Peace Research Institute (IPRI) in Oslo, the first such institute, created in January 1959 with the support of the Norwegian government.

84. See the discussion of method in Ian Bellany, "Peace Research: Means and Ends," *International Affairs* 52:1 (1976), especially 20–22.

85. Burton, *International Relations*, especially 31–86.

86. For an excellent discussion of the development of this subfield, see Buzan and Hansen, *The Evolution of International Security Studies*, 101–155.

87. Lewis Fry Richardson, *Statistics of Deadly Quarrels*, ed. Q. Wright and C. C. Lienau (London: Stevens, 1960) xxxv. On Richardson's life, see Steven A. Richardson, "Lewis Fry Richardson (1881–1953): A Personal Biography," *Journal of Conflict Resolution* 1:3 (1957), 300–304.

88. Richardson, *Statistics of Deadly Quarrels*, xliv and xxxv. For discussions of Richardson's work, see John C. Harsanyi, "Mathematical Models for the Genesis of Wars," *World Politics* 14:4 (1962), 687–699; Anatol Rapaport, "Lewis F. Richardson's Mathematical Theory of War," *Journal of Conflict Resolution* 1:3 (1957), 249–299; Ian Bellany, "The Richardson Theory of Arms Races," *British Journal of International Studies* 1:2 (1975), 119–130; and Michael Nicholson, "Lewis Fry Richardson and the Study of the Causes of War," *British Journal of Political Science* 29:3 (1999), 541–563.

89. Richardson, *Statistics of Deadly Quarrels*, xliv.

90. The "number of a state's external wars has a positive correlation of 0.77 with the number of its frontiers" (Richardson, *Statistics of Deadly Quarrels*, 297).

91. This conclusion was, of course, controversial—see Rapoport, "Lewis F. Richardson's Mathematical Theory of War," 269–270.

92. Lewis F. Richardson, *Arms and Insecurity* (London: Stevens & Sons, 1960).

93. On Richardson's posthumous impact, see Nicholson, "Lewis Fry Richardson and the Study of the Causes of War," 560–562.

94. Editorial, "Dr Paul Smoker, September 23, 1938–January 7, 1998," *International Journal of Peace Studies* 3:2 (1998), online at: http://gmu.edu/academic/ijps/vol3_2/smoker.htm.

95. Paul Smoker, "Fear in the Arms Race: A Mathematical Study," *Journal of Peace Research* 1:1 (1964), 55–64. See also his "Trade, Defence and the Richardson Theory of Arms Races: A Seven Nation Study," *Journal of Peace Research* 2:2 (1965), 161–176.

96. See, for example, Smoker's "Nation State Escalation and International Integration," *Journal of Peace Research* 4:1 (1967), 61–75; and "Small Peace," *Journal of Peace Research* 18:2 (1981), 149–157.

97. For a contemporary survey, see Michael Nicholson, *Conflict Analysis* (London: English Universities Press, 1970).

98. Peter Cooper, "The Development of the Concept of War," *Journal of Peace Research* 2:1 (1965), 1–16; Alan Coddrington, "Policies Advocated in Conflict Situations by British Newspapers," *Journal of Peace Research* 2 (1965), 398–404; and Coddrington, "Game Theory, Bargaining Theory, and Strategic Reasoning," *Journal of Peace Research* 4:1 (1967), 39–44.

99. See Adam Curle, *Education for Liberation* (London: Tavistock, 1973).

100. Michael Nicholson, "Tariff Wars and a Model of Conflict," *Journal of Peace Research* 4:1 (1967), 26–38; and his *Oligopoly and Conflict: A Dynamic Approach* (Liverpool: Liverpool University Press, 1972).

101. See M. B. Nicholson and P. A. Reynolds, "General Systems, the International System, and the Eastonian Analysis," *Political Studies* 15:1 (1967), 12–31; Michael Banks, "Systems Analysis and the Study of Regions," *International Studies Quarterly* 13:4 (1969), 335–360; and Roy E. Jones, *The Functional Analysis of Politics: An Introductory Discussion* (London: Routledge & Kegan Paul, 1967).

102. John W. Burton, *The Alternative: A Dynamic Approach to Our Relations with Asia* (Sydney: Morgans Publications 1954); and *Peace Theory: Preconditions of Disarmament* (New York: Knopf, 1962).

103. John W. Burton, "'Peace Research' and 'International Relations,'" *Journal of Conflict Resolution* 8:3 (1964), 284.

104. See, for example, Stanley Hoffmann, review of John W. Burton, *Peace Theory: Preconditions of Disarmament*, *American Journal of International Law* 58 (1964), 201–202.

105. Burton, *International Relations*, 97–140.

106. Ibid., 262.

107. Joseph Frankel, review of Charles Lindblom, *The Policy-Making Process*, etc., *International Affairs* 45:4 (1969), 685–687.

108. In a review of Burton's *Peace Theory,* Robert C. Angell observed—quite rightly—that it was "somewhat reminiscent of discussions of peaceful change before World War II" ("A Dynamic Theory of Peace: A Review," *Journal of Conflict Resolution* 8:1 (1964), 83).

109. John W. Burton, *Systems, States, Diplomacy and Rules* (Cambridge: Cambridge University Press, 1968), 1–26.

110. John W. Burton, *World Society* (Cambridge: Cambridge University Press, 1972), 28.

111. Burton, *Systems, States, Diplomacy and Rules*, 10.

112. For a discussion, see Oliver Richmond, *Peace in International Relations* (London & New York: Routledge, 2008).

113. Michael Howard, "Changes in the Use of Force, 1919–1969," in Porter (ed.), *Aberystwyth Papers*, 140.

114. Strange's first major contribution to international political economy (IPE) was the Chatham House pamphlet *The Sterling Problem and the Six* (London: RIIA, 1967). On the evolution of IPE in Britain, see Benjamin J. Cohen, *International Political Economy: An Intellectual History* (Princeton, NJ: Princeton University Press, 2008), 44–65.

115. See, for instance, Frankel's *The Changing Structure of British Foreign Policy* (London & New York: Longman, 1974).

116. For an overview of Soviet studies, see Archie Brown, "The Study of Totalitarianism and Authoritarianism," in Hayward, Barry, and Brown (eds.), *British Study of Politics*, 345–394.

CHAPTER 10

EPIGRAPH: William Wallace, "Truth and Power, Monks and Technocrats: Theory and Practice in International Relations," *Review of International Studies* 22:3 (1996), 311.

1. On American intellectuals, see—inter alia—Campbell Craig, *Glimmer of a New Leviathan: Total War in the Realism of Niebuhr, Morgenthau, and Waltz* (New York: Columbia University Press, 2003); as well as Oren, *Our Enemies and US*. On a representative French intellectual, see Bruce C. Anderson, *Raymond Aron: The Recovery of the Political* (Lanham, MD: Rowman & Littlefield, 1997).

2. Hedley Bull, "International Relations as an Academic Pursuit," 263.

3. Nicholson, "The Enigma of Martin Wight," 21.

4. P. A. Reynolds, "International Studies: Retrospect and Beyond," *Review of International Studies* 1:1 (1975), 1–19. On this point, see also Geoffrey Goodwin, "International Relations and International Studies," *Yearbook of World Affairs* 27 (1973), 383–400.

5. Reynolds, "International Studies: Retrospect and Beyond," 18.

6. The American debate on this topic is captured in Klaus Knorr and James N. Rosenau (eds.), *Contending Approaches to International Politics* (Princeton, NJ: Princeton University Press, 1969). For a later but perceptive

account of British "traditionalist" approaches from an American perspective, see Lyons, "The Study of International Relations in Great Britain."

7. These concerns are best expressed by Bull in his "Case for the Classical Approach," but see also his "International Relations as an Academic Pursuit" (1972).

8. This is clearest, perhaps, in Michael Donelan's edited collection *The Reason of States: A Study in International Political Theory* (London: George Allen & Unwin, 1978), which rallied scholars of quite different political perspectives to a common Idealist and historicist cause and conceived the role of the theorist to be one of making sense of the world or clarifying the meaning of events, rather than prescribing or advocating.

9. Jones, "The English School," 1.

10. Ibid., 7, 9.

11. Ibid., 9.

12. Ibid., 12.

13. Nicholson, "The Enigma of Martin Wight," 17–18.

14. Wight's pacifism and quietism is discussed in detail in Hall, *International Thought of Martin Wight*, especially 21–85.

15. Plato, *The Republic*, trans. Allan Bloom (New York: Basic Books, 1991), 496c–d, 176.

16. Nicholson wrote: "Now if one was absolutely certain that nothing one could do would influence the way the world went no matter what policies were carried out, then one might as well be a pacifist. Morality resides in acts alone and not in their consequences for it is not clear what a consequence would be in such a world." ("The Enigma of Martin Wight," 19).

17. Quoted in ibid.

18. Ibid.

19. Ibid., 20.

20. Alan James, "Michael Nicholson on Martin Wight: A Mind Passing in the Night," *Review of International Studies* 8:2 (1982), 120–122.

21. Ibid., 117.

22. Ibid., 119.

23. T. D Weldon, *The Vocabulary of Politics: An Enquiry into the Use and Abuse of Language in the Making of Political Theories* (Harmondsworth: Penguin, 1953).

24. The beginnings of the latter's critique can be found in Steve Smith, "Paradigm Dominance in International Relations: The Development of International Relations as a Social Science," in Hugh C. Dyer and Leon Magasarian (eds.), *The Study of International Relations: The State of the Art* (New York: St. Martin's Press and Millennium, 1989), 30–27.

25. Michael Nicholson, "Martin Wight: Enigma or Error?," *Review of International Studies* 8:2 (1982), 125–128.

26. Michael Banks, "Bucking the System: A Peace Researcher's Perspective on the Study of International Relations," in Dyer and Magasarian (eds.), *The Study of International Relations*, 370.

27. See Michael Howard, "The Relevance of Traditional Strategy," *Foreign Affairs* 51:2 (1973), 253–266; and Burton, *World Society*, ix–xi. Howard's anxieties are also evident in the downbeat conclusion to *War and the Liberal Conscience*, the lectures of which were delivered in 1977.

28. Smith, "Paradigm Dominance in International Relations," 15. For a belated riposte to this argument, see Wallace, "Truth and Power, Monks and Technocrats."

29. Hugh Thomas, *The World's Game* (London: Eyre & Spottiswoode, 1957), 203.

30. Thomas (1931–) was educated at Sherborne, Queen's College, Cambridge, and the Sorbonne. After leaving the Foreign Office he became a distinguished historian of the Hispanic world. He was made Baron Thomas of Swynnerton in 1981.

31. Thomas, *World's Game*, 203.

32. Ibid., 202.

33. Butterfield to Watson, 2 May 1949, Butterfield MS 531/W23. On the IRD, see especially Andrew Defty, *Britain, America and Anti-Communist Propaganda, 1945–53: The Information Research Department* (London & New York: Routledge, 2004). Watson served as assistant to the head of the IRD, Ralph Murray, immediately after its creation by Ernest Bevin in 1949, but soon moved to Washington to act as liaison between the IRD and its counterparts in the CIA and other US agencies. He left the IRD in 1954.

34. Armstrong was educated at Bec School and Exeter College, Oxford. He was permanent secretary to the Treasury 1962–68, and cabinet secretary 1968–74. See Kevin Theakston, "Armstrong, William, Baron Armstrong of Sanderstead (1915–1980), *Oxford Dictionary of National Biography*, online.

35. McLachlan was educated at City of London School and Magdalen College, Oxford. He worked at the *Times Educational Supplement, The Economist, The Daily Telegraph*, and was the founding editor of *The Sunday Telegraph*.

36. Palliser was educated at Wellington and Merton College, Oxford, and later became permanent under-secretary of state and head of the Foreign Office, 1975–1982.

37. Wade-Gery was educated at Winchester and New College, Oxford, and served in the Foreign Service in various capacities from 1951 to 1987.

38. These kinds of links are explored in considerable detail in Noël Annan's *Our Age: Portrait of a Generation* (London: Weidenfeld & Nicolson, 1990).

39. Winston S. Churchill, *The Second World War*, 6 vols. (London: Cassell, 1948). The construction of Churchill's history is examined in David Reynolds' *In Command of History: Churchill Fighting and Writing the Second World War* (London: Allen Lane, 2004).

40. For a pithy summary of Churchill's beliefs about foreign policy and diplomacy, see Kenneth W. Thompson, *Winston Churchill's World View: Statesmanship and Power* (Baton Rouge, LA: Louisiana State University Press, 1983).

41. See Anthony Adamthwaite, "Britain and the World, 1945–49: The View from the Foreign Office," *International Affairs* 61:2 (1985), 223–235.

42. See especially Anthony Eden's *Full Circle: The Memoirs of Anthony Eden* (Boston: Houghton Mifflin, 1960); and Wight's review, "Brutus in Foreign Policy."

43. Oliver Franks, *Britain and the Tide of World Affairs* (London: Oxford University Press, 1955), 5. Franks was educated at Bristol Grammar School and Queen's College, Oxford. He taught philosophy at Oxford and at Glasgow, and served as ambassador to Washington, 1948–52.

44. Ibid., 12.

45. For a fine exposition of this argument, see David Reynolds, *Britannia Overruled: British Policy and World Power in the 20th Century* (London & New York: Longman, 1991).

46. Churchill's advocacy of European unity was, as is well known, ambiguous: he believed Britain should promote it but not be part of it. See his 19 September 1946 speech "The Tragedy of Europe," which called for a United States of Europe with Britain as one of its "friends" and "sponsors" (available online at http://www.europa.clio-online.de/site/lang__en/ItemID__297/mid__11373/40208215/default.aspx).

47. Lord Vansittart, *Events and Shadows: A Policy for the Remnants of a Century* (London: Hutchinson & Co., 1947), 161; Edward Heath, "Realism in British Foreign Policy," *Foreign Affairs* 48:1 (1969), 39–50.

48. See Heath's memoirs, *The Course of My Life: The Autobiography of Edward Heath* (London: Coronet, 1998), which emphasize the European-ness, as it were, of his generation's minds.

49. Max Beloff, *New Dimensions in Foreign Policy: A Study in British Administrative Experience, 1947–59* (London: George Allen & Unwin, 1961), 16.

50. As Hugo Young had argued, "Throughout Whitehall, Europe was a generational, as well as an attitudinal, issue" (*This Blessed Plot: Britain and Europe from Churchill to Blair* [London: Macmillan, 1998], 177).

51. Young, *This Blessed Plot*, 173.

52. Ibid., 177. Young calls Palliser, who married the Belgian federalist Paul-Henri Spaak's daughter, "the archetypal Foreign Office European" (178).

53. For a discussion, see Chris Gifford, *The Making of Eurosceptic Britain: Identity and Economy in a Post-Imperial State* (Aldershot: Ashgate, 2008), 30–31.

54. Gaitskell (1906–63) was educated at Winchester and New College, Oxford, where he read PPE. He was elected to Parliament in 1945, appointed to his first ministry (Fuel and Power) in 1947, and became leader of the Labour Party in 1955, a post he held until his untimely death in 1963.

55. Hugh Gaitskell, *The Challenge of Co-Existence* (London: Methuen, 1957), 37.

56. Ibid., 79.

57. Beloff, *New Dimensions in Foreign Policy*, 182.

58. On these issues in general, see John W. Young, *The Labour Gov-*

ernments, 1964–1970, vol. 2: *International Policy* (Manchester: Manchester University Press, 2003), 10–14; and for a short commentary on the Plowden Report, see Max Beloff, *The Intellectual in Politics and Other Essays* (New York: The Library Press, 1971), 83–88.

59. The Duncan Committee was chaired by Val Duncan, chairman of Rio Tinto Zinc. It recommended that the Foreign Office's role in foreign policymaking be curtailed and Britain's overseas diplomatic representation cut. For a defense of the Duncan Report by one of the committee's members, see Andrew Shonfield, "The Duncan Report and Its Critics," *International Affairs* 46:2 (1970), 247–268.

60. Ibid., 252.

61. Ibid., 267.

62. Michael Donelan, "The Trade of Diplomacy," *International Affairs* 45:4 (1969), 607.

63. Ibid., 610.

64. The former diplomat Sir James Cable noted exactly that in his "The Useful Art of International Relations," *International Affairs* 57:2 (1981), 301. Cable also observed that of the four scholars of international relations who gave evidence to the Duncan and Berrill Committees were all Australians.

65. Ibid., 313.

66. Cable thought that these "symptoms of that endemic British disease: academics shrinking into the womb of 'pure' research and practitioners scorning 'theoretical' training" and that, as with other areas of knowledge, this "divorce is partly responsible for the decline of Britain in the last hundred years" (ibid., 304–305).

67. Bernstein, *Myth of Decline*.

Index

Africa, 118, 133, 135, 137, 139, 142, 143–145, 148
American Political Science Association, 9
Anderson, John, 160
Anderson, Perry, 123, 124
Angell, Norman, 54, 67, 71
anticolonialism, 12, 64, 124–126, 131–151
appeasement, 30, 33–34, 35, 37–38, 84–85, 99, 116
Armstrong, William, 178
Arnold, G. L., 38
Aron, Raymond, 90
Astor, David, 52
Attlee, Clement, 44, 118, 120, 148, 179
Austin, John, 114
Australian National University, 166
Ayson, Robert, 159

Bailey, S. H., 66, 128
Bandung conference, 137, 138, 149
Banks, Michael, 128, 129, 166, 169, 175–176
Barraclough, Geoffrey, 132
Barrett Brown, Michael, 149
Barry, Brian, 4
Beloff, Max, 2, 6, 7, 25, 27, 46, 91, 179, 181
Bentham, Jeremy, 26, 78, 110

Bentley, Michael, 88
Berki, R. N., 39
Berlin, Isaiah, 7, 44, 79
Bernal, J. D., 119
Bevan, Aneurin, 120, 121
Bevin, Ernest, 118, 120
Bevir, Mark, 4, 14, 15, 20, 21, 23–24, 25–26, 88
Birmingham University, 60
Blackett, P. M. S., 156
Bonaparte, Napoleon, 35
Booth, Ken, 31
Boulding, Kenneth, 127, 174
Brailsford, H. N., 112, 124
Brierly, J. L., 51, 52, 73, 74, 102
British Committee on the Theory of International Politics, 7, 12, 27, 100, 106, 157, 178
British International Studies Association, 3, 169, 172
Brodie, Bernard, 153, 157–158
Brogan, Denis, 8, 46
Brown, Chris, 17
Buchan, Alastair, 53, 157, 160–161, 163, 169
Bull, Hedley, 5, 7, 17, 27, 41, 46, 58, 59, 60–61, 66, 89–91, 105, 131, 140–142, 146, 152, 158–162, 163, 169, 171, 177
Bullock, Alan, 108
Burnham, James, 45

249

Burton, John W., 41, 128, 149–150, 152, 153, 163, 164, 166–168, 176
Butler, Michael, 180
Butterfield, Herbert, 7, 9, 12, 27, 33, 35, 38, 40, 41, 42, 55, 59, 60, 67, 83, 86, 88–89, 91, 95–100, 104, 105, 106, 122, 136–137, 142, 157, 177, 178
Buzan, Barry, 103
Buzzard, Anthony, 156, 158

Cable, James, 182
Callwell, C. E., 162
Campaign for Nuclear Disarmament, 112, 121–123, 124, 150, 158, 160, 165, 178
Carnegie Endowment for International Peace, 52, 157
Carr, E. H., 5, 16, 21, 22, 26, 29, 30, 31, 32–34, 38, 39, 44, 46, 49, 50, 52, 53, 62, 65–66, 67, 80, 81, 87, 90, 113, 114–117, 119, 137, 170
Carrington, C. E., 133–134, 141, 144, 147
Catlin, George, 37
Cecil, Robert, 51, 102
Centre for the Analysis of Conflict, 166
Chamberlain, Neville, 30, 32–33, 34–35, 36, 37, 99
Chatham House (Royal Institute of International Affairs), 9, 38, 46, 52–53, 72, 133, 156–157, 158, 162, 175, 178, 181
Christ Church, Oxford, 180
Churchill, Winston, 10, 16, 37, 38, 72, 76, 83, 84–85, 102, 113, 133, 134, 178–179
Claude, Inis, 161
Clutterbuck, Richard, 162
Cobban, Alfred, 68
Coddrington, Alan, 166
Cole, G. D. H., 120
Collingwood, R. G., 19, 59
Commonwealth, 133–135, 138–139, 140–141, 147, 180
Communist Party Historians' Group, 119

Communist Party of Great Britain, 119
Congress for Cultural Freedom, 162
contextualism, 14, 15, 18–19
Cooper, Duff, 112, 113
Cooper, Peter, 166
Courtney, Kathleen, 10, 74
Crick, Bernard, 6, 8
Crossman, Richard, 120, 136
Crowe, Eyre, 93–94
Crozier, Brian, 162, 163
Curle, Adam, 166
Curtis, Lionel, 48, 50, 51, 52, 67, 76, 79, 147

Darwin, J. G., 150
Dawson, Christopher, 26
Deakin, F. W., 108
decolonization, 124, 131–151
Demant, V. A., 10
Desch, C. H., 37
Deutsch, Karl, 100, 166, 167
Dickinson, Goldsworthy Lowes, 54, 112
dilemmas, 22–24
Dobb, Maurice, 119
Donelan, Michael, 17, 58, 59, 60, 182

Easton, David, 91, 128, 166, 167
Eden, Anthony, 10, 34, 139, 179
English school of international relations, 5, 17, 57, 86, 92, 105–106, 172
Ensor, R. F., 37
European Economic Community, 1, 131, 180
Exeter College, Oxford, 52

Falls, Cyril, 156
Fanon, Franz, 150
Federal Union, 76
federalism, 75–76, 81–82
Finer, S. E., 87
Foot, Michael, 120
Ford Foundation, 157, 172
Foreign Office, 53, 72, 73, 131, 142, 161, 162, 175, 177, 178, 179, 180, 181
France, 34, 116, 137, 138

Frankel, Joseph, 41, 46–47, 105, 128, 167, 169, 170
Frankland, Noble, 156, 157
Franks, Oliver, 179
Fuller, J. F. C., 154–155
functionalism, 65, 75–79, 128, 175, 179

Gaitskell, Hugh, 180–181
Gallagher, John, 147–148
Galtung, Johan, 166
Gasset, Ortega y, 77
Gathorne-Hardy, G. M., 58
Germany, 11, 16, 32, 34, 36, 38, 41, 44, 54, 83, 99, 113, 137, 155
Gibbs, Norman, 156
Gladstone, William, 39, 102
Gooch, G. P., 112
Goodwin, Geoffrey L., 39, 41, 52, 55–56, 58, 74, 79, 87–88, 90, 169
Gramsci, Antonio, 124
Green, L. C., 41
Greene, Graham, 44
Grimond, Joseph (Jo), 53, 178
Grotius, Hugo, 17, 89, 101–102, 104
Guicciardini, Francesco, 98
Gunnell, John, 19, 22, 109

Haas, Ernst, 79
Haldane, J. B. S., 119
Halliday, Fred, 150
Hancock, Keith, 7, 68, 147
Hart, H. L. A., 61
Hartley, Anthony, 117–118, 131
Haslam, Jonathan, 23
Hayek, Friedrich, 38, 50, 64, 65, 79–82
Hayward, Jack, 4
Headlam-Morley, Agnes, 10, 52, 53
Healey, Denis, 10, 45, 118, 156, 157, 180
Heath, Edward, 179
Heatley, D. P., 15, 16
Hegel, Georg, 16, 33, 44, 129
Herz, John, 66, 158, 160
Hill, Christopher, 119
Hinsley, F. H., 71, 88
Hitler, Adolf, 29, 35, 38, 137, 138
Hobbes, Thomas, 43, 58, 89, 97, 114

Hobsbawm, Eric, 119
Hobson, J. A., 124, 134, 147, 148
Hoffman, Stanley, 22, 23
Howard, Michael, 9, 154, 156, 157, 161–162, 168, 176
Hudson, G. F., 53
human nature, 35, 39
Hungary, 117, 121, 123, 130
Huntington, Samuel, 161

idealism, 16, 46
imperialism, 12, 14, 36, 118, 124–126, 138, 144, 145, 146, 147–149, 150, 151, 180
India, 118, 135, 138, 148
Information Research Department, 162, 177
Institute for the Analysis of Conflict, 166
Institute for the Study of Conflict, 162
International Institute for Strategic Studies, 9, 53, 157, 159, 162, 163, 175, 178, 181
international society, 58, 92, 101–104, 139–140, 141, 142, 143
internationalism, 11–12, 26, 64–82, 84–85, 113–115, 131, 132–136, 142, 151, 176, 178, 183

Jackson, Robert, 17
James, Alan, 174
Jebb, Gladwyn, 72
Jeffery, Renée, 19
Jennings, Ivor, 76
Jerrold, Douglas, 131
Joad, C. E. M., 76
Jones, Roy, 57, 79, 91, 105, 126, 128, 166, 172–173, 174

Kahn, Herman, 159
Kant, Immanuel, 17, 30, 89, 99, 104
Kantorowicz, Hermann, 83
Kaplan, Morton, 100, 128, 159
Kedourie, Elie, 69, 70
Keens-Soper, Maurice, 61
Kennan, George, 29, 36, 37, 177

Keynes, J. M., 112
Kiernan, V. G., 119, 148
King's College, London, 156, 163
King-Hall, Stephen, 122, 158
Kissinger, Henry, 29, 60, 159, 177
Kuhn, Thomas, 17, 26

Larkin, Philip, 1
Laski, Harold, 36, 113–115, 117, 118, 124, 147
Latham, Robert, 61
Lauterpacht, Hersch, 41, 51, 52
Lawrence, T. E., 162
Le Carré, John, 107, 111
League of Nations, 32, 48, 49, 55, 72–75, 84–85, 92, 101, 104, 112, 113, 132
Legum, Colin, 53
Lenin, V. I., 124, 129, 134, 147, 148
Lewis, Gordon, 111
Liberal Foreign Affairs Group, 53, 178
liberalism, 11–12, 26, 39, 40, 48–63, 66–68, 79–82, 131, 132–136, 142, 151
Liddell Hart, Basil, 154–155, 157
Lippmann, Walter, 5, 36
London School of Economics (LSE), 3, 8, 9, 17, 37, 41, 46, 47, 52, 55, 56–59, 60, 80, 101, 127, 137, 150, 156, 166
Lothian, Lord (Phillip Kerr), 76
Lovejoy, A. O., 17, 58
Low, David, 34
Luard, Evan, 52, 79
Lyon, Peter, 46, 59

Machiavelli, Niccolo, 8, 16, 26, 30, 33, 35, 38, 98
Mackinnon, Donald, 59
Magee, Brian, 121
Manchester University, 55
Mannheim, Karl, 22, 41, 77–78, 80
Manning, C. A. W., 7, 9, 41, 42, 51, 52, 53, 56–58, 59, 60, 61, 173
Mansergh, Nicholas, 147
Martin, Kingsley, 122
Martin, Laurence, 161, 163
Marx, Karl, 16, 26, 33, 113, 120, 129, 130

Marxism, 118–119, 123–126, 130, 144, 147, 148, 170
Maurice, Frederick, 156
Mazzini, Guiseppe, 69
McLachlan, Donald, 178
Mikardo, Ian, 120
Mill, John Stuart, 132
Miller, J. D. B., 59
Ministry of Defence, 157
Mitrany, David, 37, 65, 66, 78–79, 126, 175–176
modernist empiricism, 6, 60, 87–91, 174–175, 183
Monnet, Jean, 180
Morel, E. D., 124
Morgan, Roger, 163
Morgenthau, Hans J., 5, 7, 29, 30, 35, 36, 37, 40, 46, 58, 66, 90, 105, 115, 158
Murray, Gilbert, 31, 39, 51, 61–62, 65, 66, 67–68, 69, 71, 73–74, 75, 82, 114, 132, 133
Mussolini, Benito, 32, 35

Nairn, Tom, 123, 125
Namier, Lewis, 7, 9, 37, 38, 67, 69, 87
nationalism, 68–71, 137–141, 143
Navari, Cornelia, 44
New College, Oxford, 52
New Left, 108, 112, 119, 123–126, 131, 148–149
Nicholas, H. G., 52
Nicholson, Michael, 127, 128, 129, 166, 171, 172–174
Nicolson, Harold, 12, 86, 92–94, 102, 104, 106
Niebuhr, Reinhold, 31, 36, 37
Nitze, Paul, 159
Noel-Baker, Philip, 51, 66, 107, 121, 158–159
nonalignment, 120, 149, 167
Northedge, F. S., 1, 2, 3, 27
Nuffield College, Oxford, 52, 181

O'Neill, Con, 180
O'Neill, Robert, 161, 162

Oakeshott, Michael, 20, 59
Oldham, J. H., 40
Orwell, George, 29, 35, 38
Osgood, Robert, 159

pacifism, 10, 76, 117, 122, 149–150, 154, 162, 163, 173, 174
Paine, Thomas, 110, 115
Palliser, Michael, 178, 180
Pareto, Vilfredo, 35, 77
Parkinson, Fred, 41
Parsons, Talcott, 78, 166
peace research, 12, 27, 126, 129, 130, 152–154, 163–169, 175–176
Penrose, E. F., 152
Perham, Margery, 132, 133
Peterhouse, Cambridge, 60
philosophical Idealism, 6, 47, 51, 57, 59, 90, 102–103, 182
Political Studies Association, 9
Popper, Karl, 7, 79
Porter, Brian, 17, 58
poststructuralism, 18
Powell, Enoch, 64
Priestley, J. B., 122

Queen Mary, University of London, 166

radicalism, 12, 26, 106, 107–130, 146–150, 151, 176, 180
realism, 5, 11, 16, 17, 23, 26, 27, 29–47, 49, 81, 82, 84–85, 97–99, 116, 118, 122, 131, 135, 143, 164, 179
Rex, John, 123
Reynolds, Charles, 59
Reynolds, P. A., 9, 166, 172
Rhodes, R. A. W., 4
Richardson, Lewis Fry, 127, 128, 164–165
Robinson, John, 180
Robinson, Ronald, 147–148
Rockefeller Foundation, 7, 159, 172
Roosevelt, Franklin D., 39, 78, 80
Rose, Saul, 37
Rowse, A. L., 44
Royal United Services Institute, 157

Russell, Bertrand, 10, 34, 51, 53, 65, 66, 67, 71, 74, 75, 112, 115, 117, 122

Savigear, Peter, 60
Schelling, Thomas C., 91, 100, 159
Schmidt, Brian, 19, 22, 24
Schuman, Frederick, 5
Schuman, Robert, 180
Schwarzenberger, Georg, 16, 31, 41–43, 46–47, 52, 74, 76, 126, 166
Seton-Watson, Hugh, 135
Seton-Watson, R. W., 113
Shils, Edward, 117
Slessor, John, 158
Smith, Adam, 134
Smith, Steve, 4, 5
Smoker, Paul, 165–166
Smuts, Jan, 72
Soper, Donald, 10
Sorel, Georges, 77
Soviet Union, 1, 27, 29, 40, 61–62, 99, 111, 113, 115, 119, 120–121, 123–124, 157, 169
Spykman, Nicholas, 5, 36
St Antony's College, Oxford, 9–10, 52
Stalin, Josef, 116, 130, 137, 149
Stawell, F. Melian, 15, 16
Stedman Jones, Gareth, 125–126, 150
Strachey, John, 148, 149
Strange, Susan, 41, 53, 169, 176
strategic studies, 12, 27, 152–163
Strauss, Leo, 58
Suez crisis, 117, 121, 123, 139, 143, 179
Suganami, Hidemi, 57, 60

Taylor, A. J. P., 9, 29, 30, 43, 67, 87, 91, 107–108, 109, 112, 122, 129, 130
Temperley, Harold, 87
Temple, William, 26
terrorism, 70
Thomas, Hugh, 176–177
Thompson, E. P., 112, 119, 123
Thompson, Robert, 162
Thucydides, 22, 24, 30
Titmuss, Richard, 156

Tönnies, Ferdinand, 42
Toynbee, Arnold J., 9, 11, 22, 24, 27, 40, 49, 51, 52, 69, 70, 71, 72, 75, 76, 79, 87, 113, 114, 131, 136
traditions, 20–21
Trotsky, Leon, 110–111

United Nations, 40, 43, 52, 64, 72–75, 103, 104, 121, 132, 134, 137–138, 139, 149, 151, 175, 180
United States, 1, 5, 7, 16, 23, 27–28, 45–46, 62, 75, 80, 101, 111, 116, 118, 120–121, 124, 125, 128, 134, 138, 146, 150, 152, 157, 159, 162, 163, 172, 177
University College of Wales, Aberystwyth, 8, 9, 163
University College, London, 41, 166
University of Bradford, 127, 166
University of Cambridge, 35, 150, 177–178
University of Cardiff, 166
University of Chicago, 101
University of Kent, Canterbury, 166
University of Lancaster, 127, 165, 166
University of Manchester, 166
University of Oxford, 8, 9–10, 52, 53, 54, 55, 58, 72, 127, 133, 156, 163, 177–178
University of York, 166

Vansittart, Lord Robert, 91, 179
Vincent, R. J., 59
Voegelin, Eric, 58

Wade-Gery, Robert, 178
Wallace, William, 170

Walt, Stephen, 108–109
Waltz, Kenneth, 66, 161
Ward, Barbara, 62, 76
Watkin, Frederick, 62
Watson, Adam, 100, 104–105, 106, 141, 142–146, 147, 177
Wæver, Ole, 108–109
Weber, Max, 42
Webster, Charles, 9, 38, 51, 72–73, 74, 87, 92, 156
Wheare, Kenneth, 76
Wheeler-Bennett, John, 37, 38
whiggism, 12, 26, 83–106, 131, 178–179, 183
Wight, Martin, 8, 14, 16, 17, 21, 27, 30, 37–38, 40, 43, 50, 53, 55, 58–59, 61, 62, 64, 67, 72, 74, 79, 86, 90, 100, 101–104, 108, 131, 137–141, 142, 144, 146, 156, 160, 173, 178, 179
Wilkinson, Paul, 163
Wilkinson, Spencer, 156
Willey, Basil, 102
Williams, Raymond, 122, 123
Wilson, Woodrow, 116, 134, 138
Windsor, Philip, 157
Wohlstetter, Albert, 159
Woodhouse, C. M., 44, 53, 162
Woodward, E. L., 62
Woolf, Leonard, 51, 52, 54, 124, 147
Worsley, Peter, 123, 146, 149

Young, Hugo, 180
Younger, Kenneth, 53

Zimmern, Alfred, 7, 32, 51, 52, 54, 62, 66, 67, 70, 71, 74, 90, 114

www.ingramcontent.com/pod-product-compliance
Lightning Source LLC
Chambersburg PA
CBHW020645230426
43665CB00008B/321